Policing after th

Police Governance after the Police and Magistrates' Courts Act 1994

Trevor Jones and Tim Newburn

Policy Studies Institute

The publishing imprint of the independent
POLICY STUDIES INSTITUTE
100 Park Village East, London NW1 3SR
Tel. 0171 468 0468 Fax. 0171 388 0914

ISBN 0 85374 704 0
PS1 Report 830

Cover design by Andrew Corbett
Laserset by Oxford Publishing Services, Oxford
Printed in Great Britain by
Redwood Books, Trowbridge, Wiltshire

Contents

Acronyms and Abbreviations

ACC Assistant Chief Constable
ACPO Association of Chief Police Officers
AMA Association of Metropolitan Authorities
APT & C Administrative, Professional, Technical and Clerical Staff
BAT British American Tobacco
CAP community and police
CCTV closed circuit television
CID Criminal Investigation Department
CIMA Chartered Institute of Management Accountants
CoLPA Committee of Local Police Authorities
CPP crime prevention panel
CPS Crown Prosecution Service
DARE drugs education project
DAS District Audit Service
FFD Force Finance Director
FGPC finance and general purposes committee
FTC fixed-term contract
HMI Her Majesty's Inspector
HMIC Her Majesty's Inspectorate of Constabulary
IIP Investors in People
IT information technology
KO key objective
KPI key performance indicator
LFM local financial management
LO local objective
LPP local policing plan
NHS National Health Service
NW Neighbourhood Watch
O&D organisation and development
PACE Police and Criminal Evidence Act 1984
PACT Police and Community Team
PBO Policing by Objectives
PCCG police-community consultative group
PFI Private Finance Initiative
PI performance indicator
PLAC police liaison advisory committee
PMCA Police and Magistrates' Courts Act (1994)

PRP	performance-related pay
RCCJ	Royal Commission on Criminal Justice
RSG	revenue support grant
RTA	road traffic accident
RUC	Royal Ulster Constabulary
SLA	service-level agreement
SO	Standing Orders
SSA	standard spending assessment
STEEL	social, technological, economic, environmental, legislative
SWOT	strengths, weaknesses, opportunities, threats
TIC	other offences taken into consideration
VFM	value-for-money

Acknowledgements

First and foremost we are grateful for the financial support we received from the Economic and Social Research Council (grant no. 000236603) which made this study possible.

As with so much research we have been dependent on the goodwill and patience of a large number of people who granted us access to their organisations and staff and/or gave up their valuable time to be interviewed. We are grateful to James Sharples, the President of the Association of Chief Police Officers at the time the research began, for supporting the research and to Marcia Barton and Ian Barratt of the ACPO Secretariat for their helpful advice and their support.

Particular thanks are due to the chief constables and staff of the three forces in which the case studies were conducted, and to the chairmen, officers and members of the local police authorities in those areas. We received considerable help from staff in the Home Office, the local government associations (as they were then), and from police authorities across England and Wales. Stephen Savage read an initial draft of this book and commented most helpfully on it, as did Philip Michaelson, and senior force and police authority officers in the case study areas. At PSI, we are grateful to Sharon Collard who contributed to the analysis of the survey, to Sue Johnson, PSI's librarian, for her usual sterling service, and to Jo O'Driscoll, our highly professional publisher. Thanks are also due to Selina Cohen, who copy-edited, and much improved, our original typescript.

Introduction

In this book we examine the emerging effects of the reforms brought about by the 1994 Police and Magistrates' Courts Act (PMCA), without doubt the most significant reform of police governance since the 1964 Police Act. Critics of the reforms argued that their most important consequence would be to extend further centralization of control over British policing – a process, they argued, that has been in train since at least the Second World War. Supporters of the reforms presented them as a genuine attempt to enhance local influence over policing, albeit within a broad national framework. Presenting data from the first major study of local police authorities since the passage of the legislation, we consider why the proposed reforms were interpreted in such dramatically different ways, and which of the conflicting positions appears to fit the emerging system of police governance most closely.

We build upon a large body of research and writing on police accountability as it has developed in England and Wales over the last 20 years (*inter alia* Grimshaw 1984; Lustgarten 1986) and particularly on our recent study of the relationship between policing and democratic institutions (Jones et al., 1994). Within the wider body of work, authors have, from different perspectives, examined the nature of the relationship between policing and democratic concepts and institutions. Until the mid-1980s, the core of the discussion focused on the balance between effective community supervision of the police service on the one hand, and safeguards for impartial law enforcement and prevention of partisan control over the police on the other. Since then, a further crucial element has emerged and, some would argue, come to dominate, the debate – the concern, now common to all state-provided services, that public resources be used efficiently and effectively, and that 'consumers' receive proper standards of service.

Our overall objective is to describe and analyse emerging effects of the PMCA on the system of police governance in England and Wales – what has most usually been referred to as the 'tripartite structure'. Our concerns are with the impact of the changes on the roles of the Home Secretary, chief constables and the local police authorities within this structure. In relation to policing at the local level, we have three particular objectives:

- to assess the influence of the new police authorities, including the contribution of the new 'independent members' on these authorities;
- to examine the development of local policing plans and the relationship between national and local objectives; and

- to examine the relationship between force-wide corporate objectives and policing at a local level.

Much academic and political debate about local governance of the police has stressed the importance of 'democratic' controls or influences over this most powerful of public services. As we have argued elsewhere (Jones et al., 1994), many authors writing in this field have used the term 'democracy' in a largely unthinking or uncritical way. We have therefore tried to apply the lessons of our previous research to the results of this study, particularly our earlier thinking about democracy and its normative content.

The study on which this book is based was carried out during 1996. It was composed of three main parts.

First, given the controversial nature of the legislation and the often wildly differing views of the intentions behind it, we carried out a series of interviews with key national-level actors. These interviews allowed us to explore the history of the reforms as seen through the eyes of many of those closely involved. By charting the history of (and changes to) the White Paper on Police Reform and the subsequent Police and Magistrates' Courts Bill, we are able to develop a more refined understanding of the underlying aims of this legislation that has caused so much controversy. As part of this process, we conducted interviews with key Home Office officials concerned with framing the legislation, politicians involved in the national debate, members of the secretariat of the Association of Chief Police Officers (ACPO), local authority associations, and representatives of Her Majesty's Inspectorate of Constabulary (HMIC) and of the Audit Commission. These interviews also gave us an opportunity to explore perceptions at the national level about the early effects of the reforms.

Given that one of the main purposes of the PMCA was to reform local police authorities, the second part of the study was an analysis of the early impact of the key reforms across the provincial police authorities of England and Wales. This contained two main elements – an analysis of the published policing plans for 1995 and 1996 of 41 provincial police forces in England and Wales, and a telephone survey of police authority secretariats. The aim of the telephone survey was to collect information about the operation of the new police authorities, their involvement in planning and other aspects of the reforms. Most of the interviews were carried out with clerks, although in some cases the clerk nominated an assistant clerk to answer the questions. The interviews were undertaken with clerks' officers, rather than with police authority chairpersons or representatives of police forces, because they were considered the best placed to give an informed view of how the pre-1995 police authorities operated and of any changes that may have occurred in the relationship between the police authority and the chief constable. The interviews were semi-structured and lasted between 30 minutes and one hour. It was agreed that no individual authority would be identified in the report and, given this condition, most interviewees were happy for the interview to be tape-recorded.

The third part of the research followed the approach successfully adopted in our earlier study of the making of police policy. To supplement the general picture built up through the analysis of policing plans and the telephone survey, we undertook detailed case studies of the effects of the reforms in three force areas. The intention was to examine policy-making at all levels of the police organisation. As in our previous work, we are concerned with the 'middle range' of the term 'policing policy'. That is, we do not focus on the fine grain of policing on the ground, but neither do we restrict ourselves to statements of policy at force level. While there are clearly limits to the extent to which one can generalise from case studies, and we make no claims about the representativeness of our three case studies to the situation nationally, we did try to allow for a range of experience by focusing on forces in three geographically dissimilar areas. These included a shire force (previously administered by a single county police authority), a police force covering more than one county (a former combined-authority force), and a metropolitan force (where the police authority was a joint board). We chose the particular force areas for inclusion after consultation with ACPO and the police authority associations. Moreover, two of the forces had been used in our recent study of the pre-1994 situation, which provided a benchmark for comparison over time. In each of the force areas, this element of the research involved various stages. First, semi-structured interviews with leading members and officers of the police authority, along with analysis of minutes of authority meetings over the past year and observation of at least one police authority meeting. Second, interviews with police staff at all levels within the organisation, particularly with chief constables, officers and civilians in the force management team, local operational commanders, and lower ranking police officers at the local level. Third, we collated and analysed force reports and other documents relating to new policing priorities.

In Chapter 1, in which we briefly consider the history of local governance of police, we set out the broad background of reforms that are central to the study and give historical reasons for why centralisation and constabulary independence are so critical to debates about police accountability. In Chapter 2, we move on to the more specific area of the background to the Police and Magistrates' Courts Act 1994. Here we examine alternative views of the intentions underlying the reforms, look at the passage of the legislation, including the key amendments made to the original proposals, and provide an overview of the eventual statute. One of the most significant changes brought about by the PMCA was the requirement that local police authorities produce and publish a policing plan for their area. Chapter 3 looks in detail at these plans and the results of our analysis of plans for 1996/7. Chapter 4 presents the results of the telephone survey of police authorities in England and Wales, providing data about the operation of the new arrangements across all 41 provincial police forces. Chapters 5 to 7 present the results of the detailed case studies of the three police forces in which we explored the impact of the reforms locally. In Chapter 8, we provide an overview of the findings of the study. In this final chapter, we return to the key debates outlined in Chapter 1 – the relationship between the three 'actors' in the tripartite structure since the PMCA; the extent to which managerialism and value for money can be said to have taken over from questions of the nature and direction of local policing services as the business of police authorities; the implications of the changes brought about by the PMCA for 'democratic' control over policing; and, relatedly, how an understanding of the normative content of the idea of democracy can aid an evaluation of recent changes to the operation of police authorities. Finally, on the basis of the above discussion, we conclude by offering some policy recommendations for the future of police governance.

Chapter 1

The Governance of Police

The reforms introduced by the Police and Magistrates' Courts Act 1994 (PMCA) came into force in April 1995. In this chapter we place these reforms in the context of three key debates in British policing. The first debate concerns the changing system of police governance and the tensions between local and national control over policing. The second focuses on the wider discussion about efficiency, effectiveness and value-for-money in policing. The third key debate is that surrounding the nature and meaning of democracy in the context of a unique public service such as policing.

POLICE GOVERNANCE AND THE GROWTH OF CENTRALISATION

The 'modern' system of policing is generally thought to begin in 1829 when Sir Robert Peel established the Metropolitan Police. Its accountability was, and remains, via the Home Secretary to parliament. Provincial police forces only developed some time later and, as they grew, they were accompanied by two distinct systems of local accountability. The first, created by the Municipal Corporations Act of 1835, created what were known as Watch Committees, made up of elected local councillors, and which possessed powers to appoint officers and establish regulations for the running of the town forces. The Local Government Act of 1888 established county councils and, under their aegis, standing joint committees, consisting of two-thirds elected councillors and one-third local magistrates, were to provide the police authority for county forces. This arrangement was applied to all police authorities by the Police Act of 1964, and it is with this Act that our discussion of police governance begins.

The 1964 Police Act laid down the powers and responsibilities of the three parties forming the 'tripartite structure' of police governance (Loveday, 1991; Lustgarten, 1986; Morgan, 1986; Morgan and Maggs, 1985; Reiner, 1992).[1] For the 41 provincial police forces in England and Wales, the Act divided responsibility for the framing and monitoring of policing policy between local police authorities (consisting of two-thirds elected councillors and one-third magistrates), chief constables, and the Home Office.

---

1. A number of works include detailed discussion of the development of the system of police governance prior to 1964. See, for example, Lustgarten 1986; Jones et al., 1994; Reiner 1992.

1

The local axis: chief constables and police authorities

A central part of the debate about police accountability has focused on the part that local elected representatives play in the framing and formulation of policing policy. In the late 1970s differences began to emerge between those who argued that the 'operational independence' of chief constables needed to be defended from partisan political interference, and others who felt that the police should be more directly accountable to local elected representatives.

The legal basis for this notion of 'operational independence' is found in the well-established doctrine of 'constabulary independence'. The case most commonly referred to as establishing the model of constabulary independence is that of *Fisher v. Oldham Corporation* ([1930] 2 KB 364). Having been arrested in a case of mistaken identity, and then released after the charges had been dropped, Fisher sued the Oldham Corporation and the Watch Committee (the precursor of the modern police authority) for wrongful imprisonment. The judge ruled against Fisher arguing that there could be no 'master–servant' relationship between the corporation or Watch Committee and a police officer. The judge also referred to *Stanbury v. Exeter Corporation* ([1905] 2KB 838), where the ruling was that if an official is mandated to perform public and national functions, local government should not be made liable for his actions. Another argument used in the Fisher case was that, because police constables have authority conferred directly on them, they are not subject to the directions of control of their paymsters.[2] For current purposes it is sufficient to note that since this time the doctrine of constabulary independence became established and progressively entrenched. Even if we accept the legal basis for such constabulary independence – and Lustgarten (1986) shows this to be dubious – it is important to note that it concerns the independence of the individual constable. It would protect a constable from the direction and control of senior police officers, as much as it protects them from influences external to the police organisation. In particular, the notion of unfettered discretion of the individual constable is a very different concept from the 'operational independence' of chief constables.

As Lustgarten (1986) noted, prior to the 1920s there was no tradition that politicians could not direct chief police officers in matters of general policy. For example, borough forces were directed in some detail by their Watch Committees, and the Metropolitan Police received directions in policy from the Home Secretary. The case most central to the extension of discretion from that of the individual constable to that of the independence of the chief constable in 'operational matters' was *R v. Metropolitan Police Commissioner, ex parte* Blackburn[3] (a case in which the Metropolitan Police Commissioner's

---

2. For a more detailed assessment of the legal arguments in these cases, see Lustgarten (1986).
3. [1968] 1 All E.R. 763.

discretion in not enforcing certain gaming laws was challenged). In his judgement, the Master of the Rolls, Lord Denning, outlined what he took to be the chief constable's position:

> I hold it to be the duty of the Commissioner of Police, as it is of every chief constable, to enforce the law of the land. He must take steps to post his men so that crimes may be detected; and that honest citizens may go about their affairs in peace. He must decide whether or not suspected persons are to be prosecuted and, if need be, bring the prosecution or see that it is brought; but in all these things, he is not the servant of anyone, save of the law itself. No Minister of the Crown can tell him that he must or must not keep observation of this place or that; or that he must or must not prosecute this man or that one. Nor can any police authority tell him so. The responsibility for law enforcement lies on him. He is answerable to the law and to the law alone.

'Operational matters' have never been defined in statute, but in practice have been interpreted widely to include matters of general policy, rather than narrowly as decisions in particular cases. Even though Denning's judgement has come to be quoted in all legal discussions about police accountability, Lustgarten convincingly argues that it was filled with errors. In fact, the legal grounds for operational independence of chief constables have never been clear.[4] Geoffrey Marshall argued in favour of independent police chiefs on practical grounds, in so far as 'civil liberties and impartial justice are more to be expected from chief constables than from elected politicians' (Marshall, 1978: 61). Marshall accepted, however, that there was no legal principle that forbade police authorities from intervening in general prosecutions policy, and certainly no *legal* reason why they should not direct matters in general policy regarding law enforcement outside the area of prosecutions. Marshall's notion of operational independence did not preclude the requirement that chief constables explain policy to their police authorities. Rather, it meant that police authorities could not issue directions to their chiefs. Thus, in Marshall's terms, the mode of accountability was 'explanatory and cooperative' rather than 'subordinate and obedient'.

Discussions about operational independence and police accountability remained largely the preserve of the police themselves, and a few academics, until the late 1970s. However, after that time the bipartisan consensus, which had existed about policing, quickly broke down (Rawlings, 1991). The 1980s was a decade of polarisation, conflict and radical social change. The police service found itself embroiled in political and industrial conflict (Reiner, 1992). Arguments reached a peak in the early to mid-1980s, when Labour-

---

4. See also, for example, *R v. Oxford ex parte Levey* (1986) *Times*, 1 November; *R v. Chief Constable of Sussex ex parte International Traders' Ferry Ltd* [1995] 4All E.R. 364; [1997] 2All E.R. 65.

dominated police authorities in the metropolitan areas tried to assert their influence over policing policy, although chief constables successfully resisted this development. These conflicts continued during the miners' strike of 1984–5, when a number of police authorities challenged their forces' participation in the mutual aid arrangements set up to facilitate the anti-picket operation. In all of these disputes, the courts ruled in favour of the chief constable (Lloyd, 1985). Moreover, this time also saw the disappearance of the metropolitan councils, which were abolished in 1985 and their police authorities replaced with what, in the eyes of some commentators, were more compliant joint boards (Loveday, 1987).

Some writers have used these developments to argue that the 1964 Police Act, or certainly the subsequent legal interpretation of it, gave little substantive influence to police authorities in the tripartite structure for police governance. This lack of influence was related not only to the distribution of statutory powers, but also to the fact that many police authorities failed to use the powers that they did have – thus, the narrow way in which police authorities interpreted their own role significantly contributed to their lack of influence (see Regan, 1983; Morgan and Swift, 1987; Day and Klein, 1987; Audit Commission 1990a). Our research on the pre-1994 system of police governance also found that self-limitation was a significant factor, leading us to describe some authorities as 'architects of their own decline' (Jones et al., 1994). Our study suggested a further series of factors that limited police authority influence, including the cumbersome size and structure of many police authorities, the relative lack of information and expertise of the membership, and the scale at which police authorities operated. A further crucial influence was the approach of the chief constable. Some chief officers clearly viewed the police authority as playing an important role in *post hoc* democratic accountability, and sought to provide them with detailed information, and consulted them before taking major policy decisions. Other chief constables took a more bullish approach to their police authorities, and allowed them little real influence.

Reiner's (1991) research on chief constables found that most made efforts to establish close working relationships with their police authorities, and thus elected members had some influence in day-to-day matters. However, when 'push came to shove' and matters of real significance arose, Reiner argued that the chief constable's view would inevitably prevail. Thus, the police authority could have influence, but only so much as the chief constable (and the Home Office) would allow them to have.

Local consultation
An important amendment to the tripartite structure occurred with the development of local consultative mechanisms during the early 1980s. Following the Brixton riots in 1981, Lord Scarman's influential report criticised the insufficient formal liaison between the black community and the police in and around Brixton, and argued that the absence of such communication was both

a symptom and a cause of the 'withdrawal of consent' that underpinned the policing problems in the area (Morgan, 1992). His view was that police authorities could act more effectively if there were better arrangements for local consultation in areas considerably smaller than those covered by whole forces. He favoured the introduction of a statutory duty to make such arrangements at police divisional or subdivisional levels.

This recommendation was quickly followed by a Home Office Circular (54/1982) supporting such arrangements and a large number of police authorities, in the main supported by their chief constables, established such committees in their areas. Statutory provision for the making of arrangements 'in each police area for obtaining the views of the people in that area about matters concerning the policing of the area and for obtaining their cooperation with the police in preventing crime in the area' were introduced under s.106 of the Police and Criminal Evidence Act 1984 (PACE). As a consequence, police community consultative committees are often also referred to as s.106 committees (though with the passage of consolidating legislation it is now s.96 of the Police Act 1996 that provides the basis for such groups).

Morgan (1992) has argued that police community consultative groups (PCCGs) have, at least in the minds of officials, four major objectives. The first is as a forum in which consumers of police services may articulate and communicate to the providers of the service what it is they want. This is related to Scarman's view that effective policing can only be maintained if the police are aware of public concerns and priorities. The second aim is the perceived need to educate the public. This arises from the simple observation that, given that police resources are finite, they need to be rationed in some fashion. Consequently, one way of avoiding the widespread alienation that would follow from the police continually failing to meet public expectations, is to persuade the public, through education, to temper the demands they make on the police. The third function of PCCGs, he suggests, is to resolve conflict. Given that policing involves coercive powers and, indeed, that the communities being policed may impose conflicting demands on the police (Smith, 1987), it is necessary to have forums in which disputes can be resolved. Finally, he suggests, the hope was that PCCGs would form the basis for police-public cooperation for crime-preventive activities.

A growing body of work has examined how PCCGs operate in practice. The work of Morgan and colleagues (Morgan and Maggs, 1985; Morgan, 1986; Morgan, 1987; Morgan, 1992) in the mid-1980s found that public attendance at PCCG meetings was poor, that the agenda at meetings tended to be dominated by 'police business', that 'few PCCG members have ever had adversarial contact with the police nor are they the sort of people who normally meet people who have' (Morgan, 1992). Few members have any experience that might enable them to question effectively or challenge police viewpoints, and members tend to be overwhelmingly positive in their views of the police. Indeed, Morgan (1992) has recently argued that PCCGs have played a vital symbolic role in changing the face of local police–public politics. No longer, he suggests, is there significant conflict between chief constables and local representatives, for the latter, through their membership of PCCGs and through lay visiting, have largely been 'incorporated' into the police view of the everyday realities of policing. Thus, Morgan concludes, the unintended consequence of the introduction of PCCGs has been to undermine 'the case for radical constitutional reform', and not only this but 'it may have done so without fundamentally repairing the policing practices that gave rise to the calls for reform'. This would explain, he suggests, why so much effort is being devoted by the Home Office in encouraging PCCGs despite the absence of any evidence that they have achieved any of their primary objectives.

Accountability to the centre: the Home Office
As suggested above, the orthodox defence of the operational independence of chief constables was that the coercive powers of the state should be used impartially, and should be protected from partisan political control. During the turbulent years of the early and mid-1980s, it was radical Labour police authorities who were presented as the greatest threat to this independence. However, in all cases of conflict between chief constables and police authorities, the former prevailed. In recent years, the more potent threat to the operational independence of chief constables has often been seen as central, rather than local, government. During the miners' strike, there were suggestions that the Home Secretary was influencing the police anti-picket operations via the National Reporting Centre at New Scotland Yard, although this was strongly denied by the Home Office. Less dramatic, but arguably more salient, has been the gradual growth in central influences over a longer period. As Lustgarten (1986) observed, 'the key paradox is that, while the Home Office exercises enormous influence over policing, it does so without directly infringing the independence of chief constables, which it genuinely respects.' In some ways, this represents an even greater exercise of power than open compulsion, since the Home Office can exert major influence without generally having to resort to direct command.

A key part of the growing influence of the Home Office is exercised via Home Office circulars. These are officially advisory, but since the late 1970s have grown in number and become more policy-specific. Our previous research found Home Office circulars to have been vital influences for change in all the main policy areas studied (Jones et al., 1994). One of the reasons for this is that the Home Office consults widely before issuing a circular, and in many cases the police staff associations and local authority associations were given an opportunity to comment in detail on drafts. In some cases, the Association of Chief Police Officers (ACPO) was such an important influence over the content that we described them as 'joint authors' of the circular. Thus, it was hardly surprising that chief officers tended to follow the advice laid out in the circulars. A further aspect of centralisation has been the role of Her Majesty's

Inspectorate of Constabulary. The inspection process has been made more systematic, with HMIs often further encouraging forces to follow Home Office circular advice. In addition, the annual inspection reports are now published. The Home Office has also increased its influence over the training of senior police officers, who are now far more likely to share a common perspective.

Of course, if the Home Office did have to resort to direct command, the 1964 Police Act provided it with clear and significant powers to do so. For example, the Home Secretary could require a chief constable to resign in the interests of efficiency, could call for reports into any aspect of policing an area, set up a local enquiry into a policing matter, and had the power of approval over many police authority appointments. Most significant of all, the Home Office exercised detailed controls over the staffing and funding of the police, which provided the main lever of influence in encouraging value-for-money measures from the mid-1980s onwards.

Under the pre-1994 arrangements, the Home Office paid 51 per cent of the police budgets for each force, and the police authority paid 49 per cent. However, the central government share has in practice been much higher, given the high proportion of local government expenditure funded by the revenue support grant (RSG) paid to local authorities by the Department of the Environment. Thus, although the Home Office has contributed 51 per cent of local policing budgets, when the RSG is included the total central government contribution has, in recent years, amounted to over 76 per cent. Given the fact that the business rate also raises local money, this leaves only about 10 per cent of policing paid for by council tax contributions. As will be discussed in the following chapter, this was a key pressure for greater central government controls over police expenditure, and effectiveness and efficiency. Local expenditure on the police has not historically been subject to cash limits. Once the local police authority had set the police budget, the Home Office was therefore obliged to pay its share, and the contribution by the Department of the Environment was determined by a complex formula, which took account (among many other things) of the number of police officers, but not of the number of civilians, within the local police service.

Clearly, the Home Office could in theory refuse to pay its share of the police budget where a certificate of efficiency is refused by HMIC. This has proved to be rather an empty threat, because until comparatively recently, all forces have been certified as efficient. Although in 1992 and again in 1993, HMIC refused to certify Derbyshire police force as efficient, in practice the police grant continued to be paid. The only effective kinds of financial control available to the Home Office before 1994 were therefore via the use of its power to approve police officer establishment, control of police pay by means of nationally negotiated agreements, and central controls over capital expenditure. Police authorities could not increase the police officer establishment without Home Office approval, and therefore they could not increase the number of police officers employed once the establishment had been reached.

There was no parallel control by the Home Office of the numbers of civilians employed within the police service. Consequently, the Home Office had to use bargaining over police establishment as a means of increasing the number of posts filled by civilians.

Centralisation and the Police and Magistrates' Courts Act
One of the key issues in the background to the PMCA was centralisation and the potential for its further extension. In summary, we have outlined four strands in the brief history of police governance that bear on this issue.

- First, the idea of 'constabulary independence' and its variant, 'operational independence', have become progressively entrenched and, in some ways, broadened, with the result that local police authorities have been gradually stripped of many of the limited powers that remained with them.
- Second, in the 1980s the national police operation mounted in response to the miners' strike, together with the conflictual relationships between police authorities and chief constables in some metropolitan areas, resulted in a further transfer of power to the centre. This was most visibly illustrated by the Local Government Act (1985), which killed off the metropolitan police authorities and replaced them with joint boards that were less likely to take issue with their chief constables.
- Third, so unwilling have local police authorities been to use the powers they have available to them that rarely have they been more than uncomplaining bystanders as they have been asset-stripped by a Home Office hungry for ever-greater control.
- Finally, as increasing emphasis has been placed on efficiency (as we shall see below) so the fact that controlling police budgets has largely taken place at the centre has also served to undermine the role of the local police authority. It is this issue we turn to now.

EFFICIENCY, EFFECTIVENESS AND NEW PUBLIC MANAGEMENT

In the second half of 1993 three separate reviews of policing were published; the Royal Commission on Criminal Justice (RCCJ, 1993), the Sheehy Inquiry into Police Responsibilities and Rewards (Inquiry into Police Responsibilities and Rewards, 1993), and the Home Secretary's White Paper on Police Reform (Home Office, 1993). Each recommended fairly radical change in the structure and functioning of policing. In addition, late 1993 saw the setting up of yet another official enquiry into policing. The Home Office *Core and Ancillary Tasks Review* was to look at the cost-effectiveness of various tasks undertaken by the police service, and examine opportunities for hiving off ancillary tasks. The police service interpreted this review as the precursor to a radical programme of privatisation and contracting out, although, in the event, the final recommendations were largely pragmatic and uncontentious (see Morgan and Newburn, 1997).

Arguably, these reviews and enquiries were part of a wider process of official concern about the effectiveness of the police, which has its roots in the early 1980s. In 1983, the Home Office issued circular 114/83, entitled *Manpower, Effectiveness and Efficiency in the Police Service*. This signalled the extension of the government's financial management initiative, which sought to promote value-for-money across a range of government departments and public services, to the police. The circular outlined potential new management strategies for the police – now generally referred to as 'Policing by Objectives' (PBO) – many of which had influential supporters within the police. Kenneth Newman, for example, had introduced very similar initiatives into the Metropolitan Police before the circular was published. Nevertheless, both ACPO and the Police Federation were, on occasion, very hostile to the new emphasis on 'value for money'. The core issue in this conflict has been summed up by Rawlings (1991: 46) as the then government's view that while:

> PBO will lead to a more efficient and effective use of resources and, almost as a by-product, will tend to hold down the numbers of police officers and so reduce costs, police organisations regard its primary objective as being the cutting of expenditure through a reduction in the number of police officers without any real concern about the effect this may have on policing.

One of the instructions in Home Office Circular 114/83 directed at chief constables and police authorities suggested that clear priorities and objectives for forces should be established and that these should reflect the needs and wishes of the public. Forces were then asked to put in place systems that would enable assessment of whether objectives had been achieved. A subsequent circular made increases in force establishments conditional on their ability to demonstrate 'where possible [by] quantified output and performance measures, that objectives were being met' (Home Office, 1995). The outcome of this in most cases was the issuing of mission statements by most forces, followed by the establishment of management systems designed to link the mission statement to specific local objectives 'aimed at generating purposeful, planned activity by junior operational officers and at measuring the results of that activity' (Weatheritt, 1993). These management systems were almost all some form of variant of 'policing by objectives' (PBO), itself derived from Drucker's theory of 'management by objectives'.

During the 1980s the Home Office issued a series of circulars (105 and 106/88, and 81/89), which further tightened the financial management of the police service. The process began by tying bids for establishment increases to demonstrations that existing resources were being used effectively. With a growing emphasis on performance review, and efficiency and value for money in evaluating and assessing police work, an increasingly important institution, and one that stands outside the 'tripartite structure', is the Audit Commission. Weatheritt (1993) has argued that 'the future form and content and, indeed, precise purposes of inspection have been made more relevant and pressing by the entry of the Audit Commission onto the policing scene.' Created by the Local Government Act 1982 to monitor and promote economy, efficiency and effectiveness in the management of local government, it has subjected a number of aspects of police performance to rigorous scrutiny. From the mid-1980s onwards, the Audit Commission began to publish a series of papers which applied private sector business management principles to policing. From the early 1990s, largely as a result of increasing Audit Commission influence, value-for-money (VFM) principles have increasingly been applied to the police. The basic aim has been to encourage the police to link resources to outputs, to measure performance more effectively, and to consider what its core functions, and therefore central organisational objectives, are. The central pressures for all this activity is clearly a concern with effective use of resources (see Audit Commission, 1989, 1990a, 1990b, 1990c, 1991a, 1991b, 1991c, 1992, 1993, 1994, 1996). In general, the Audit Commission's approach has been to recommend the delayering or flattening of police organisational structures, together with the devolvement of responsibility and financial delegation. What has become known as local financial management has been increasingly pressed by the Audit Commission, though it has not been without its critics (Chatterton et al., 1996). Much of this change parallels the broader introduction of 'new public management' principles by the Thatcher and Major administrations in the 1980s and 1990s (Dunleavy and Hood, 1994). While Audit Commission reports have been highly influential in general terms over police management, their recommendations have also been incorporated into the 'Audit Guides' used by the District Audit Service (DAS) when they audit individual police forces, which provides a more direct lever of influence at the local level.

In the early 1980s, the Thatcher government embarked on a radical programme of social change, which led to considerable opposition and conflict. Public services faced both privatisation and rationalisation, and the growth of public expenditure was drastically cut back. However, the Conservatives kept their 1979 manifesto promise to 'spend more on fighting crime while we economise elsewhere'.[5] Thus, the police service largely escaped the immediate cuts in public expenditure and restructuring, which were applied to most other public services. Indeed, expenditure on the police expanded rapidly in real terms, largely as a result of increases in police staffing and improvements in pay. However, as crime rates continued to rise throughout the 1980s, concerns grew within government about the returns they were getting for their investment (see the discussion in Morgan and Newburn, 1997, Chapter 2). It is this that underpins much of the recent debate about the central functions of the police.

There remains considerable confusion about the proper role and function of the police, in public opinion as well as in official documents (see discussion in

---

5. Conservative Party Manifesto, 1979 (p. 19).

Independent Committee of Inquiry Report into the Role and Responsibilities of the Police, 1996). The models of policing outlined in both the White Paper and the Review of Core and Ancillary Tasks (Home Office, 1995) depart from much previous thinking on this matter. The White Paper on Police Reform, for example, takes the very narrow view that 'fighting crime should be the priority for police officers ... a priority that local communities should share.' This was widely criticised, especially in the context of increased pressures on police managers to work to specific performance indicators. Since 1995, the Audit Commission has published annual comparisons between police forces on standard performance indicators. Although it was stressed that these should not be seen as 'league tables', it was feared that such developments would encourage police managers to chase statistical targets that reflected the Home Secretary's narrow 'crime-fighting' conception of policing. In fact, the Audit Commission indicators measure policing across a broad range, and do not appear to be overly skewed towards narrow detection type indicators, although the inherent difficulty in measuring prevention activity remains a problem. Perhaps the greater concern about overly-narrowing the role of the police was raised with regard to the Home Secretary's national objectives published in the wake of the PMCA.

As we describe in the following chapter, the Sheehy Inquiry proved to be the most controversial of all the above-mentioned reviews of policing, and was the target of substantial hostility from the police service itself. The Report of the Inquiry, published in July 1993, led to a chorus of criticism from the police staff associations, although they varied in their opposition to different proposals. The most controversial proposals included:

- the introduction of ten-year fixed-term contracts for new police recruits;
- the introduction of performance-related pay (PRP) with up to 30 per cent of salaries of ACPO-level officers linked to performance-related bonuses;
- the reduction of starting pay and linking pay to median non-manual private sector earnings;
- the ending of many forms of overtime payment;
- the freezing of housing allowances for currently serving officers and the abolition of such allowances for new recruits; and
- the raising of the retirement age from 55 to 60, with the qualifying period for full pensions raised from 30 to 40 years.

In the face of strong opposition from the police service, a much watered-down version of the Sheehy proposals was finally introduced, the details of which are explored in the next chapter.

In addition to the increasing imposition of private sector principles of management and finance to the police service, recent years have seen growing speculation about the possibility of the privatisation of some aspects of the police service. Moreover, some authors have highlighted the growth of a 'privatisation mentality' within the police service (Johnston, 1996). The growth of the private security industry (Jones and Newburn, forthcoming) and the proliferation of 'providers' of policing services on the ground has added to the concerns about the market for policing. Thus, although concerns about governance of police have tended to focus on the central direction of policing and, more particularly, on national policing objectives, it is perfectly possible that there may be equally important tensions between force-wide objectives and the priorities identified by local command units at the sub-force level.

After centralisation, the second and related general trend that can be identified in relation to the governance of police, therefore, is the move away from 'political' accountability (though we should never lose sight of the historical limits of political accountability) towards 'financial' and 'managerial' accountability. The most significant way in which the Home Office has gained control is through imposing a quasi-private sector management model on to the police. The trend towards management or financial accountability, in which performance is judged against targets often set centrally rather than locally, and which are evaluated by the centre (HMIC), is one that allows the doctrine of constabulary independence to remain apparently unchanged while imposing a large variety of very particular constraints on the degree to which that independence is likely to be utilised. As Reiner (1993b) has observed, chief constables in exercising their powers according to their professional judgement in individual cases, 'will be acutely aware, however, that their performance must reach the specified targets'. This issue was again central to debates around the PMCA.

DEMOCRACY AND POLICING POLICY

In introducing the Police Bill to the House of Commons in 1963, the then Home Secretary said that 'one of the lessons of modern times is that a police system, instituted to defend freedom and maintain law and order, must itself be under effective control.' For most of the history of 'modern' policing, it has been assumed that a significant element of this 'effective control' should be organised 'democratically'. The Metropolitan Police has always been answerable to parliament via the Home Secretary (though this has often been argued to be insufficiently 'democratic'), and from 1888 to 1994 two-thirds of the membership of all provincial police authorities in England and Wales was locally elected. The idea of 'democracy', therefore, has long been central to questions of governance of police. This was perhaps best illustrated, as we will show in Chapter 2, in the debates over the 1993 White Paper on Police Reform and the subsequent Police and Magistrates' Courts Bill in which several commentators suggested that the proposed reforms constituted an attack on local democracy. Our third broad aim in this book is to explore the realities behind such charges. To do so, however, we have to be much clearer than most commentators are as to what we mean by the term 'democracy' and how it is to be applied to policing.

In our recent research we examined in detail the relationship between external influences and changes in the pattern of policing, including studies of the making of policing policy in England (Jones et al., 1994), in France (Horton, 1995) and the Netherlands (Jones, 1995). The research aimed to examine how and why policing *policy* changes, what the major influences over such changes are, and what this implies for the relationship between policing and democratic institutions. The focus was upon the intermediate level of policing policy rather than restricting attention to written policy statements on the one hand, or the details of 'ground-level' policing on the other.

The first study in this series (Jones et al., 1994) focused on the making of policing policy in England. It described and analysed how the bodies involved in making policing policy – which in England included police forces, the Home Office/Home Secretary, Her Majesty's Inspectorate of Constabulary, police authorities, pressure and community groups, political parties, and the media – interact to bring about changes in the style, organisation or operation of policing on the ground. The study focused on three specific areas of policy in which there had been important developments over recent years: the development of crime prevention, new policing responses to crimes against women and children, and civilianisation in the police service. The research found that important developments had occurred in all three areas of policing policy, and located these changes within a framework provided by an analysis of the notion of democracy in political theory.

Democratic theorists may broadly be divided between those who define 'democracy' in normative terms, and those who see the term as denoting a particular set of political institutions. This latter conceptualisation was particularly important in theories of democracy developed by North American political scientists after the last war. They observed that the US political system had little in common with the polity envisaged in 'classical' democratic theory, and defined democracy in terms of a particular set of political institutions that afforded only limited participation of the majority of citizens. One noted supporter of the latter approach, Joseph Schumpeter, defined democracy as 'that institutional arrangement for arriving at political decisions in which individuals acquire the power to decide by means of a competitive struggle for the peoples' vote' (Schumpeter, 1961: 269).

However, further analysis of the concept led us to the conclusion that 'democracy' denoted more than a specific set of political institutions, and that 'discussions about democracy are ultimately concerned with values' (Jones et al., 1994: 43). Although discussions of police accountability are crucially about the application of democratic values to policing policy, the meaning of democracy is rarely made explicit, often being uncritically equated with control by local elected bodies. However, we have argued that the concept of democracy is essentially normative. Therefore, rather than focus on describing particular institutions, we argued that a more helpful approach to examining the meaning of democracy would be to analyse the range of values

underpinning those institutions and processes. To do so, the following set of
criteria were distilled in relation to policing:

- *Equity.* In so far as the police are delivering services, these should be
  distributed fairly between groups and individuals. In so far as the police are
  enforcing the law in their adversarial role, the pattern of enforcement
  should be fair.
- *Delivery of service.* The police should deliver the appropriate services (as
  determined on other criteria) effectively and efficiently.
- *Responsiveness.* In determining the order of priorities, the allocation of
  resources between different activities and objectives, and the choice of
  policing methods, the police should be responsive to the views of representative bodies.
- *Distribution of power.* Power to determine policing policy should not be
  concentrated but distributed between a number of different bodies.
- *Information* should be regularly published on funding, expenditure, activity, and outputs. Representative bodies should be able to engage in a continuing dialogue with the professional managers of the police force so as to
  become better informed and to elicit relevant information through a
  sequence of interactions.
- *Redress.* It should be possible for a representative body to dismiss an
  incompetent or corrupt chief officer, or one who exceeds his or her powers.
  There should be means of redress for unlawful or unreasonable treatment
  by individual officers. Redress may also involve the possibility of achieving a reversal of policy where such a policy is deemed to be ineffective or
  unfair.
- *Participation.* As far as possible, citizens should participate in discussion
  of policing policy with police managers.

Although participation is the element most commonly stressed in popular discussions of democracy, we suggested that the possibilities of widespread participation in the making of policing policy were limited and that, in practice,
other democratic values were of more importance in the field of policing.
Nevertheless, the image of 'participatory democracy' (Pateman, 1985;
Poulantzas, 1980) is still an enduring one in popular rhetoric, as the debate
surrounding the passage of the Police and Magistrates' Courts Bill recently
illustrated (see Chapter 2).

The overall conclusion in our previous work was that developments in
British policing policy could be seen as the outcome of 'democratic' processes, but that some elements of democracy were clearly more important than
others. For example, the principles of equity, of improved service delivery,
and the provision of information were relatively important. In addition, despite
the Home Office clearly being the most influential player, power was perhaps
more dispersed in the system than some commentators have suggested. How-

ever, the formal democratic institutions that are supposed to frame policing – police authorities, consultative committees, parliament – appear to have played a limited role in the development of policy. This suggested that the principles of participation and responsiveness, with which these institutions are associated, were much less important in bringing about change. This does not mean that developments in policy were necessarily 'undemocratic', but rather suggests that democracy is not only or primarily about governmental institutions, but more generally about the openness of a society and its capacity to respond flexibly to new demands and pressures. However, the findings also suggested that the role of the formal 'democratic' institutions that are supposed to frame policing policy is one that could, and arguably should, be enhanced.

Different models of reform give different weights to different elements of democracy. The dominant model behind recent government reform of the police (and other public services) is one that emphasises effective service delivery, information (defined in market terms – performance outputs and so on) and defines participation in terms of consumers' purchasing services. It places less emphasis on responsiveness to elected bodies, and direct participation in policy-making. Policing is presented as a politically-neutral technical exercise – its outputs can be measured and thus its performance judged. This has led to the emphasising of objectives, performance indicators, efficiency, customer service and public satisfaction surveys over the more traditional institutional forms of accountability.

As we shall show, the 1994 reform of police governance represents a new departure in local *democratic* input into public service provision. Although the operation of non-elected 'quangos' in other areas of public service provision has been widely criticised (Association of Metropolitan Authorities, 1994), the new, somewhat hybrid, police authorities represent something of a compromise between a government keen on 'quangoisation', and a range of bodies defending (for differing reasons) local electoral representation. Reiner (1993a) has argued that recent developments in police governance represent a shift in emphasis away from formal 'political' modes of accountability towards what he calls a 'calculative and contractual' mode. This is visible in the application of business management techniques to the police service, decentralisation, financial devolution, performance measurement and the use of public attitude surveys. Our final concern in this study, therefore, is to explore the extent to which the changes brought about by the PMCA may realistically be characterised in this manner, and to assess the extent to which contractual modes of accountability have either supplanted or enhanced more traditional institutional or political forms of accountability. In doing this, we use the 'democratic criteria' developed in our previous work as a means of assessing the changes that have been taking place in the governance of police.

Chapter 2

The Police and Magistrates' Courts Act

'I am inclined to the view that we are witnessing a move, perhaps unintended, for national control of the police by central government.'

Sir John Smith, President of ACPO, speech to local authority associations' conference, 4 February 1994

'This is not the centralisation of policing, as is often suggested. It is precisely the reverse. ... It is enabling policing to be done locally, to be the responsibility of local people, and for policing to be accountable to local people.'

Lord Mackay, introducing the Police and Magistrates' Courts Bill, House of Lords, 18 January 1994

In this chapter, we consider the background to the Police and Magistrates' Courts Act 1994 (PMCA), using material from interviews with politicians, civil servants and other professionals, as well as official and media reports of the events that took place. Providing a more detailed history of the background to the Act is necessary for two reasons. First, as the two quotations above illustrate, there are significant areas of difference in the ways in which the nature and impact of the legislation are perceived and presented. Second, such a history should allow a more refined understanding of the thinking behind these reforms and of the essential compromise which the final legislation represented in practice. We begin by looking at the Sheehy Inquiry into Police Responsibilities and Rewards and end with a consideration of the detail of the PMCA, together with an account of some of the speculation about the likely effects of the amended Act.

BACKGROUND TO THE REFORMS

The campaign against Sheehy

We begin with the Sheehy Inquiry because it was first and foremost in stimulating controversy in the early 1990s about future government policy toward the police and, indeed, about the future of the police. As outlined in the previous chapter, it was the Sheehy Inquiry rather than the White Paper on Police Reform that appeared to cause the most concern in the police service itself, and that set in motion a campaign of opposition. This campaign simply gained momentum when the White Paper and the Police and Magistrates' Courts Bill emerged, uniting a broader coalition of interests.

The Inquiry, chaired by Sir Patrick Sheehy, the chairman of BAT industries,

16

was announced at the Police Federation conference in May 1992. Its terms of reference were 'to examine the rank structure, remuneration, and conditions of the police service in England and Wales, in Scotland and in Northern Ireland, and to recommend what changes, if any, would be sensible.' It reported on 1 July 1993 (Inquiry into Police Responsibilities and Rewards, 1993) two days after the publication of the White Paper. It made 272 recommendations in all, designed, it was suggested, to 'reward good performance and penalise bad'. These included:

- hiring new recruits to the police on ten-year fixed-term contracts, which would be considered for renewal subsequently every five years;
- abolishing the ranks of deputy chief constable, chief superintendent and chief inspector;
- introducing a severance programme to enable the termination of the contracts of up to 5000 middle-ranking and senior officers;
- introducing performance-related pay, with up to 30 per cent of the salaries of chief constables and their assistants being linked to performance-related bonuses; reducing starting pay and linking pay rates to non-manual private sector earnings; and
- ending many forms of overtime payment and the freezing of housing allowances.

Initial reactions to the Sheehy Inquiry Report were varied. The Police Federation reacted negatively, arguing that the recommendations would remove the vocational aspect of the work, turning it into a 'job like any other job' ('Police threaten "open conflict"', *Financial Times*, 1 July 1993). The Superintendents' Association echoed this sentiment, suggesting that recruitment, retention and motivation would all be hit by the proposals, though there was cautious approval from some quarters – ACPO for example – for the financial and structural reorganisation heralded by the Report. *The Times*, in its editorial under the headline 'Fat Blue Line', argued that 'the police were the least affected by Mrs Thatcher's radical re-examination of the state. Sir Patrick Sheehy's report, coupled with Tuesday's White Paper on police reorganisation constitute an overdue blueprint for change' (1 July 1993). That there would inevitably be conflict was anticipated by one of the Inquiry team, Eric Caines, who was quoted as saying that the public sector was 'notorious' in its attitude to change, and that there were many hurdles to be overcome before the Inquiry's recommendations could be implemented.

Though ACPO had been fairly cautious when the Inquiry first reported, its criticism of the report gathered steam in the coming weeks. The then president of the association, John Burrow, said that the report would damage the morale and ethos of the service, and the commissioner of the Metropolitan Police said that his own position might become untenable if the Inquiry's recommendations were acted upon (he was joined in this by the head of the Royal Ulster

Constabulary (RUC), Hugh Annersley, and the chief constable of Derbyshire, John Newing). In its formal response to the Inquiry's recommendations, ACPO supported fixed-term contracts for senior officers, but rejected the idea that they were appropriate for the majority of officers. It opposed the proposal to link lower ranking officers' pay to performance and was also critical of the proposals for increasing the retirement age and changing the rules over pensions, and those to reduce the number of ranks in the service. The biggest show of anti-Sheehy sentiment, however, came on 20 July at Wembley conference centre when nearly 17,000 officers gathered at a rally organised to protest at the Inquiry's proposals.

As the protests gathered momentum, including, the *Daily Telegraph* (23 August 1993) implied, protest from civil servants in the Home Office, there were suggestions from the Home Office that the new Home Secretary, Michael Howard, might not implement all the recommendations. As Duncan Campbell put it in the *Guardian* (21 August 1993), 'Howard has obviously decided to play Detective Sergeant Nice to Clarke's Detective Constable Nasty. ... He has let it be known that he is a "listening" Home Secretary. There have been well-publicised trips to police stations to show him doing just that and he has been anxious to reassure the police that he will consult them all before anything is done.' By the end of August, 'close colleagues' of the Home Secretary were being quoted as saying that he would not be implementing proposals for fixed-term contracts and performance-related pay ('Police reforms to be abandoned', *Independent*, 27 August 1993).

The following month, ACPO presented its official response to Sheehy. It sought to lower the temperature of the debate, which in recent weeks had become increasingly acrimonious, and distance itself from the Police Federation. John Burrow said, 'At no point did we reject the report out of hand like the Federation did. We are not at one with the Federation' ('Chiefs differ with ranks on Sheehy', *Guardian*, 21 September 1993). Given that ACPO's critical stance on Sheehy initially had done much to lend credence to the oppositional stance taken by the Police Federation, this was an interesting development and signalled a new phase in the debate over the future structure and organisation of the service. In its response to Sheehy, ACPO accepted the need for performance-related pay, though it rejected the scheme Sheehy put forward and rejected the idea of disposing of the ranks of chief inspector and chief superintendent.

Both the Home Secretary and senior police officers, then, had signalled their willingness to compromise over elements of Sheehy. At the end of October 1993, the Home Secretary made his position clear. Fixed-term contracts and performance-related pay were not to be introduced for lower ranking officers, the particular matrix suggested by Sheehy for determining performance-related pay was rejected, as was the proposal to reduce starting salaries. A working party was set up to consider appraisal-related pay for senior officers, although this idea was later also to be dropped. The proposal to reduce the number of ranks by three was accepted, as was the linking of pay to non-manual private sector pay settlements, though how levels of pay were to be determined was left unclear. Predictably, the scaled-down version of Sheehy announced by the Home Secretary was greeted relatively favourably by police spokespersons, though John Smith, the new president of ACPO, said that 'there were lots of arguments yet to come. The surface has only just been scratched' ('Small print disconcerts police', *Guardian*, 30 October 1993).

What really concerned most commentators, however, was the juxtaposition of some of the Sheehy-inspired proposals and those contained in the White Paper on Police Reform. As Vernon Bogdanor put it ('It's an unfair cop, minister', *Guardian*, 1 November 1993):

> taken in conjunction with the proposals for police reform in the June White Paper, the new arrangements [for fixed-term contracts and performance-related pay for senior officers] portend a national police force without the checks and balances needed to ensure the freedom of the chief constable from political interference. ... Will a chief constable whose contract comes up for renewal within, say, 18 months, be in a strong position to resist the advice of his chairman?

The White Paper on Police Reform

By the early 1990s, a largely 'service-based, consumerist' view of policing had come to dominate discourse among senior police managers' (Reiner, 1992). However, this process of internal reorganisation and re-presentation was never likely to prove sufficiently radical for a Home Secretary such as Kenneth Clarke. As early as June 1992, Clarke had indicated that he hoped to bring the principles that guided his reforms in health and education to bear on the police service. The *Independent* (21 September 1992), reporting on the Superintendents' Association conference, suggested that, although Clarke 'was committed to local involvement in policing, he was not convinced that the current system of police authorities was entirely the best method'.

The thinking became clearer in January 1993 when the Home Office leaked plans for what the papers referred to as 'a radical reorganisation of the police' (*Financial Times*, 8 January 1993). These, it was suggested, would result in a virtual nationalisation of police authorities in England and Wales, with government appointees replacing councillors as the majority on the committees, and police funding coming direct from central government. The leaked ideas sparked immediate controversy. ACPO announced that it would be holding an emergency conference to consider the proposals and, with a twist of irony given what was to happen later, it was reported that Cabinet had been unable to agree the proposal in December 1992 because of opposition from the then Environment Minister, Michael Howard. Indeed, the *Local Government Chronicle* (8 January 1993) quoted Mr Howard as saying, 'elected members do a much more diligent job than any appointed members could do.' The

Prime Minister, it was reported, had to step in to chair the Cabinet sub-committee considering the proposals in order to calm the row between Clarke and Howard. In interview, however, Clarke strongly denied that he wished to bring the police under greater control from the centre:

> I have taken a pretty consistent approach to the public services I was made responsible for. Contrary to popular belief I'm not a centraliser; I strongly believe in delegating responsibility out of Whitehall Departments which I actually regard as quite incapable of running a nationwide service from the centre, and I would not wish or try to do so. But you do need to have at the local level people charged with the responsibility, knowing what standards of performance they are meant to be delivering and properly accountable to someone who can hold them to account for whether or not they are delivering it. So in very broad brush terms that is what led me to start advocating changes to the police authorities which got put into effect.

Having hurriedly met to consider the proposals, ACPO held a press conference at which they criticised both the Home Secretary's apparent lack of desire to consult about the changes, and the speed with which they were moved, despite the possibility of other far-reaching proposals emanating from the Royal Commission and the Sheehy Inquiry. The president of ACPO, John Burrow, said that the 'plans have been drawn up in the corridors of Queen Anne's Gate [the Home Office]. We have not been involved. . . . We are not opposed to certain changes, but we are concerned about the extent and timing' (*Guardian*, 12 January 1993).

The following day, the papers suggested that both the Foreign Secretary, Douglas Hurd, and the public service minister, William Waldegrave, opposed the plans to dilute local control, though there was no opposition to reducing the number of forces from 43 to, perhaps, 25. At this stage, however, all was just speculation; there had still been no official announcement about government proposals for the police. As *The Economist* summarised the situation: 'Mr Clarke is spoiling for a fight. The chief constables, happy to provide one, have jumped on him in the hope of preventing the crime before it is committed. But Mr Clarke is a dangerous man, with a record as long as your arm' (23 January 1993).

Speculation continued throughout February and into March, though increasingly it was suggested that the intervention of the Prime Minister, with the thrashing out of some compromises in Cabinet, had reduced Michael Howard's opposition to Kenneth Clarke's plans. The same could not be said for the police, who particularly resented what they perceived to be a reluctance to discuss the proposals in advance of their public announcement. In a letter to the *Guardian* (13 March 1993), signed by the presidents of ACPO and the Superintendents' Association and the chairman of the Police Federation, they said:

> We find it astonishing that despite a series of well-informed leaks to the media, the Home Secretary has not asked the police staff associations for their views.

Mr Clarke has said that when he is ready to put forward his proposals there will be a period of consultation. It is now obvious that this will be a curtailed procedure and by then it will be too late to make any significant difference. What we find inexplicable is the current refusal to listen to our views before considering options and formulating proposals that will inevitably lead to a new Police Act.

Clarke, of course, was by this time well-known for having strongly-held views and for driving them through, often in the face of entrenched opposition. As far as consultation on possible changes to the police service were concerned, a senior official in the Police Department of the Home Office at the time reported that the Home Secretary was reluctant to have detailed discussions about change with a range of interested parties, prior to deciding the broad direction of reform, because 'it lets the rats get at everything'. Or, as Clarke put it himself:

My experience of consultation was you got completely bogged down for six months whilst absolutely everybody came together to resist any change whatever, which is the usual result of a process of consultation in this country. I think it was true of health actually. Once you have made the changes it's amazing how people can't remember even that they wanted it to stay as it was.

The long-awaited announcement eventually came on 23 March in the House of Commons. Clarke argued (*Hansard*, 23 March 1993, col.765) that so significant had been the changing demands made on the police in the 30 years since the 1964 Act that reforms were now necessary to improve the service. Enabling, he said, the police service to give of its best meant:

giving police authorities and police forces greater freedom to decide for themselves how best to spend their money; creating more powerful and businesslike police authorities which will give more leadership to the local police service and ensure that money is spent more effectively; creating a new police authority for the Metropolitan Police in line with the new national pattern, thereby strengthening local accountability in the capital. It also means setting key national objectives for police activity; complementing local objectives agreed by the police authority; measuring performance against these objectives and publishing the results so that the public know what their force has delivered and how well their police force is doing compared to others; reforming the funding arrangements to get the best out of the money spent on policing; and simplifying the procedures for forces to be amalgamated when the time is right.

In fleshing out his proposals, he suggested that in future police authorities should comprise half local councillors and half an amalgam of magistrates and local people nominated by the Home Secretary. Moreover, the chairman of the authority would be nominated by the Home Secretary from among the authority's membership. Not only were there to be national policing objectives, but local police authorities would be expected to set local objectives as well. According to Clarke, his reasons for proposing reform of local police authorities were as follows:

> I started from the point that in my opinion most of the existing police authorities were ineffective. That's unfair to a few good ones, but the majority struck me as wholly ritual organisations, exercising no effective control over the service at all and taking very few real decisions. Their relationship with local government allegedly gave democratic accountability, but in practice I think that was mythical. I don't think the average member of the public knew who the Chairman of the local police authority was and the average member of the police authority did not regard himself or herself as being accountable to the public for any of the things they did. Local authority members did not fight to get on to the police authority, so you were lucky if you had a good smattering of high quality councillors on the police authority, and on the poorest you had the risk of getting some real duffers who couldn't be put on anything else. ... One interesting thing in formulating my views was to ask members of police authorities what they thought the police authority was for and what they did, and you could find among the magistrates as well as the local government members a rather distressing absence of clear replies to that. ... In some places because of the local government connection it got drawn in the local party-political battle and to that extent everyone just wasted their time issuing party-political statements about comparatively parish pump issues locally and what you didn't find – like the old health authorities before I reformed them – was authorities which spent their time discussing issues that really mattered to the chief constable and the people responsible for delivering the service in the locality. Some chief constables were only too happy that it should be like that. And then you had all the muddled accountability for the money and the finance.

Under Clarke's proposals, the joint funding arrangement for policing was to remain largely unchanged, though police authorities would become freestanding precepting bodies and expenditure on the police would be cash-limited. Interviews with senior Home Office officials revealed that a number of options for reforming the funding system for the police had been considered. These all involved the complex process of understanding and combining elements of two very different funding systems of the Home Office and Department of the Environment respectively. In this sense, the funding of the police service has always reflected the peculiar complexities of a quasi-national, locally administered public service. Reformers were basically faced with three options. First, to fund the police service in a straightforward local government funding manner, via the revenue support grant (RSG) and council tax. However, this was not possible given that the police authorities were to become independent precepting bodies. The second option was to make the police entirely funded by central government, and locally administered, similar to the funding system for the National Health Service. This had the benefit of simplicity, especially since about 90 per cent of police funding comes from central government in some form or another. However, with all the furore about a national police force this was not considered to be a politically-viable option. The third option, and the one eventually chosen, was to continue with the 'hybrid' form of funding, but with cash-limited police grant for the 51 per cent accounted for by the Home Office. The remaining 49 per cent could then be made up of RSG, council tax and business rates.

Although threats of a direct 'nationalisation' of the system of police funding receded, there remained real fears that the reforms would provide the Home Office with the necessary powers to 'regionalise' force structure, via amalgamations. Indeed, Kenneth Clarke suggested that there may no longer be a need to maintain 43 separate police forces, but demurred from suggesting how many were necessary or when any amalgamations might take place. The proposals, he said, would be further developed in the coming months when a White Paper would be published. Simon Jenkins, *The Times* columnist, was particularly outspoken on this subject, however, arguing that 'Clarke was shameless in his contempt for local government of any sort. He left no chief constable in any doubt that he wanted a nationalized police force. He set about trying to create one' (Jenkins, 1995: 101). As we have seen, Clarke himself strongly denied that his underlying aim was to introduce a national police force, and discussions with senior Home Office officials supported this. For example, officials accepted that the introduction of a national police force had been considered during the late 1980s, but that Kenneth Clarke dropped it from his reforming agenda at quite an early stage. Indeed, it was reported that officials could find no strong evidence that larger forces were necessarily more efficient or effective than smaller ones.

There was a mixed response to the House of Commons announcement. The police appeared relieved that there were no immediate plans to amalgamate forces, and there was broad support for the proposal to give police authorities greater budgetary control. However, the police, the local authority associations and opposition politicians criticised the proposed changes to the membership and chairmanship of police authorities. John Burrow, the president of ACPO, described the Home Office appointment of the authority chairman as 'a dangerous shift of power to the centre' (*Independent*, 24 March 1993). Simon Jenkins in *The Times* said, 'As for Mr Clarke deciding personally to nominate every police authority chairman – a banana republic touch even by Home Office standards – what use will Labour make of this powerful tool in the Home Secretary's hand?' (24 March 1993).

According to senior Home Office officials, although there was ministerial concern about police effectiveness and about police misconduct, and a perception that police authorities were becoming less and less effective, the primary driving force behind the proposed changes was Treasury-inspired worries about burgeoning police expenditure.[1] Police expenditure was not cash-limited, the police grant was the result of a complicated set of arrangements in which the final amount the Treasury had to pay out was uncertain, and Home Office controls over police establishments and capital spending were considered to be indirect and complex – indeed, a 'surrogate' for proper controls. Even before the White Paper was published, however, further leaks suggested that the Treasury wished to go even further than the Home Secretary's announcement in the Commons and engage in some full-scale privatisation of some police functions. A story in the *Guardian* suggested that the Treasury was interested in some fairly radical proposals being made by the Adam Smith Institute, such as using private security firms to patrol housing estates, but 'Whitehall sources believe the Home Office is prepared to support the privatisation of fringe police activities such as escorting heavy loads on the roads and issuing shotgun certificates but is resisting much of the Adam Smith agenda' (*Guardian*, 7 April 1993).

Although at first there had been strong support for an independent police authority for London, within two months of the initial announcement in the Commons it was being reported that the Home Secretary had abandoned such plans. Newspaper reports suggested that the strongest opposition had come from backbench Conservative MPs who 'feared town hall involvement in the Yard's national or specialist policing functions' (*Independent*, 26 May 1993). When a month later the Home Secretary introduced the proposals that were to be contained in the White Paper, earlier speculation about the absence of an independent police authority for London proved correct.

In the main, the Home Secretary's statement on 28 June contained the general proposals he had flagged up in March. They included changing police authorities to 16-person committees comprising eight councillors, three magistrates and five 'independent' members appointed by the Home Secretary 'to ensure that each police authority contains within its overall membership a range of people with the experience, skills, motivation and energy which the authority will need' (1994: 21). These new police authorities were to be freestanding corporate bodies with their own standard spending assessment, and responsible for drawing up an annual costed policing plan for its force. However, he also proposed giving chief constables greater financial control over local budgets while also introducing strict cash limits, and moving the focus of policing from force headquarters to local or basic command units. For London, Clarke aimed to introduce an advisory body to help the Home Secretary 'oversee the performance' of the Metropolitan Police. 'Because of the special national interest in the work of the Metropolitan Police, both in policing the capital and because of its wider role, for example in combating

---

1. Growing criticisms of the police within senior Conservative circles at this time have been well documented in Kenneth Bakers' memoirs (Baker, 1993).

terrorism, all the members of the new authority will be appointed by and directly accountable to the Home Secretary' (1994: 44). He further proposed to introduce national league performance tables utilising approximately six key objectives set by the Home Secretary, which 'will provide the strategic framework within which police authorities and chief constables will operate' (Home Office, 1993: 24). Finally, the proposals suggested the need for amalgamating, at some stage in the future, an unspecified number of forces.

Changing the composition of police authorities was perhaps the most controversial of the measures proposed. Clarke described the reasons for the proposed changes in the following way:

> I thought there should be room on the authorities for people who could bring particular skills and expertise on to the authority. In making a contribution to the responsible body for a big public service it did not seem to me that it should only be people who happen to have the time to go through the party-political process of getting elected to a local council. I think there are very, very good people on both sides of politics who emerge from being candidates and winning seats. But if you're administering millions of pounds for a huge service I wouldn't say they were the only people capable of making a contribution are those who happen to have gone into politics. Hence in health authorities, whereas they used to be all local political poobahs, they're now all people appointed for their individual contribution, and there's scope for that on a police authority. Magistrates tend to come from a broader range of backgrounds – of course there are magistrates and councillors from every walk of life – but there are people who do not have the time to be a magistrate, don't want to be a county councillor, still capable of making a very worthwhile contribution to a police authority. I thought there was scope for appointing some as a result.

As to why he felt it necessary for the appointments of the independent members and the chairperson of the authority to be made by the Home Secretary, Clarke said that it was:

> to establish some accountability to the centre for overall performance, so that the authority was accountable to somebody and to try to avoid chairmen emerging from the local political, with a small 'p', process. Again, that was what I had done in the health authorities with exactly the same row about it, and as far as I am aware nobody would now go back on the arrangements in the health service. It gives the chairman some separate status of his own *vis-à-vis* the authority. He's not constantly having to keep one eye over his shoulder to keep his popularity with his members. He merely has to keep his eye over his shoulder at the Home Secretary who's just keeping an eye on how well this authority is delivering.

Those concerned about the proposals were given until September to consider them. Reactions from the police staff associations were mixed. The Police Federation was critical of the proposal to redesign police authorities and appoint their chairpersons, Alan Eastwood suggesting that it was a blow for local democracy. The Superintendents' Association opposed the proposal to introduce national league tables on the grounds that there was a risk that they would simply measure quantity rather than quality, and might fail to take account of local differences. By contrast, John Burrow, ACPO president at the time, welcomed elements of the statement – particularly the proposals for greater financial freedom for senior officers and for the new pay formula, though he too was critical of the plans for police authorities and argued strongly that there was a need for a genuine dialogue on the proposals. ACPO's position was set out in its written response to the White Paper in which it said (ACPO, 1993):

> The Association believes an argument of principle can be made for individuals other than elected members and magistrates to sit on the police authority to give 'added value'. But ACPO shares the concerns of the local authorities about the Government's proposals for the Home Secretary to appoint such members. To ensure real added value to the police authority those appointed must have not only a skill to contribute, but must be acceptable to the local community. ... The proposal that the Home Secretary should appoint the chairman of the police authority continues to be a matter of extreme concern. ... These proposals provide an unacceptable shift of power to the centre.

Although ACPO voiced concerns about the centralisation of policing, arguably this was related more to fundamental fears about the potential threats to the 'operational independence' of chief constables, which the reforms were perceived to contain. In particular, they expressed worries about the introduction of performance-related pay (PRP) and fixed-term contracts (FTCs) in conjunction with the new power of the Home Secretary to set national policing objectives. However, they also had concerns about possible threats to independence coming from the police authority, although these received less attention in the debate. They campaigned strongly for the legislation to lay down that the local policing plan should be the product of a joint agreement between the chief constable and the police authority. However, ACPO secretariat officials accepted that they 'didn't win on that one' and the final legislation clearly gave ownership of the plan to the police authority.

In the main, the proposals contained in both the Sheehy Inquiry Report and the White Paper were discussed together by the national press, and one academic commentator suggested that 'though separate, these two initiatives must be regarded as a single centralising package' (P. A. J. Waddington, 'The case of the hidden agenda', *Independent*, 1 July 1993). His argument was that the White Paper's proposal to reduce local authority representation on police authorities and the Sheehy Inquiry's support for the introduction of fixed-term contracts that would be reviewed by the Home Office was merely another element in a century long process involving the 'gradual accretion of central control over the police'. This was certainly the implication drawn in relation to the White Paper by *Police Review* (2 July 1993), whose editorial comment concluded: 'This White Paper is committed to devolving command to basic units while it creates a strong central control system. It could be named the "Home Office Rules".'

An early indication of the view the local authority associations were likely to take was given at a conference organised by the largest local government associations in July 1993. Ominously entitled 'Control of the police: democracy at risk', it was attended by the leaders of 40 of the 41 police authorities of England and Wales, and included speeches by several critics of the White Paper proposals. Key among them was Tony Blair, then shadow Home Secretary, who said that he was 'deeply concerned about the White Paper's proposals to allow the Home Secretary to nominate five members of the police authority, and most worryingly the decision to nominate the chairman of the authority' (speech to the joint AMA/ACC conference, 21 July 1993). He also voiced concern that the introduction of national objectives set by the Home Secretary in conjunction with the Sheehy committee's proposals for judging the performance of chief constables illustrated that 'the dangers of over-centralisation are very clear'. He concluded by arguing, to great applause, that 'the White Paper has little to offer in the fight against crime, it seems more concerned to attack local democracy'.

The Police and Magistrates' Courts Bill

As already noted, Kenneth Clarke had acquired a reputation as a radical reforming minister who was not afraid to take on established interests, and who had brought about far-reaching changes to the health and education sectors. However, as we have outlined above, the government's proposals for reforming the police service met with a highly effective campaign of resistance, which was already in motion by the time the bill outlining the proposed reforms was published. A key stage of the campaign came with the debates over the bill in the House of Lords. One of the key movers in this campaign of opposition at this stage, the Liberal Democrat peer, Lord Harris of Greenwich, suggested that it was the proposals that emerged from the Sheehy Inquiry that first set off the alarm bells.

> [The Home Secretary] appointed an extremely insensitive businessman and a group of people who, with the exception of Paul Fox who had been on the Royal Commission on Criminal Procedure, had no experience of policing at all. ... Tory MPs then started getting cold feet, because they started getting pressure from significant numbers of the constituents who were police officers. So that was the first time that they started going into reverse.

The Police and Magistrates' Courts Bill was published in December 1993 and, unusually, was introduced in the House of Lords. This, Harris described, as a 'fatal error'. He went on:

> There were two big Bills in that parliamentary session. ... Obviously Howard had been told that having two Bills going through the House of Commons at

the same time was out of the question. ... So [the Lords] had the Second Reading and it quickly became obvious that they were in very grave political trouble. Now if the Bill had been introduced in the Commons, they'd have been able to use the argument that it was the will of the elected house. But of course it hadn't been introduced in the Commons. We were doing it first which gave this House an infinitely stronger position. ... Members of the House of Commons, Ministers, know nothing about this place at all. They don't begin to understand the difference between a Bill introduced in the Lords and one that is introduced in the Commons. By this time, a very senior member of this House, a Conservative, had told the Prime Minister that Howard was going to be in a disastrous position. The Prime Minister basically said the law must take its course or so be it. ... All part of the ignorance about the sort of people who are here. This House does feel that it has certain responsibilites as far as constitutional propriety is concerned. This idea that you were handing over the police to appointees of Ministers was simply an absurdity.

Senior Home Office officials who had drafted the bill accepted that they faced an effective lobbying effort from the police service and local authority associations. One senior official said that the debates in the Lords reflected a 'very well-organised campaign by the local authority associations onto which ACPO climbed'. Though ACPO was by no means opposed to all aspects of the changes, it was prepared to enter a 'marriage of convenience' with the local authorities to campaign against those aspects it found most worrying. Representatives of ACPO's secretariat said that they directed an 'intensive lobbying effort' at the House of Lords, although in the event many senior peers did not take a lot of persuading against some of the more radical elements of the bill. It was reported that ACPO had 'many good friends' in the Upper House, as numerous interventions in the subsequent debates were to prove.

The second reading took place on 18 January 1994 and was introduced by the Lord Chancellor, Lord McKay of Clashfern. As stated at the beginning of this chapter, he presented the main purpose of the bill as being the decentralisation of real power to local police authorities: 'It is giving away to police authorities and to chief constables various powers which the Home Secretary presently has. It is making those local police authorities stronger, more independent and more influential' (col.458). The overall aim, he said, was 'to improve the management and organisation of the police service, so that it is better able to combat crime' (col.457).

A series of eminent speakers rose to deliver a stinging attack on the proposed legislation. A central voice among them was that of Viscount Whitelaw, ex-Conservative Home Secretary and, at that time, still an *éminence grise* of the Party. The main foci of his ire were the proposals that the Home Secretary appoint the chairmen of police authorities and that the membership of authorities be changed. On the day before the bill was read in the House of Lords the Home Secretary, responding to criticism, announced that the chairmen of police authorities would be appointed by him, but only after a shortlist had been drawn up by local recruitment consultants in conjunction with the Lord Lieutenant of the relevant county. If the intention of the announcement was to convince critics that there was to be some independence in the appointments procedure, it failed in relation to Whitelaw, who in the second reading debate said (cols.479–80):

> The chairman will surely be regarded as the Home Secretary's man, particularly in moments of stress in policing operations. This arrangement would surely run the risk of involving the Home Secretary directly . . . in police operations and that, if I may say so, has always been carefully avoided in the past and, I pray, will always be carefully avoided in the future.

He then went on (cols.480–1) to question the prudence of changing the size and balance of police authorities: 'Is it really wise substantially to reduce their size in every case? Is it really wise to replace local authority members with the Home Secretary's nominees? Will the nominees really know more about their areas than the people from local authorities already do? It is extremely doubtful.' He was followed by two further ex-Home Secretaries, Lord Callaghan of Cardiff and Lord Carr of Hadley, both similarly critical. Lord Carr, though not nearly as sceptical as some about either the idea of having appointed independent members or the proposal to reduce the size of authorities, nevertheless said that, in his view, policing ought to be locally controlled and it was on this count that the bill gave him cause for concern. Although 'Opposition spokesmen went a little overboard in some of their opposition', he said, 'I believe the Government have gone overboard on some of their proposals' (col. 492). Lord Knights, a former chief constable, argued that the threat to constabulary independence was extremely serious, particularly when some of the proposals were considered together. He suggested that the imposition of national objectives added 'to the fact that [the chief constable] will be on a fixed-term appointment, the continuation of which is in the discretion of the police authority, and through it that of the Home Secretary. One can imagine the political pressure that could be placed on him as gets towards the time of the renewal of that appointment' (col.494) .

Traditionally, second readings in the Lords not to go to a vote and therefore the bill remained unchanged. However, it was immediately clear to the government that there would be considerable resistance to the legislation and, given Michael Howard's announcement prior to the House of Lords debate, further concessions were expected. Within a week there was speculation in the press that police authorities might be allowed to continue to elect their own chairmen. Two days after the second reading, the Home Secretary had met Lord Whitelaw to discuss the latter's concerns about the bill and, it was suggested, Michael Howard was so concerned to keep the proposal for five independent members that there might be some horsetrading over the chairmanship issue.

The announcement came on 2 February. In a written answer in the Commons, the Home Secretary said that amendments to the bill would be tabled as

soon as possible. The effects of these amendments would be that the chairman
of a police authority would be appointed by the members of the authority; that
independent members should be shortlisted by regional panels consisting of a
professional recruitment consultant and 'two people independent of government' (Written answers, 17 January 1994: 377) and then chosen from the
shortlist by the Home Secretary; and that police authorities would not necessarily be limited to 16 members. In cases where the Home Secretary author-
ised a larger number of members, one half would be councillors and not more
than one-third would be independent members (Written answers, 2 February
1994: 711–12). Simon Jenkins argues that it was an 'open secret' in Whitehall
than the shortlist passed by the selection panel would be vetted by the government's whips office 'for political reliability' (Jenkins, 1995: 104). With further
tests awaiting the legislation in the Lords, commentators were beginning to
ask awkward questions about the future of the Home Secretary's career. The
Daily Telegraph (4 February 1994), under the headline 'The trials of a law-
man', suggested it was:

> difficult to see the general thrust of his proposals as anything other than an
> expression of the distrust of local authorities characteristic of this Government,
> and as evidence of the Government's desire to exercise more control from the
> centre. . . . But it is doubtful if Mr Howard's choices will be more in tune with
> local opinion, and he does not seem to realise how greatly the centralising
> tendencies of this Government are resented. Any Tory minister who provokes
> public dissent from Lord Whitelaw is living in a dangerously narrow world.

The following day, in what *The Times* (5 February 1994) described as 'one of
the strongest attacks mounted on government policy by a senior serving
officer', Sir John Smith 'denounced Michael Howard's plan to set national
objectives for the police as a "superficial approach" to dealing with crime',
and dismissed it as a 'bean-counting culture', which might improve response
times but would not improve policing. He went on, 'this superficial approach,
undermining a constitutional concept which Home Secretaries have assidu-
ously sought to protect, this Elastoplast culture which merely masks the
wound from public view while failing to heal it, is not going to produce what
society seeks.' Sir John prefaced his remarks, as we were told he did all his
critical comments at this point, by remarking that criticising the government
was not something that came easily to police officers, and certainly didn't to
him. 'Make no mistake', he said, 'I would rather not be in this position. It is a
mark of the depth of our very real concerns that I am prepared to speak out
against what we believe to be an ill conceived and publicly unacceptable
package of measures' (*Guardian*, 5 February 1994).

The next debate on the bill took place on 15 February. Not only did the proposed legislation come in for extensive criticism – despite the amendements
tabled by Earl Ferrers on behalf of the Home Secretary – but, once again, the
most serious damage was done by Tory peers. Lord Rippon of Hexham

repeated a statement he had made in the original Lords debate on the White Paper. 'There is a comparison', he said, 'with the national socialists in Germany who said that a locally-elected mayor like Adenauer does not represent the wishes and interests of the people of Cologne as well as perhaps an appointed businessman by the name of Krupp. That may be pushing it too far, but there are real dangers in giving a Home Secretary of any party the powers suggested in this Bill' (*Hansard*, 15 February 1994, col.119).

Lord Renton, another former Conservative minister, was also highly critical. He focused first and foremost on the role of elected members on police authorities. He argued that it is 'of vital importance to the successful operation of the police that they should have the cooperation of the public. They are much more likely to get it if democratically elected representatives of the public are well represented, indeed are in a majority at least on the police authority.' He concluded, 'As Members of the Committee know, I am a keen and sympathetic supporter of the Government, but on this occasion I think we are entitled to ask them to think again' (*Hansard*, 15 February 1994, col.124–5). At the end of the session an unusual step was announced by Earl Ferrers who said that several of the clauses relating to local authority representation were being stood down in order to allow for a short period of consultation with concerned parties before the clauses were brought back to committee.

By 17 February, the first signs that further emasculation of the bill might be prevented began to emerge. In its leader column that day, under the heading 'The Lords should delay the police reforms no longer', *The Times* said:

> Two weeks ago, the Government yielded to the objections of a group in the Lords, led by Lord Whitelaw, to the proposed composition of the new police authorities. Michael Howard agreed that authorities could have more than 16 members where appropriate and that their chairmen should not be centrally-appointed. These were sensible concessions, consistent with the Bill's devolutionary purpose. In the pressure it brought to bear on the Home Secretary, the House of Lords was true to its constitutional role as quality controller of the law. This week, however, a more mischievous revolt has broken out in the Upper House over the distribution of places on the new authorities. ... Two former Conservative Cabinet ministers, Lord Renton and Lord Rippon, have joined the Labour and cross-bench rebellion. Significantly, however, Lord Whitelaw has not. His decision to speak in favour of the bill in amended form should have sent a signal to their lordships that it no longer represents a constitutional threat.

As one of the peers central to the campaign against the bill put it, 'Willie was got at' – the suggestion being that Lord Whitelaw was persuaded by the Home Secretary's office at this stage to withdraw his active support for those attempting to amend the bill. Where perhaps *The Times* misread the situation, was in placing too great an emphasis on Whitelaw's role in the campaign. Though his presence as a critic in the second reading debate was of great symbolic importance to the campaign against the bill, Whitelaw was never central to 'the campaign team' and, by the time he withdrew from active participation, the campaign was so well-established, and had so many other major establishment figures supporting it, that there was little chance that the momentum would be lost.

So this proved. When the committee stage began again there were a series of fresh assaults on the bill. The first defeat was a rebel Tory amendment to the bill moved by Lord Bethell, an advisor to the Police Federation, who successfully sought to avoid attempts by the government to repeal those sections of PACE that prevent officers being subject to a disciplinary hearing for offences over which they have been cleared by the courts. Worse was to come, however, for the Home Secretary was, as the *Financial Times* (1 March 1994) put it, 'forced into a humiliating climbdown' over the appointment of independent members. This was a reference to the announcement of yet another new, and again somewhat cumbersome, system for selecting independent members. The new proposal was for the establishment of local selection panels consisting of three people who would sift applications from people wishing to serve as independent members. This panel would then submit a shortlist of up to 20 candidates to the Home Secretary, who would then whittle this down to ten, from which the police authority would select its five independents. It was reported that the announcement of the new procedure in the House of Lords by Earl Ferrers was greeted by laughter, and Lord Jenkins said that they were 'the most complicated and elaborate procedures that one could possibly imagine' (*Police Review*, 11 March 1994). Jenkins went on to say that the procedure was 'not an aid to police efficiency but an expensive piece of sticking plaster for such bits of the Government face as are still in place'. The general view of the new process was summed up by Robin Wendt, secretary of the Association of County Councils, who said that 'though the process was convoluted it ensured the independent members would be co-opted locally rather than be ministerial appointees' (*The Times*, 4 March 1994). Though backbench Tory peers continued to press to have the balance of police authorities further restored towards elected members, this was not pushed to a vote – with over 20 amendments having been passed there had already been sufficient embarrassment for the government – and, eventually, the new compromise proposals from the Home Office were accepted by the House of Lords. Even in the House of Commons the revised bill was not immune from criticism from the Conservative backbenches, but it emerged without further radical change and became law in July 1994.

THE SYSTEM REFORMED: THE POLICE AND MAGISTRATES' COURTS ACT 1994

The roles of all three parties in the tripartite structure have been recast by the PMCA, which became operational in April 1995. Given the extent to which the original proposals contained in the White Paper on Police Reform and the

Police and Magistrates' Courts Bill were amended in parliament, it is worth briefly outlining the main components of the PMCA, before moving on to consider the implications of the Act for the governance of police.

Police authorities and chief constables

The size of police authorities was reduced, most now being limited to a maximum of 17 members (although the legislation allows the Home Secretary to grant exceptions to this). Perhaps, most controversially, the Act allows for the appointment of 'independent members' to police authorities. The majority of police authorities now consist of nine local councillors, three magistrates and five appointees. Although the original proposal was that independent members should be directly appointed by the Home Office, a complicated selection procedure was introduced, in which a selection board comprising one person nominated by the local police authority, one by the Home Office, and a third person nominated by the first two, shortlists up to 20 candidates from all those who apply. This list is then halved by the Home Office, from which the local selection panel chooses the successful candidates.

The Act made significant changes to the statutory powers and responsibilities of police authorities. All police authorities became independent pre-cepting bodies and, in general terms, the Act represented an attempt to introduce the 'purchaser-provider' split into policing arrangements. The new financial regulations are set out in the financial management code of practice (Home Office, 1995). One of the most important codes is number three, which states: 'Unless there are good reasons to the contrary, police authorities should delegate financial management to the chief constable so that, as far as possible, the financial management of a force takes place within that force.' Thus, whereas prior to the Act some police authorities exercised quite detailed controls over issues such as regradings of civilian staff, capital investments in buildings and so on, this is now the clear responsibility of the chief constable. The police authority, however, retains a monitoring role.

The primary duty of a police authority under the Act is to secure the maintenance of an 'efficient and effective police force for its area'. In doing this, they are required to determine objectives for the policing of the authority's area during the forthcoming financial year; to issue a plan setting out the proposed arrangements for the policing of the authority's area for the year ('the local policing plan'); and to include in the local policing plan a statement of the authority's priorities for the year, of the resources expected to be available and of the intended allocation of those resources. The chief constable is to draft the plan, and the police authority must consult with him or her before making changes. However, the legislation clearly identifies the police authority as having the ownership of the plan, and the responsibility for consulting the local community prior to setting objectives.

As we outlined above, the PMCA requires police authorities 'before the beginning of the financial year to determine objectives for the policing of the authority's area during that year'. In doing so, the authority must '*consult* the chief constable for the area' and 'consider any views obtained by it in accordance with arrangements made under s.106 of PACE'. The local policing plan shall include a statement of 'any objectives determined by the Secretary of State', 'any objectives determined by the authority' and 'any performance targets established by the authority'. The PMCA consequently places greater emphasis on police–community consultation than had previously been the case. At the end of the year, the police authority is required to produce an annual report, giving performance against the objectives.

The Act allowed for the introduction of fixed-term contracts for ACPO rank officers, and also paved the way for the introduction of PRP. Section 24 allows local authorities to contract with police forces for the deployment of extra police staff. Such agreements may provide specific definitions of the roles and functions of such designated officers and could, in theory, bring into sharper focus the local 'market' for policing services, in which local authorities may consider the respective merits of hiring private security patrols, extra police constables, or setting up their own community patrol forces, such as the one that operates in Sedgefield (l'Anson and Wiles, 1995).

The Home Office

As we described in Chapter 1, one of the key links between the Home Office and the police authorities is via the funding of policing. Under the amended arrangements, each new police authority receives a police grant, consisting of a limited amount of cash, and continues to receive funding through the revenue support grant, non-domestic rates and council tax. Under the new system, the Home Secretary no longer decides on police officer establishments of provincial forces, that being decided by the chief constable and police authority. They will decide how to allocate the total between officers, civilian staff, vehicles, buildings and equipment. While this will give local police authorities and chief constable greater freedom *within* the budget, the Home Office can now exercise greater control over *total* spending. Importantly, the Act provides the Home Secretary with a new power to direct police authorities to spend above a certain amount – that is to increase any precept that is made. It seems likely that such a measure has been introduced at least partially after the recent experience of Derbyshire Constabulary, which has twice been refused a certificate of efficiency after local disagreements over a realistic budget for the force. The Home Office minister, Charles Wardle, described Derbyshire County Council as having made 'adverse spending choices', and the new powers will allow the Home Office to dictate, where it considers necessary, increased expenditure on policing against the will of the local police authority.

The Act gives the Home Secretary powers to order force amalgamations. Because the proposals over the constitution of local police authorities dominated the political debate at the time, the issue of force amalgamations –

touted so strongly prior to Sheehy – was largely overlooked. The Home Secretary said that he had no immediate plans for amalgamating forces and yet the PMCA includes striking new powers. It gives the Home Secretary power to amalgamate forces without having any form of local inquiry, as would be the case under the 1964 Police Act, and contains no requirement on him to justify his plans before an independent inspector, or even to do more than give reasons to those who have objections to his proposals. This certainly represents a significant concentration of power centrally over decisions about the structure of local forces.

The Home Secretary will be able to issue codes of practice for the new authorities, and local policing plans will be governed by these codes and by directions to be issued by the Home Secretary. Thus, as one commentator has argued, the context of the functions of police authorities is to be substantially different, for it may reasonably be inferred that part of HMIC's function in future will include reporting on the performance of the authority's duties as well as those of the force (*Police Review*, 24 December 1993).

One of the issues the Act has not resolved is the anomalous position of the Metropolitan Police. The Home Secretary remains the police authority for the capital despite his predecessor's view that 'London needs a police authority, and the arrangement whereby the Home Secretary is in theory the police authority for London is not adequate if we are to hold the Metropolitan Police to account, and if we are to assist them by giving clearer guidance on priorities' (Kenneth Clarke, 1993, quoted in *Hansard*, 18 January 1994). An advisory body has been appointed to act in support of the Home Secretary in relation to the effective and efficient running of the Metropolitan Police, but this falls some way short of a full-scale police authority for London.[2]

National objectives: central direction of policing?

With the defeat of the proposals to allow the Home Secretary to appoint both the 'independent members' to police authorities, as well as their chairmen, perhaps the most far-reaching change to the role of the Home Office brought about by the Act was the introduction of national objectives for policing. Local police authorities must now give regard to national objectives when setting local policing priorities.

The first set of objectives were announced by the Home Secretary in 1994 and have changed little since (although, as we discuss later, various 'concerns' have been added to the objectives system, which have caused some confusion). The objectives were as follows:

---

2. The capital city's other police force – the City of London Police – did not come under the remit of the PMCA. However, its police authority decided voluntarily to follow the spirit of the Act and, accordingly, reduced their members to 17 and produced a policing plan.

- to maintain, and if possible increase, the number of detections for violent crimes;
- to increase the number of detections for burglaries of people's homes;
- to target and prevent crimes that are a particular local problem in partnership with the public and local agencies;
- to provide high visibility policing so as to reassure the public; and
- to respond promptly to emergency calls from the public.

Although the key performance indicators attached to the first two of these objectives have been criticised for their focus on numbers of detections (rather than prevention), it is difficult to see how general objectives such as these will seriously undermine the possibility of responding to local policing needs. Indeed, as later chapters show, the national objectives were considered rather uncontroversial both by senior police officers and local police authorities. However, the principle of the Home Secretary being allowed to set policing objectives still caused concern in some quarters. In the words of one chief constable we interviewed, 'the existence of national objectives poses the greatest threat to the smooth running of the tripartite structure' (interview, June 1996). In practice, it has not been the substantive content of the published national objectives that has raised concern among chief constables, but rather the thought of what a future Home Secretary might choose as key objectives.

Section 28A of the Act states that the Home Secretary may determine objectives for the policing of all the areas of police authorities established under the Act. However, it also states that before doing this the Home Secretary must consult 'persons whom he considers to represent the interests of police authorities' and also 'persons whom he considers to represent the interests of chief constables of forces maintained by those authorities'. Representatives of the ACPO secretariat reported that this provision for consultation with chief constables about the national objectives was inserted after pressure from ACPO. The objectives are to be set by statutory order laid before parliament, although in practice the Home Secretary has, to date, simply published the national objectives in an annual letter to police authorities and chief constables.

The actual objectives emerged from an *ad hoc* working party within the Home Office, which included representatives of the Home Office, police authority associations, and the ACPO quality of service committee. Interviews with representatives of all these bodies seemed to suggest that there was little opposition to the objectives that were chosen. The Home Office was very concerned, first, to limit the number of objectives, and second, to keep them relatively constant over time (so that improvements in performance over a period of several years could be measured). Senior Home Office officials reported that there had been some pressure from other central government departments to add to the national objectives issues that concerned them. However, the pressure to 'hang more baubles on the Christmas tree' (in the words of a senior official) was successfully resisted. The senior Home Office official involved with drafting the Act remained aware that political pressures could change this in the future, and noted that a great deal of care would need to be exercised to prevent the objectives becoming a 'political football', the outcome most feared by the police service. That said, members of the ACPO secretariat said that the current objectives were regarded as 'mother and apple pie', and they accepted that they reflected the main concerns of the public about policing. At the national level, national objectives were perceived as very influential. ACPO representatives saw them as 'significant drivers' of the annual policing plans, although one could not tell if this was because they were set by the Home Secretary, or because they were considered appropriate by chief constables and police authorities.

Clearly, the local authority representatives retained significant misgivings about the principle of national objectives. Again, however, they largely supported the subject areas of those who were chosen.[3] A senior CoLPA[4] official, for example, described them as 'fairly sensible objectives'. Nonetheless, they clearly detected the potential for further centralisation, and future problems relating to such a power in the Home Secretary's hands. In the words of a second senior CoLPA representative, the objectives arose from an inter-departmental negotiating process rather than a 'democratic' one. Although the Home Office had successfully resisted political additions so far, there was no guarantee that it would continue to do so in the future.

Senior Home Office officials underlined that they were taking a 'softly softly' approach to the setting of national objectives. In particular, they were intended to provide a 'broad steer' to the police service, rather than give particular directions. As we outlined earlier, this view is borne out by analysis of the objectives themselves, which appear to cover the main areas of police work. The key performance indicators (KPIs) have been strongly criticised, in that the first two unambiguously emphasise numbers of detections per officer. The logic of including these is not apparent, especially given the work being developed by the Audit Commission emphasising officer effectiveness (primary clear ups per officer). Home Office officials reported that these were deliberately chosen as measures of officer productivity, in order to complement rather than replicate the Audit Commission indicators. However, this begs the question of why for the fourth and fifth national objectives the Home Office simply adopted Audit Commission PIs. It remains to be seen how far the Home Office is prepared to exert pressure on police forces to follow

---

3. Representatives of the (then) AMA police committee reported that they had pressed rather unsuccessfully for the concept of crime prevention and reduction to be given more weight in the national objectives, although they accepted that one of the reasons for this was that prevention was very difficult to measure.

4. The Committee of Local Police Authorities later merged with the Association of Metropolitan Authorities Police Committee, following the establishment of the Local Government Association, which covers all local authorities.

national objectives, either directly via its powers to set target ranges for police authorities, or indirectly through HMIC. In the two years after the Act became operational, the Home Secretary's power to set target ranges was not utilised, although the potential clearly remains. Moreover, given the expressed concerns in relation to the 'potential' of national objectives, it remains to be seen whether the nature of the national objectives becomes more specific and perhaps more contentious in future years.

THE REFORMS: AN INITIAL ASSESSMENT

The outcome of the protracted campaign of resistance to many of the original proposals was, then, a much-amended final Act. The original intention behind the reforms seemed to be clear. Kenneth Clarke was quite explicit that he wanted to give real powers of performance monitoring, and devolved responsibilities to local police authorities. At the same time, police authorities were to be focused on technical issues of policing objectives and monitoring performance, and not concern themselves with the wider 'political' questions surrounding policing. It seems clear that within this managerialist view of the role of police authorities, there was a genuine intention to give them real powers and influence. The flip side of this was of course, greater control over police authorities by the centre, with the appointment of chairmen and independent members. In the event, the Act retained the significant powers devolved to police authorities, and yet its provisions gave fewer central controls over the local police authority than had been originally intended. The crucial amendments in this regard gave local authorities authorities a significant input into the selection of appointed members, and allowed them to elect their own chairpersons. Coupled with the relinquishment by the Home Office of detailed controls over capital spending and staffing, it was clear that there was strong potential within the Act for an increasing level of local influence. The Act also had the potential further to encourage the trend towards financial devolution within police organisations and, in theory at least, to give more freedom to local police managers (Audit Commission, 1994). The new arrangements thus have far-reaching implications for the power balance within the tripartite structure, although their ultimate effect on the overall nexus of control is far from clear.

Some critics clearly felt that the amendments, although welcome, had not gone far enough, and that the eventual result would still be a further centralisation of control over policing. For example, it was argued that 'independent' police authorities will become distanced from local government, mainly on the basis of the belief that previous single county police authorities were more effective because of their integration into the local authority structure (Loveday 1987). It was also suggested that the new smaller police authorities would be unable to reflect the local political balance, particularly in the larger police areas. Despite changes to the selection procedure, the specific criticism of the introduction of appointed members remained. In particular, it was suggested that they would be unlikely to improve the contribution of local police authorities to policing policy and would still be more attuned to central concerns. As we shall see later, the new selection procedure has not prevented accusations of party-political 'interference' in the selection of independent members, in particular that Conservative Central Office has been consulted in an attempt to ensure that 'suitable' candidates are selected (Loveday, 1995).

Despite these criticisms of the Act, we have argued that it also contains provisions that could in theory enhance local influence over policing (Jones and Newburn, 1995). The most significant change is the new statutory requirement for the police authority (not the chief constable and not the Home Office) to publish a local policing plan laying down objectives, priorities and performance targets for the coming year. As noted in later chapters, there are important constraints on this power in that the chief constable drafts the plan and the police authority cannot make substantive changes without consulting him or her first. Furthermore, the statutory inclusion of national policing objectives (see below) has been used to argue that much of the plan will be centrally determined. Nevertheless, the thinking behind the reforms seems clear in that it is the police authority that is unambiguously given the responsibility for, and ownership of, this plan.

Though there can be no doubt that the Secretary of State has the power to set objectives, and that a police authority is required to print these in its local policing plan, it does not necessarily follow that these therefore become *de facto* objectives for the local police. Section 4.2.a of the Act says merely that the police authority 'shall have regard to any objectives determined by the Secretary of State'. More important, perhaps, is that s.5. of the PMCA states that 'in discharging his functions, every chief constable shall *have regard* to the local policing plan issued by the police authority for his area'.

At the committee stage of the bill in the House of Lords, Lord Knights referred to a Home Office memorandum that had been sent to the Delegated Powers Scrutiny Committee of the House. This stated that, 'although police authorities and police forces are to be required to have regard to such objectives, they represent a framework for the exercise by those authorities of their statutory responsibilities, and are not a tightly drawn regulatory framework'. In his reply to questioning, Earl Ferrers, on behalf of the government, said 'a chief constable will be free *not* to meet the key objectives or any related performance targets if, in his view, other operational considerations are of overriding importance.'

Though the phrase 'have regard' has not yet been tested, it is likely that it allows police authorities to state reasons why they are not going to meet all of the Home Secretary's published objectives. Alternatively, it almost certainly allows chief constables, under certain circumstances, to ignore local policing plans (and all that is contained in them including the Home Secretary's key objectives). It is likely that any chief doing so would need to argue that 'operational considerations' required such actions. The idea of constabulary (operational) independence is now so well established in the minds of politicians and police authority members (even if it has a dubious constitutional basis – see Chapter 1) that this would no doubt be a solid defence. Though Earl Ferrers's words are not included in the Act, it is likely that they too could be used to support the above interpretation.

With objectives as broadly consensual as it appears the initial ones were generally perceived to be, none of this is likely to arise. However, in the event of a future Secretary of State issuing objectives that do not command general support, there is an escape clause, which appears not only to protect the independence of chief constables but may also allow local police authorities to ignore one or more national objectives. As the chairman of ACPO's quality of service committee put it to us:

> Now, the Act also requires police authorities to set local objectives, and police authorities if they are doing their job properly must reflect the wishes of their community and it may well be that the community say that we're not worried about the level of burglary, but we are worried about the level of car crime or we are concerned about the street nuisances. . . . Now the fascinating thing about this is that the chief constable doing his job right, hearing the views of the community, as does the authority – and they put up a policing plan – he drafts it and he says we're not going to do anything on the Home Secretary's key objectives, what matters here in Bluntshire is this, this and this, not the Home Secretary's key objectives. The police authority hearing what the public are saying and listening to the chief constable, say 'we agree' and they adopt the plan. The Home Secretary says, 'hang on a tick you're not doing anything on that', and the chief constable says, 'nothing to do with me Home Secretary it is the police authority's plan. They've adopted it, I merely proposed it'. Fight between police authority and Home Secretary. It's going to come . . . It's the recipe for a really good argument, and one in which the chief constable can stand on the side and watch.

That said, there is much in the legislation that has given rise to the charge that it is still, fundamentally, a centralising measure. Simon Jenkins, for example, has argued that while for the best part of a century there has been an ongoing tug of war between local and central government over the police, 'slowly central government edged ahead. In 1994 it justifiably called itself the winner' (Jenkins, 1995: 89). Similarly, Loveday (1994) has argued that it may be 'appropriate to view the Act as a further example of a long-term trend of centralisation of the police service which has taken place throughout the twentieth century'. Indeed, we have argued elsewhere (Jones and Newburn, 1995) that there can be little doubt about the potential for centralisation under the new arrangements. However, we depart from many other commentators in that we are also of the view that the word *potential* is important here and, therefore, the important question for us is: to what extent is this potential being operationalised?

CONCLUSION

In Chapter 1, we outlined the three broad themes underpinning our consideration of the system of police governance. These concerned the shifting power balance in the tripartite structure, the growing concerns with efficiency and effectiveness in service delivery, and the nature and meaning of 'democracy' in the context of policing. Depending on how it is operationalised, the PMCA has far-reaching implications for all of these areas.

First of all, it is clear that the new Act sought to bring about changes in the operation of police authorities and in the nature of the relationships between the Home Office, local police authorities and police forces. We have argued that the Act contains both the potential for further centralisation of control over the direction of policing, and provisions that could in theory enhance local influence over policing. The most significant of the latter concern the new statutory requirement for police authorities (not chief constables or the Home Office) to publish local policing plans laying down objectives, priorities and performance targets for the coming year. As we will describe in later chapters, there are important limits to this power; the chief constable, for example, drafts the plan and the police authority cannot make substantive changes without consulting him or her first, and the statutory inclusion of national policing objectives may more than counterbalance the local influences on policing plans.

The crucial question is how is this being played out in practice, and what is the nature of the new relationships that are being established? Only by examining this in detail can we come to a judgement about the centralising or localising tendencies in the legislation. Second, by creating stand-alone pre-cepting bodies with powers to set objectives, impose performance targets, delegate financial powers and so on, the PMCA also has very important potential consequences for the managerial or contractual aspects of police governance. More particularly, there is the question of whether such changes have resulted, as some commentators suspect, in a further move from 'political' forms of accountability to 'calculative and contractual' modes (Reiner and Spencer, 1993: 177). Finally, we should not forget that the Police and Magistrates' Courts Bill was greeted by critics as heralding a further decline in local democracy. Loader (1996: 11), for example, has argued that 'local democratic influence over policing seems set to recede to the point of insignificance'. We have outlined what we take to be a sophisticated means of analysing the 'democratic' content of the system of police governance and, in the following chapters, we build on this previous work in assessing the changes brought about by the PMCA. We begin with a detailed examination of the introduction of published local policing plans.

Chapter 3

Reinvigorating Local Governance?
Local Policing Plans 1996/7

One of the key changes in the statutory powers of parties within the tripartite structure is the requirement that police authorities publish a local policing plan (LPP). Section 4B of the PMCA states that 'the local policing plan shall include a statement of the authority's priorities for the year, of the financial resources expected to be available, and of the proposed allocation of those resources'. The Act also lays down that the plan should 'give particulars of' national objectives laid down by the Home Secretary, local objectives determined by the police authority, and any performance targets stipulated by the authority.

As discussed in Chapter 1, a central part of the debate over police accountability has concerned the degree to which police authorities have the power to influence general policing policies. Although the doctrine of constabulary independence clearly circumscribed the powers of police authorities in individual cases, and in matters pertaining to prosecution policy, the legal justifications for limited police authority involvement in general policy are less clear. Even latterly strong supporters of the 'operational independence' principle, such as Geoffrey Marshall, argued initially that local politicians should be able to influence the chief constable in matters of general policy. He later changed this view, and argued on practical grounds that the protection of civil liberties and justice were better left to chief constables than to local politicians. However, he accepted that there remained a *legal* justification for policing policy to be broadly determined by local police authorities. As noted in Chapter 1, subsequent legal rulings and the practical actions of most chief constables confirmed a broad notion of 'operational matters', which have generally been taken to include issues of general policy, as well as more particular executive decisions.

Thus, giving the police authority the statutory responsibility for production of an annual policing plan could be a highly significant shift of powers. We have argued that it could even tip the balance of powers within the tripartite structure back towards the local police authorities (Jones and Newburn, 1995).

Of course, the Act includes many safeguards. First, the plan is to be *drafted*[1] by the chief constable and the police authority may only introduce changes after consulting him or her. There are a number of grey areas here, especially about what happens if the chief constable strongly objects to changes made by the police authority. Second, both the Act and the Home Office circular on policing plans (27/94) state that the chief constable shall 'have regard' to the plan in undertaking his or her responsibilities. The circular goes further and explicitly states that the chief will not necessarily be bound by the plan and can depart from it if deemed necessary in his or her operational judgement. But if this does occur, the chief constable is expected to set out reasons for the police authority. Third, one might argue that the requirement to include national key objectives will mean in practice that much of policing is directed from the centre, rather than locally-driven. Despite these safeguards, it is reasonable to argue that, in terms of statutory powers at least, the changes represent a limited but important shift towards local police authorities. Both the Act and the circular make it clear that it is the *police authority*'s policing plan and that the *police authority* shall determine priorities, after consulting the chief and the local community. Tony Butler has argued that a key distinction is between *what* the force is expected to achieve, and *how* it goes about achieving it (Butler, 1996). In his view, the former is the proper concern of the police authority, but the latter is an operational matter for the force.

Of what then do the plans consist? How specific are they? And what model of policing do they suggest? To answer these questions and others, we conducted a detailed analysis of the published policing plans for 1996/7. This analysis provides information about the published plans for all 41 local police authorities across England and Wales, assessing how the plans have been presented and what they contain. A particular focus was on how plans dealt with national objectives, and on how many and what kinds of local objectives have been set. It is important to remember Weatheritt's cautionary note that we are here analysing outcomes, and that outcomes are only a partial indicator of *process* (Weatheritt, 1996). The published policing plans provide important clues about the varied influences of the different interested parties on the final document. However, it is ultimately the planning process with which we are primarily concerned; the telephone survey of police authority clerks and the three case studies will provide deeper insights into the kinds of processes that led to the final published plans.

PRESENTATION

As in 1995/6, the published policing plans vary a great deal in the way they

---

1. This word is italicised here because of its importance to later discussions. We will argue that the word 'draft' has perhaps taken on a meaning that was not originally intended when the legislation was itself drafted.

are presented. However, a 'typical' format for a policing plan appears to be emerging which follows the framework laid down by Circular 27/94. This includes the following features: glossy A4 format, foreword(s) by both the chairperson of the police authority and the chief constable, some reference to the policing environment (broad demographic and workload indicators), some mention of local consultation and partnership, a section of policing objectives for the coming year in which the national policing objectives take a prominent position, performance targets against these objectives, and some general income and expenditure analysis.

Nearly all the main plans[2] were published in A4 format (only three out of the 41 were published in a smaller booklet format). There is a great deal of variation in the density of text, the use of photographs and the employment of illustrations such as graphs and pie charts, which take up a lot of page space. Thus, the analysis of the length of the plans in terms of number of pages is only an approximate indicator of variations in the amount of information they contain.[3] As in the previous year, there is a big variation in numbers of pages, with the shortest plans being just five pages long and the longest one exceeding 90 pages. The average length of main plans is just over 29 pages.

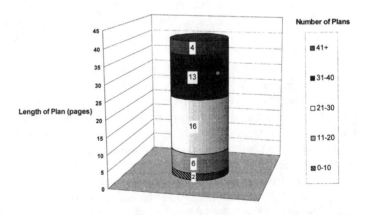

Figure 3.1 Length of policing plans (number of pages)

The majority of plans include some background information about the area in which the force is located and the demands on police organisation. This mostly

---

2. A number of police authorities also published a shorter summary of the main plan in the form of a booklet.
3. Plans for the Welsh police authorities were published in both Welsh and English which, of course, doubled their number of pages. This analysis includes the figures for the number of pages in one language only.

takes the form of some general details about the physical and demographic features of the area. Examples of this kind of information include motorway mileage, population size and structure, main types of employment and industry, and unemployment rates. A number of plans include details of the main demands on policing resources in terms of recorded crime and incidents, and policing problems related to particular events or developments in the force area (for example, the Reading Rock Festival in Thames Valley, or the Channel Tunnel links in Kent). One or two plans place such information in a 'public relations' context, presenting the police as struggling against overwhelming odds and resource limitations. A few plans provide predictive information about local events or developments during the coming year that will have implications for policing. These include developments that are likely to become a focus for public demonstrations, such as the Newbury bypass in Thames Valley, or the Brightlingsea animal export protests in Essex. They also include major industrial or infrastructure developments, such as plans to build new leisure parks, or shopping complexes, which will attract people into the force area. Very few plans give any background information about the previous year's objectives or performance, as a context for the current year's plan. However, one plan (North Wales) provides some data on crime rates and workload in the form of 'control charts', which show variation in rates over time. Only one plan explicitly mentions performance against the previous year's objectives.

OWNERSHIP

Weatheritt (1996) notes that firm conclusions about ownership of policing plans cannot be drawn by studying the contents of plans alone. However, she identifies a number of features that may indicate the degree to which the police authority is taking ownership of the plans. These include to whom the plan is formally attributed on the front cover, who contributes the foreword, how the authority is linked to statements made in the plan, whether and how the chairperson and other members of the authority are identified, the information given about the role and activities of the police authority, and whether or not a contact point for the police authority is given.

The first thing that any reader sees of the plan is, of course, the front cover. In 1995/6, Weatheritt noted that the front covers of a small minority of plans (three) formally attributed the plan to the police force rather than the police authority. This has been replaced in 1996/7 with attribution to the police authority in nearly all plans. A joint approach is suggested by the fact that many of the plans also have the police force identified on the front cover. This is either done by way of the force logo, or more explicitly by reference to partnership: '– police authority in partnership with – constabulary' (Merseyside and West Mercia follow this example, in fact, the latter has as its title 'Joint Policing Plan').

The majority of plans include either a joint foreword, signed by both the police authority chairperson and the chief constable, or a foreword by each. In most, the police authority chairperson's foreword comes first. There is, however, a good deal of variation in the amount of coverage the police authority receives after this in the plans. Some include a large amount of coverage of the police authority and its activities, explaining its role in the tripartite structure, and giving details of activities and forthcoming meetings. Some also include lists of police authority members, accompanied in some cases by photographs, addresses and telephone numbers. In only a minority of plans is the police authority given a high profile in the way that the plan is drafted, with regular references to the police authority in discussions of force objectives or priorities for the coming year. For example, in a few plans, references such as 'the police authority and chief constable plan to . . . . '; or 'the police authority will prioritise . . . '; are commonplace. However, this approach is unusual and, in the majority of plans, the police authority is rarely mentioned after the background information. In one plan, the police authority is not mentioned at all after the foreword. The overall picture still suggests that it is the force rather than the police authority that takes the lead in producing the plan (which our telephone survey of police authority secretariats subsequently confirmed).

CONSULTATION

Most plans include some reference to consultation within the force area, usually emphasising how important it has been in setting objectives. With the important exception of Northumbria, few plans give anything more than very broad details about what this consultation actually entails, and almost none explicitly link it to stated policing objectives. For each of its stated objectives, the plan includes a target, performance indicators and a statement of origin. A number of the 'origins' include reference to priorities identified in community consultation. Nearly all plans have at least a sentence saying that consultation is important, and that the police authority and/or the force have consulted widely prior to publishing the plan. A number of plans give examples of the kinds of organisations consulted prior to the plan. Common examples include local authorities (particularly district and parish councils), chambers of commerce, neighbourhood watch groups, voluntary and community groups, schools, section 106 committees, and other agencies. A few plans give more detail about consultation, for example mentioning the different types of consultation employed.

A number of plans mention the use of public attitude surveys, although the term 'survey' appears to cover a multitude of developments ranging from satisfaction questionnaires left in police stations to more proactive telephone and postal surveys, and even some specific structured interviewing of particular groups. A number of plans mention the development of new forms of consultation such as consumer panels, focus groups and special public meetings or seminars designed to discuss policing priorities for the coming year. One police authority set up a free-phone telephone line through which to receive suggestions from the public. Only a minority of forces mention consultation within the force, with police officers and civilian staff, prior to publication of the plan. A minority of plans give details about the general themes highlighted by the consultation process and, in some, these are mirrored in the choice of local objectives. However, only in a few plans are the outcomes of consultation explicitly linked to the choice of local objectives in the plan. A number of plans request feedback on the contents, and provide a contact address for the police authority to which the public are asked to send comments and suggestions for the plan via a tear-off slip and freepost address.

As in 1995/6, references to partnership are rather limited. A large number of plans have some reference to the importance of a range of agencies working in partnerships to combat crime, but only a few of these actually list examples of partnership projects.

THE KEY NATIONAL OBJECTIVES

The key national objectives for 1996/7 changed only slightly from the previous year. Local policing plans are required to 'give particulars' of these and, indeed, all plans included key objectives (KOs) in some form or another. However, a number of different approaches towards dealing with national objectives in policing plans were identified, which may indicate the priority given to the KOs by police authorities and police forces. The existence of KOs led some commentators to question the extent to which the policing plan is an expression of local needs and priorities. Loveday (1994: 8), for example, has argued that 'the status of the Local Plan and local priorities will clearly be subordinate to the Key Objectives set by government. ... Chief Officers will know that when 90 per cent of police funding comes from the Centre, Key National Objectives will assume a somewhat greater salience than those emanating from either Local Plans or police community liaison panels.'

While we not wish to place too much reliance on the analysis of the written plans, it is nevertheless important that there is no clear evidence from the analysis that national considerations dominate local ones. Although national objectives have clearly been important in that they are present in some form in all plans, they by no means dominate all the plans. In considering the plans for 1996/7, we found there to be a basic dichotomy between those plans in which the KOs were explicit and dominant, and a slightly larger group of plans in which KOs were much less prominent.

National objectives dominant

Of the 41 policing plans in England and Wales for 1996/7, 19 gave prominence to the national objectives. This impression is created in a variety of ways. First, it is created by the *number of local objectives* determined. As we show below, a number of policing plans identify only one or two local objectives. Thus, in terms of sheer weight of numbers, national objectives appear more important. Second, it is created by *order of appearance*. In many of the plans in this group, national objectives appear in a separate section prior to any discussion of local objectives. Third, it is created by the way in which these objectives are *identified and worded*. National objectives are identified as such and quoted in exactly the same wording as laid down in the Home Secretary's letter. Perhaps the best example of this kind of plan is that of Nottinghamshire, for it focused very much on national objectives and contained only one local objective. Other plans, such as that for South Wales, focused on the national objectives by stating that the KOs echo the main priorities for policing arising from local consultation.

National objectives less prominent

In one or more ways, national objectives seem less prominent in 22 of the policing plans. In the majority of plans in this category, KOs are still identified as such (by means of an asterix or in red ink), but are incorporated or subsumed under a larger number of broader objectives or service areas. In one or two plans, KOs are simply listed and then not mentioned again. In one, the KOs appear in an appendix. In some, the order of the KOs is changed. In a minority (for example, Surrey and Warwickshire), some or all the KOs are rephrased or revised to give a slightly different emphasis. In these plans, the subject matter of national objectives is included and identified as such, but the actual form the objectives take is different (for example, to reduce the incidence of violent crime rather than to increase the detections per 100 officers). A number of plans in this category add local objectives (LOs) to the same broad subject area as the KOs, but again with a different emphasis (for example, Greater Manchester includes an LO that aims to prevent burglary alongside a KO that aims to increase detections).

Key performance indicators

Although in some form or other all plans contain the key objectives set by the Home Secretary, they do not all contain the corresponding key performance indicators (KPIs). This is because not all plans contain KPIs 1 and 2, which consist of detections per 100 officers for domestic burglary and violent crime (all plans contain KPIs 4 and 5). KPI 3 has been dealt with in a variety of ways, partly because the objective is framed in such a broad manner (to target and prevent crimes that are of particular local concern). However, as noted above, specific subject areas in terms of both drugs and repeat victimisation were mentioned, and a drugs performance indicator (PI) was suggested (arrests and disposals under the Misuse of Drugs Act) and a substantial number of plans contain this.

KPIs 1 and 2

Most plans give the KPIs as set for the first two national objectives. However, a number omit these KPIs and replace them with different indicators (most usually with detection rates, or total number of crimes reported). Seven plans come into this category, namely Avon and Somerset, Bedfordshire, Hertfordshire, Kent, Northamptonshire, Thames Valley, and Warwickshire. In all cases bar one (Bedfordshire), the KPIs are replaced by detection rates for domestic burglary and violent crime. Two of the seven also measure the total number of burglaries per 1000 dwellings, and two use a victim satisfaction measure.

Although the majority of policing plans include KPIs 1 and 2, most indicate that a range of indicators will be used. Some plans explicitly indicate that although the KPIs are there, the priority will be on the actual incidence of crime rather than numbers of detections (for example, North Wales). Seven plans appear to use only the KPIs for the first two national objectives.

KPI 3
This is a difficult one to assess because a number of forces have framed objectives under this title as local objectives, many of which are connected with the policing of drugs. However, numerous plans adopted KPI 3 (the number of arrests/disposals under the Misuse of Drugs Act) as set down in the Home Secretary's letter. In a number of plans this objective was supplemented with other enforcement-based objectives related to the value of drugs seizures or search warrants executed, and some introduced prevention-type indicators such as the numbers of multi-agency drug prevention groups set up.

KPIs 4 and 5
These appear to be the most unproblematic of the performance indicators and are included in all the plans bar one. Their almost universal adoption perhaps relates to the fact that these PIs were simply lifted from those of the Audit Commission, against which forces were already required to publish their performance. Just over half the plans (23) simply set the KPIs on their own; a further 11 give additional PIs for KPI 4 (high visibility policing). Most of these PIs are to do with the amount of officer time spent on patrol, though some plans have PIs relating to the special constabulary (total number, ratio to regular force, or hours of patrol duty by specials). One plan has the additional PI of number of permanent beat officers, and aims to measure the ratio of police officers on duty per 1000 population.

LOCAL OBJECTIVES AND INDICATORS

A number of difficulties arise when trying to analyse the number and type of local policing objectives. First, as noted above, the plans have dealt with objective-setting in different ways, and there is not always a clear demarcation between the national and local objectives. As we saw earlier, in some plans there is considerable overlap between local and national objectives. Some simply adopt certain national objectives as local objectives. In the subsequent analysis, when local objectives are simply the national objectives listed verbatim, such objectives will be regarded as national objectives, even if described as local objectives in the plan. A number of plans contain local objectives concerning drug-related criminality, and some plans make reference to addressing repeat victimisation. Both these are mentioned specifically under the Home Secretary's third key objective for 1996/7. Nevertheless, these will still be regarded as local objectives where they are stated as such. Although such a classification may appear somewhat arbitrary, the rationale is that KO3 is much more loosely-worded, raising the importance of dealing with local problems, with drugs and repeat victimisation being given more as examples than as directives.

Table 3.1 Numbers of local objectives set in force plans for 1996/7

Number of local objectives	Number of policing plans
1	3
2	7
3–5	18
6–10	7
>10	6
Total	41

A final problem with analysing the objectives as written in the plans is that it is not always clear what counts as an objective. Some plans identify particular objectives, then list a number of other 'areas of concern' that will be addressed in the coming year. We have addressed this by only analysing areas specifically framed as local policing objectives, rather than additional priorities or areas of concern. Because of the varied approaches taken in different plans, we have not included particular divisional objectives in the analysis. This is because some plans provide local, as in force-wide, objectives, and then state that divisional commanders will set objectives that are local to their areas. Only a few of these plans actually identify these divisional objectives. Thus, in this analysis, 'local' objectives are taken to mean 'force-wide' policing objectives.

Weatheritt's (1996) analysis of local objectives uses the following categories: crime, disorder and nuisance, drugs, road traffic, responding to customers and developing relationships with the community, and managerial objectives. We have used a slightly larger number of categories to explore the subject matter of the objectives. The analysis below uses 11 categories to explore the range of subjects covered by local objectives. Figure 3.2 illustrates the frequency with which different subjects appear within the local objectives in policing plans.

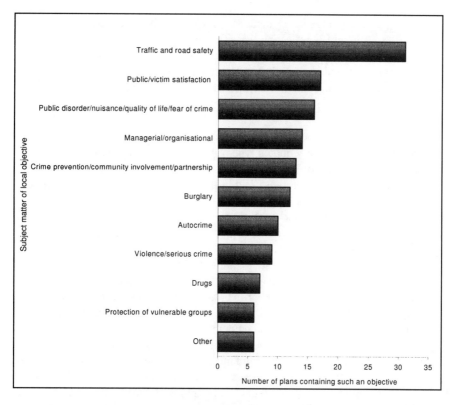

Figure 3.2 Subjects covered by local objectives in policing plans for 1996/7

Traffic and road safety

The concern of many chief constables that the national objectives failed to mention traffic policing is reflected in the fact that traffic was the most frequent subject chosen for a local objective. Some plans actually include a traffic objective under the list of national objectives, citing the Department of Transport's national objective of reducing road traffic accident casualties by the year 2000. This is the most frequent form taken by traffic policing objectives, and refers to the reduction in the number of traffic accidents and/or casualties resulting from traffic accidents (18 plans contain objectives of this sort). The traffic objectives sometimes take on a different form; in seven plans the objective is framed more generally in terms of improving road safety. Five plans contain objectives that target specific forms of driver behaviour associated with accidents, including drink driving and speeding. Finally, three of the plans include objectives aimed at an improved service for victims of road traffic accidents (RTAs) and their relatives. The PIs attached to these traffic objectives reflect these differing emphases. The most commonly-used PI concerns the number of RTA deaths/injuries, or total numbers of casualties. A few plans restrict these measurements to a set number of accident blackspots.

Plans containing objectives focused on specific forms of driver behaviour include additional PIs reflecting these; for example, the number of breath tests or speeding tickets administered, the number of prosecutions arising from speed cameras, and the number of sites at which cameras are in place. Two plans (West Midlands and Surrey) include traffic-related objectives, but do not attach specific PIs.

Public satisfaction/improved service to victims

The next most frequently quoted type of local objective concerns either overall public satisfaction with (or public support for) the police and, more specifically, the satisfaction of victims. Within this broad category, the most frequent type of objective relates to general public satisfaction. Some objectives are phrased in terms of 'public confidence' in or 'public support' for the police, but most are simply phrased in terms of raising levels of satisfaction with police services. A few plans identify particular customers for whom the aim is to raise satisfaction levels. In some plans this refers to people who make non-emergency calls. In a larger number of plans, this kind of objective is specifically linked to victims of crime (and in one or two of these, the kind of crime is specified). Two plans include objectives that aim to keep victims and/or callers informed of the outcome of their case. Again, the chosen indicators reflect the nature of these objectives. All forces now undertake satisfaction surveys of some sort and most plans reflect this (even those that do not include further local objectives concerned with public satisfaction or service to victims). Most of the PIs are framed in terms of percentage of public/customers who express satisfaction. Some identify a particular group of customers (such as the victims of racial violence, domestic violence, burglary and violent crime, callers to the police station, or visitors to the front office). One PI measures the percentage of force staff from ethnic minority groups. Two plans include PIs under the broad category of monitoring the number and type of complaints against police officers.

Public disorder and nuisance

The third most popular kind of local objective concerns public disorder and nuisance. Two plans contain this kind of objective framed in a very general way, such as 'maintaining the peace', 'to increase public tranquillity', or 'to cooperate with schools, young people, parents and residents to promote community harmony'. The majority of plans containing such objectives are slightly more specific, referring explicitly to public disorder, nuisance, vandalism and noise. One objective highlights alcohol-related incidents in particular. A number of plans make references to such things as residents' 'quality of life'. Four plans include objectives explicitly concerned with tackling public order. One of these (Thames Valley) is concerned with dealing effectively with 'serious' outbreaks of disorder (perhaps related to demonstrations at Newbury). In addition, Cleveland's objective to deal more effectively with public disorder appears to be focused on town centre disorder. Two plans include objectives aimed at reducing fear of crime. These are very difficult areas to measure in terms of hard PIs, and this is reflected in the plans. Four plans do not identify PIs for these kinds of objective (Lancashire, South Yorkshire, Essex, Hampshire – this plan indicates that work will be undertaken to develop a useful PI). A number of plans give the PI as some measure of levels of public nuisance/disorder – for example, Cheshire intends to measure the 'level of public disturbance reduction' in a range of ways, including the percentage of complainants satisfied, and other 'identified criteria' (which are actually not identified in the plan). Suffolk's PI is the number of public disorder incidents per 1000 population. Merseyside intends to monitor the number of command and control incidents classified as public disorder. Northamptonshire's PI for its rather broad objective to increase the level of public tranquillity is simply the level of recorded crime. Greater Manchester Police's PI on this is the number of complaints received about youths causing nuisance by 1000 population. Cleveland intends to measure the number of operations carried out to deal with town centre disorder. Finally, objectives that aim to deal with fear of crime tend to have PIs expressed in terms of public satisfaction with patrol levels, although one plan has a PI expressed in terms of fear of crime as measured by public surveys.

Management and organisation

Although 14 plans include local objectives specifically concerned with managerial and organisational issues, these issues are not completely ignored in other plans. Most plans include sections on organisational strategies in support of the main objectives, which cover matters of management and internal organisational support, even though they are not always framed explicitly as objectives. This analysis is confined to plans that specifically framed local objectives of this type. Within this general category, there is quite a lot of variation. Some plans include general objectives of this type (for example, 'To implement the Kent policing model' or 'To continue to develop Surrey's policing system'). Another plan (Essex) includes a general objective to increase the economy, efficiency and effectiveness with which the constabulary is managed. A number of plans make reference to improved deployment of operational resources, in particular to the more effective use of the special constabulary. A few plans include objectives concerning better quality of investigations, or improved technical support for detectives.

Two plans include objectives that aim to improve the quality of case files or evidence submitted to the Crown Prosecution Service (CPS). One plan has an objective to improve the information systems within the force, three include objectives about training and personnel matters and two include an objective to devolve budgets and decision-making to lower levels in the organisation. The PIs attached to this range of objectives vary a great deal. Some plans do not set PIs for internal/organisational objectives. This is clearly the case when the objectives are so broad as to defy measurement (see Kent and Surrey). Some of the internal standards are more amenable to measurement. For example, the improvement in quality of CPS files has a PI that will monitor the percentage of prosecution files meeting an agreed standard, and the percentage sent within particular time limits. Another PI is the percentage of detections via fingerprint identification (attached to the objective to improve technical support for detections). Humberside set a range of internal objectives and its was the only plan to include an objective and measure aimed at marketing the policing plan within the force. The PI given for this is the percentage of staff aware of their role in delivering the plan (which presumably will be measured by surveys). The plan also included PIs for numbers of connections with the computer network, for percentage of budget devolved, for number of police posts civilianised and for numbers of days lost through sickness.

Crime prevention, community involvement and partnership
Within this general category there is again some variation between plans in the way objectives are framed. On the one hand, there are general objectives with a sometimes rather vague meaning, such as 'to deliver a community-based police service' (Warwickshire). Several plans include objectives specifically mentioning partnerships, though again these are somewhat general. Examples of these are 'to work in partnership to promote community safety', or 'to work more effectively with other organisations' (West Yorkshire). Some objectives are more specific. North Yorkshire, for example, states that the police will progress with joint police/local authority closed-circuit television (CCTV) initiatives. Two objectives are concerned with increasing public participation, one by increasing the number of neighbourhood watch (NW) schemes (Devon and Cornwall) and the other by increasing participation in NW and the special constabulary. Two objectives focus on the need to improve consultation and, in this sense, should be seen as objectives for the police authority rather than the force. One of these (West Midlands) particularly concerns the police community consultative groups, whereas the other simply aims to 'improve the police authority consultation process'. Given the broad nature of this general category and the naturally less 'measurement-friendly' aspects of the subject areas, a range of PIs have been adopted. The broader objectives tend not to have PIs (as in Warwickshire), but more specific ones do. These include such things as measuring the level of public awareness of consultation mechanisms, or the numbers of people who attend PCCGs; numbers of NW schemes or percentage of households covered by NW; numbers of CCTV schemes in operation and percentage of population reporting feeling reassured by CCTV; and numbers of partnerships supporting local policing initiatives.

Burglary
Although one of the national objectives is concerned with burglary, a number of plans include additional local objectives with this focus, though they have a

different emphasis from the national objective. Indeed, on the surface, some of these local objectives could be seen as contradicting or undercutting the national objective. The national objective focuses on increasing the numbers of detections per 100 officers. In theory, a successful initiative to reduce the overall incidence of burglary will reduce the chance of performing against the national objective, there being fewer burglaries to detect. The majority of plans containing local objectives on burglary focus on the numbers of burglaries: 11 specifically aim to reduce the incidence of burglary (of which one aims both to reduce the number of offences and to increase detections). One plan focuses in particular on commercial burglary. Another includes an objective that aims to increase the detection rate for domestic burglary. The most popular PI attached to local burglary objectives is the number of domestic burglaries per 1000 dwellings, though some plans identify other measures of incidence such as total number of burglaries, or burglaries as a percentage of total crime. A few plans also identify the detection rate for burglary as a PI, and one (West Yorkshire) adds the number of primary detections as an additional PI. The plan that includes commercial burglary as a local objective simply mirrors the KPI for domestic burglary (detections per 100 officers), but adds the total number of commercial burglaries as another PI. It should be noted that almost all plans included similar additional PIs for the national key objective concerned with domestic burglary. This may have the same effect as introducing a particular local objective to reduce total incidence rather than increase numbers of detections. However, the inclusion of an additional local objective on burglary could be interpreted in some quarters as a recognition of the limitations of the KO and KPI in this regard.

Car crime

Ten plans include objectives relating to theft of and/or from motor vehicles. Within this category, objectives are divided between those that emphasise prevention or reduced incidence of autocrime and those that stress increasing detections. Two of the plans include objectives aimed at reducing the overall incidence of car crime, and four have objectives to increase the number or proportion of detections. Two plans (Avon and Somerset and Staffordshire) include objectives that simultaneously aim to reduce the incidence and increase the number of detections. The South Yorkshire plan has a general objective to tackle car crime, introduced under KO3, but not specified in the Home Secretary's letter and therefore treated here as a local objective. In terms of the PIs, most plans with autocrime local objectives include more than one PI, measuring both total recorded crime and detection rates. Three plans adapt the national KPI 1, and include a PI of autocrime detections per 100 officers. One plan (Northumbria) has as the PI the total number of autocrimes (reflecting the crime prevention and reduction nature of the objective), and one plan does not set a hard PI for its autocrime objective.

Violent and serious crime

Nine plans include local objectives on violent crime in addition to the national objective, which is concerned with increasing the number of detections per 100 officers. Once again, this can be interpreted as a way of introducing a subtly different goal, which is aimed at prevention and reduction rather than primarily at detection. Five of the plans include objectives that specifically aim to prevent and/or reduce the incidence of violent crime (Merseyside, West Yorkshire, Dorset, Gloucestershire, Norfolk). One plan concentrates on detections, but aims to increase the detection rate rather than numbers of detections (Sussex). Another plan (Avon and Somerset) aims to target and arrest offenders who persistently commit serious and violent crimes in the force area, and another (West Mercia) aims to protect the police and public from armed criminals. The plan for Durham includes a local objective to improve the personal safety of police officers. Similar arguments apply to the local objectives concerned with violent crime as applied to those about domestic burglary. Part of the rationale behind stating a local objective on the same broad subject as the key national objective may be to give a different emphasis. This may be achieved implicitly by the large number of plans that do not contain specific local objectives on violent crime, yet add a number of PIs to the KPI (and, in some cases, state that total incidence would take priority). Nevertheless, plans that include specific local objectives about violent crime, attach PIs that give a different emphasis from the KPI. The most popular is total number of recorded violent crimes per 1000 population (although two plans just use total recorded violent crime). One plan (Sussex) uses the PI of the detection rate for violent crime, and two others include victim satisfaction as additional PIs. In Durham, the objective focused on officer safety has a number of PIs attached; these include the numbers of assaults on officers and the percentage of staff taking sick leave due to assault.

Drugs

Although drugs are referred to in the third key national objective (KO3), seven plans include specific local objectives relating to this subject (Greater Manchester, Merseyside, West Yorkshire, Cleveland, Dyfed-Powys, Surrey, Staffordshire). Two of these objectives are framed in a general way – 'to tackle the misuse of drugs' (Cleveland) and 'to address and tackle the incidence of drug dealing and abuse' (Merseyside). Two plans include two local objectives focused on drugs, one concerned with enforcement and the other with prevention/education. For example, in one objective the Greater Manchester plan aims to target drug dealers and in another to encourage and promote drug prevention initiatives. Similarly, in Dyfed-Powys, one objective is to enforce the law rigorously against the misuse of drugs and another is to encourage multi-agency partnerships to prevent drugs misuse. Staffordshire, through having a local drugs objective, combines both enforcement and prevention aims. It is sometimes difficult to distinguish between national and local objectives in the area of drugs because of their mention under KO3. This is partly reflected in the fact that although only seven plans include local objectives framed around drugs, a much larger number of plans include PIs on the subject of drugs. Of all 41 plans, ten do not include a specific performance indicator for drugs, and a further three include performance indicators for prevention only. The remaining 28 plans include enforcement-based drugs PIs, the most common being the numbers of arrests and disposals under the Misuse of Drugs Act, although some include other enforcement type indicators such as the value of drugs seizures and the number of search warrants executed in relation to drugs. A few of these plans include prevention indicators, such as the number of anti-drugs talks given in schools, or the number of multi-agency drugs prevention teams set up. One plan (Hampshire) explicitly refuses to employ the nationally-set enforcement based PI. A number of the plans that do not set a drugs PI refer to PIs being set on division, or to work in progress to develop a useful indicator in this area of policing.

Protection of vulnerable groups

When the national objectives were introduced, some commentators argued that there would be a skewing of activity towards areas that are more measurable by hard data (such as arrests and detections) and away from the more complex areas of policing that take up a lot of time and resources and, more often than not, produce little in the way of concrete statistical 'results'. Two areas of policing often referred to in this regard are domestic violence and racial violence and harassment. Six policing plans contain objectives of this sort. Again, some of the objectives chosen are at a general level, such as Derbyshire's 'to protect people's rights and freedoms' (although the plan makes clear that divisional objectives coming out of this force objective have concerned issues such as stop and search policy and racial incidents, which are considered central to policing among ethnic minorities).

Cleveland is slightly more specific in that it includes a local objective to 'protect vulnerable people, especially ethnic minority groups'. West Midlands has the broader aim of promoting good relations between people of different ethnic minority groups. The local objective in Northumbria is to take positive action to reduce all forms of racism, measured by the percentage of reported racial incidents where further police action is taken. In West Yorkshire, the objective is to increase the percentage of racial incidents that are reported to the police. However, no PI is identified in the main plan for this objective. The South Yorkshire plan includes local objectives on both domestic and racial violence, introduced as local priorities under the KO1 on increasing detections for violent crime. One of these objectives aims to reduce the incidence of repeat victimisation related to domestic violence (which would in fact reduce the number of detections and therefore does not really complement the KO), and the other aims to improve the level of service provided to victims of racial incidents. The South Yorkshire plan does not identify any PIs as such, only targets. However, the nature of some of the targets make clear what the PI is (for example, if the target is to increase the detection rate to x per cent, then the PI is the detection rate). However, the targets for most of these local objectives do not allow us to imply a PI. In fact, they are framed more as objectives, first to implement the recording and monitoring system for domestic violence and second to develop multi-agency policy for dealing with racial incidents. Only in Northumbria does the plan contain a 'hard' PI attached to the objective, namely the percentage of reported racial incidents where further police action is taken. In Derbyshire, there is no force-wide PI for the broad local objective about protecting people's rights, but the divisional plans have specific PIs attached.

Other local objectives

A number of plans include local objectives that do not fit easily into any of the above categories. In some cases these are very broad, such as the West Midlands' objective 'to promote good citizenship'. Some include plans to look at all crime. For example, Northamptonshire has a local objective to reduce overall crime, Sussex has one to obtain a 30 per cent overall detection rate and West Mercia has one to reduce the number of crime victims. North Yorkshire plans to target criminals travelling into the force area.

FUNCTIONAL ANALYSIS OF LOCAL OBJECTIVES

Although the categorisation we have used here provides a useful way of exploring the range of subjects covered by the local objectives, it is unable to tell us whether there is a clear skew in the nature of the objectives. For example, under drugs we have both enforcement and education/prevention oriented objectives classified together.

It was suggested that police forces might be encouraged to prioritise crime-fighting approaches at the expense of other areas of policing, given that arrests and detections have proved easier to measure than prevention or community affairs. This fear was partly encouraged by the fact that the first three key performance indicators concern numbers of detections, or numbers of arrests. In Table 3.2, we have therefore analysed the distribution of local objectives between five broad areas of policing: crime investigation/detection, crime prevention/reduction, public order and reassurance, traffic, and other.

It is not immediately apparent from this analysis that in terms of adopted local objectives there has been a shift towards enforcement and crime-fighting. A larger number of local objectives concerned prevention and reduction, quality of service to victims or the public in general, and traffic policing (mainly the reduction of road traffic accident casualties). By far the biggest single category concerned matters of internal organisation and management. We would suggest it is reasonable to infer that this category of local objectives was heavily influenced by chief constables, for police authorities have traditionally shown little interest in (and been allowed little influence over) matters of internal force organisation. This suggests two things. First, that many local objectives are strongly influenced or entirely set by chief constables. Second, that matters of internal organisation and managerial efficiency are seen as a vitally important part of the policing plan. Here we are perhaps seeing a shift towards contractual and managerial forms of accountability more typical of business planning, whereas objectives directly concerning the style and approach of policing, or directing resources towards particular areas, might be seen as more in the realm of 'political' accountability.

Table 3.2 Distribution of local objectives between policing functions

Policing function	Number of local objectives
Crime investigation/detection	26[4]
Crime prevention/reduction	38[5]
Public order and reassurance	21
Traffic	36
Other	124
(internal organisation and management)	(54)
(quality of service)	(33)
(partnerships and community affairs)	(28)[6]

ACTION PLANS

The majority of plans include at least some reference to the actions that will be taken to meet the stated objectives. However, only in a relatively small number of plans (nine) are such action plans given in any detail, and in a substantial minority of plans (16) there is no reference at all to how the objectives will be achieved. In this, the plans are similar to those from the previous year (Weatheritt, 1996).

PERFORMANCE TARGETS

Virtually all the 1996/7 plans set specific performance targets for at least some of the objectives. There are only two exceptions to this (Dorset and North Wales), where the plans explicitly explain that no target has been set because the information systems to make such targets meaningful are not yet in place. Both plans indicate that the force will work to address this problem in the coming year, so that specific targets can be set in the next plan. Although most plans set specific targets where possible (i.e. to increase detections per 100

---

4. This includes four objectives that mention both detection and prevention, plus two that mention drugs enforcement and partnerships to reduce drug misuse.
5. This includes the four objectives that include both detection and prevention.
6. This includes the two objectives that mention both partnerships and drugs law enforcement.

officers by x), some opt for general targets (i.e. to increase detections, to do better than last year). In those plans where the first two national objectives were modified, either by adding a particular local objective on the same subject or using a different PI, the targets reflect this. For example, in Wiltshire, as well as having a target set for KPI 1, targets are also set to reduce the actual incidence of crime and to increase the detection rate. Presumably, those indicators which have targets specified take priority over those which do not. A large number of plans aim to monitor 'service-standards' as well as the more quantifiable indicators. These are usually measured in terms of the satisfaction of the public in general (or of particular groups such as victims) and, in Nottinghamshire, appeared to be seen as a 'qualitative' balance to the 'quantitative' measurements in the performance system.

MONITORING

Although the majority of the plans make at least some reference to the monitoring of performance against the plan, about ten do not make clear the ways in which performance will be monitored. Of those that do mention monitoring, this is most usually framed in terms of regular reports from the chief constable to the police authority. The majority of these mention quarterly reports, although three plans refer to more regular monitoring reports (every one or two months), and one refers to a six-monthly performance review report to the police authority. Some of these plans identify a particular sub-committee of the police authority with responsibility for monitoring, for example, the 'audit and performance review' committee in one police authority and the 'audit panel' in another. Two plans refer to internal police force monitoring as a performance review by headquarters departments of police divisional or departmental managers. Six refer to monitoring only in a very general way. They mention the police authority's annual report, or refer to the police authority as one of a range of bodies, such as HMIC and the Audit Commission, with responsibility for monitoring performance.

FINANCIAL INFORMATION

Different approaches have emerged on the costing of policing plans. Although the Home Office circular 27/1994 refers to 'costed' policing plans, the Police and Magistrates' Courts Act itself makes no such references. Furthermore, the circular explicitly recognises that many forces will not have developed the appropriate financial information and budgetary systems to allow them to 'cost' objectives in terms of costing policing 'outputs'. However, it does state that 'in the longer term, it is envisaged that forces will move to a more sophisticated system of costing to show the distribution of resources by output'. The published plans for 1996/7 indicate that the majority of police forces do not have sufficiently sophisticated financial information systems to allow output costing. Most plans include only the most basic 'costing' in terms of the minimal information required by the circular – namely a summary of normal income and expenditure details. In general, policing plans for 1996/7 continued to include broad financial information that was not closely linked to the rest of the plan or to its stated objectives.

The level of financial detail varies between plans. Some opt for a brief summary of expenditure and income, along with an outline of the capital programme for the coming year. Most, however, provide more detail than this. A large number give a breakdown of the force staffing, while others include details of the civilianisation programme. Some provide an analysis of income sources (for example, council taxes, business rates, Home Office cash-limited grants, rate support grants, service charges and other fees). A number include a broad breakdown of expenditure by service area (for example, a pie chart divided into categories such as traffic, crime, responding to calls and patrol). Within this, some include the allocation of total resources to divisions and departments. As noted above, only a few plans actually relate financial information to the rest of the plan in any detail. Devon and Cornwall, Hampshire, Kent and Northumbria were the only ones to make any explicit attempt to provide cost estimates for objectives. Perhaps the most detailed of these is Hampshire, in which each objective comes with an estimated costing of different elements. A number of plans explicitly outline the difficulties involved in output costing in a service like policing, and some indicate that initiatives will be developed to improve systems in this regard. For example, the Cleveland plan reports that the force will develop its activity-based costing system over the coming year. The Norfolk plan also refers to developments in financial information systems, as does the plan in North Wales. The Thames Valley and West Mercia plans include some broad activity analysis.

CHANGES FROM PREVIOUS YEAR'S PLAN

In general, most plans are similar in size and content to those produced in 1995/6. One change has been towards setting targets – seven plans that did not set performance targets in 1995/6 did so in 1996/7. The majority of the others do not appear to have changed a great deal over the two years. A few became more streamlined in the second year of planning. For example, Nottinghamshire's plan identified a range of local policing objectives in 1995/6, but for 1996/7 there is only one, concerning traffic. Hertfordshire's 1995/6 plan was much longer than its 1996/7 one. Similarly, Bedfordshire's very professionally produced and generously illustrated A4 glossy booklet for 1995/6 has, following Northamptonshire's lead in 1996/7, become a five-page fold-out summary. To a lesser extent, Cheshire has also shortened its plan. In most cases, the national and local objectives have changed little. However, in a small number of plans, the local objectives have been modified, or in some cases new ones have been added. Thus, for example, in Cumbria there was no local objective set in the plan for 1995/6, but in the current plan there is a local objective on dealing with nuisance incidents. The overall impression is one of continuity over the first two years of local policing plans.

CONCLUSIONS

Our central questions in this chapter concerned the content of local policing plans, in particular how specific they were in setting objectives for the local service and what model of policing they implied. Underpinning these questions are the wider concerns we set out in the first two chapters, namely exploring the nature of the balance between local and central controls over policing, and the balance between political and managerial forms of accountability. What conclusions can we draw from the analysis of policing plans?

First, it seems clear that in the second year of planning since the PMCA came into operation, there is still a considerable amount of local variation in presentation and content (though most police authorities and forces now tend to follow the guidance laid down in the Home Office circular 27/1994). While some central features of the plans appear to be widely shared, in terms of some aspects of content, length, presentation and production they do not appear in any way to be uniform documents. Given their status as *local* plans, this is perhaps to be expected and welcomed.

Second, although it is clear that police authorities have made more efforts to express themselves as 'owners' of the policing plans in 1996/7 than they were either willing or able to do previously, analysis of the objectives still suggests that, in terms of their substantive content, the police service drives the plans. The largest single subject category of local objectives continues to concern internal managerial and organisational objectives. These, we feel confident, are much more likely to have come from the forces themselves than from police authorities. Two conclusions may be drawn from this. First, as we have argued, the 'balance of power' still seems to favour forces over authorities in the drafting of plans. And second, perhaps because of this, the emphasis in local objectives is managerial rather than strategic.

Third, there is no clear evidence yet that plans are becoming dominated or driven by central concerns. Although a large number of plans give prominence to national objectives, an even greater number do not. Moreover, some of the plans that prioritise the KOs do so, they report, because they were found to reflect local concerns. Though under certain circumstances this could sound disingenuous, in this case it is lent some credence by the senior officers and local authority representatives in the study who described the Home Secretary's objectives as being largely uncontentious. The majority of plans give the impression, whether deliberately or not, that planning is not driven primarily by national concerns. The KOs are included, as is the statutory requirement, but they are not given special weight and are often subsumed or incorporated into a broader set of local objectives. Moreover, some plans appear to rephrase or revise the KOs in order to give them a different emphasis (in terms of prevention rather than detection for example).

Fourth, the analysis of national and local objectives provides little clear evidence that performance objectives and PIs have led to a skewing of emphasis towards crime and, in particular, enforcement-type functions. Though this concern has been expressed for some time, it is not borne out by the analysis of the published plans. The functional analysis of local objectives suggested that many police authorities/forces took the opportunity to identify local objectives concerned with crime prevention/reduction, public order and reassurance, and traffic. Of course, the written plans by themselves do not tell us what priority these local objectives received compared with the crime-oriented ones.

Finally, although one of the government's intentions in introducing policing plans was to provide the basis for a finely-graded costing of policing services, there is little evidence so far that police authorities and forces are at all close to being able to produce plans with 'output costed' objectives or, indeed, that there is much enthusiasm for doing so. It seems that the financial information systems are simply not sophisticated enough for complex activity analysis and costing. This provides one important limit on the move to full-scale managerialism. Thus, although performance is increasingly measured in ever more subtle ways, and 'success' or 'failure' can in theory be linked to financial resources, most authorities/forces are a considerable distance from being able to tie the performance of discrete functions to expenditure.

Chapter 4

Accountability after the Act:
The View from the Police Authorities

The core of the research reported in this book came from case studies in three police force areas. However, it is vital to locate these data within the broader national picture of changes taking place in police authorities. To gather information about the national situation, in the summer of 1996 we conducted a telephone survey of representatives from the other 38 provincial police authority secretariats. We were thus able to combine questions that elicited straightforward factual information with more subjective material on how the new authorities were operating in practice. The use of case studies allowed us to explore some of the issues highlighted by the survey is greater depth.

In conducting the survey, it was only practical to undertake a single interview in each police authority area. There were two obvious candidates for such interviews – the chairperson and the clerk of the relevant police authority. As we mentioned in Chapter 1, we decided to interview the clerk (or in some cases the deputy clerk), for it was felt that clerks were best placed to provide the descriptive, factual information we required, and were also the most likely to provide a relatively 'neutral' (at least non-party-political) view of the changes that had taken place. That said, when considering the more subjective areas covered by the survey (such as changes in a new police authority's effectiveness and influence, or the impact of independent members), the reader should always bear in mind the position of the interviewee. It is likely, of course, that police authority chairpersons, other police authority members or representatives of the police force may have held very different views from those expressed by the clerks. For example, it may well be the case that clerks would have a natural preference for smaller police authorities because the clerking of such bodies (managing the committee process, circulating reports and papers, and organising business) becomes an easier task.

In this chapter we look at the data derived from the telephone survey of 38 police authority secretariats, combined with data from interviews with police authority secretariats in the three case study forces. The analysis that follows therefore covers all 41 police authorities in England and Wales.

THE SIZE AND STRUCTURE OF NEW POLICE AUTHORITIES

Of the new police authorities, the Home Secretary granted three permission to expand their size from the usual 17 members. A further 19 police authorities unsuccessfully applied to the Home Office for an increase in size. The effect of reducing the size of police authorities, coupled with the reduction in the number of elected members, resulted in a redistribution of chairs between political parties during the first year of the reforms, and led to some critical comment. A survey in early 1995 found that although Labour chaired 23 of the 41 provincial police authorities in England and Wales prior to 1995, elections to the shadow authorities revealed that this had been reduced to 17, with the Liberal Democrats and Conservatives having eight chairs each ('Labour buffeted by police chair losses', *Local Government Chronicle*, 17 February 1995). The number of police authorities chaired by magistrate members increased from two to seven. Table 4.1 suggests that by 1996 the Labour and Conservative share of chairs had remained roughly constant, with fewer Liberal Democrat chairs, and two police authorities chaired by appointed independent members.

Table 4.1 Distribution of chairs of police authorities (summer 1996)

Police authority chair	Number of police authorities
Labour councillor	16
Conservative councillor	9
Liberal Democrat councillor	5
Other councillor	1
Magistrate	8
Independent member	2

As we saw in Chapter 2, according to Kenneth Clarke, one of the intentions of the Police and Magistrates' Courts Act 1994 was to weaken the influence of party politics on police authorities, and thus reduce the number of authorities dominated by a single political grouping. This was, of course, an almost inevitable effect of reducing the number of elected members to nine (in most cases). Table 4.2 shows the political distribution of the *elected part* of the 41 provincial police authorities in England and Wales in 1996. It is important to note that given the reduced proportion of the police authority taken up by councillors, the question of whether or not one party or the other has a majority within the elected part will inevitably be less important than it would have been under the pre-1995 arrangements.

The most marked dominance of a single party came in four police authorities where the Labour Party held eight of the nine councillor seats. A further five authorities had seven Labour councillors and five also had six councillors from the Labour Party. However, in no police authority was there a built-in majority for a single political party (i.e. one party holding all nine seats, or ten seats in the case of the three larger authorities).

Table 4.2 Political distribution of elected component in police authorities (summer 1996)

Political balance (elected element of police authority only)	Number of police authorities
No single party with majority	21
Labour majority	16
Liberal Democrat majority	3
'Other' majority	1

In assessing effectiveness, a number of clerks specifically referred to the new smaller size of the police authorities, which most felt made them more effective. As the clerk of a combined police authority reported, 'There's a smaller number of people, actually going out and meeting the public face-to-face, and that I think is a plus. It is a smaller body, and that means it can't carry passengers, they participate pretty evenly, and they have to be pretty knowledgeable because they are going to have to stand up and give an answer.' Another combined police authority clerk also felt that the smaller size had some positive effects: 'I personally think that the change to 17 (members) ... although we think it's a little on the small side for an authority of our size, has actually helped the conduct of business very much.' Another shire police authority clerk said: 'It's easier to manage of course as a smaller body, so you tend to get a more sensible discussion.' One shire police authority clerk felt that the smaller size of police authority had led to a closer relationship with the chief constable: 'Because the authority is smaller I think the relationship [between the authority and the chief] has got closer. I think that is inevitable. He can arrange more events that involve all the authority because its a manageable size.' We should again note the point made earlier about the possibility of a 'natural preference' among clerks for smaller authorities.

However, a number of clerks clearly felt that the smaller size had made the police authority less effective. As one clerk from a metropolitan police authority said: 'The main problem with the new authority is that a big authority, as it was, allowed representation of a lot of areas and a lot of interests. And it's fundamentally too small now, and it puts demands on members for things like evening panel meetings and lay visiting which can be quite difficult.' Another metropolitan police authority clerk complained that the smaller size of the new police authority had left large districts of the force area 'unrepresented' on the police authority. This feeling was not restricted to metropolitan areas, for the clerk of a large rural shire police authority said that: 'The main concern of the authority still is that nine elected members do not adequately represent the population of this area, and they are concerned that the authority is too small.' In these areas, councillors were seen as very much representing the people of their local area on the police authority. This contrasts with the 'stewardship' emphasis underlying the new police authorities; the main role was to be as effective overseers of service-delivery. That they had some elected representatives among them was considered sufficient 'democratic value', and members were supposed to be on the police authority for the benefit of all people across the force area, not representing the interests of a particular part of the area. This tension was later to come out quite strongly in the case studies.

OPERATION OF NEW POLICE AUTHORITIES

Support services for the new authorities

Police authorities require a range of support services, including clerking and committee secretariat, legal and financial advice, management services, pay-roll and personnel functions, and architectural services. The reforms contained in the PMCA, along with requirements to put some services out to competitive tender, means that there are growing pressures to change the way support services are provided. The survey collected some very general information about the level of, and changes in, support services to the new police authorities. We had hoped to collect financial information, in order to compare the proportion of police authority budgets spent on support services for the police authority. However, the first few interviews with clerks showed that this was going to be an impossible task. As they pointed out, obtaining comparable figures cannot be done because of the many ways in which support is organised, including a range of contracts with councils, with outside agencies and with police forces, many of which involve buying segments of people's time and calling upon people employed by local authorities, police authorities and police forces.

As expected, we found that the combined and metropolitan police authorities introduced fewer changes in how they organised their support services. This is because the police authorities in these areas have been independent precepting bodies for some years. In the metropolitan areas, the new police authorities on the whole continued to receive their support services from the 'lead authority' in the area. One exception was a metropolitan police authority that made use of a 'joint secretariat' of 60 people, which had existed since the abolition of the metropolitan county councils in 1985. This joint secretariat provided support services for four 'joint boards', including the one that administered the police, and recharged the costs to constituent councils. In the combined police authorities, there were changes in a few areas. In one, for example, staff employed by the police force now undertook the clerking and financial services previously provided by councils. Three of the combined police authorities reported having support staff based at police HQ, which is where the authority meets. One combined police authority had relocated to new accommodation, which the clerk reported was situated between the county hall (where they had met previously) and the force HQ.

It was in the shire police authorities that the major changes were occurring as a result of the Act and that police authorities were gradually becoming independent of the county councils of which they had once been a part. This was happening to varying extents across England and Wales. In the majority of police authorities, the support services continued to come largely from the county councils, often with service-level agreements (SLAs). In most cases, as a result of the shift in financial management responsibilities to the police force, financial services were less dependent on county councils. The majority of police authorities still had as clerk the chief executive of a constituent local authority. However, most clerks reported that this was under review and a few explicitly predicted a move in the future either to independent clerking and support services or to clerking by employees of the force. Some police authorities had already moved along this route. About seven reported that the police authority support and meetings were based at police HQ. Only one police authority reported having moved its clerking services and meeting place to independent accommodation, i.e. to buildings owned neither by the force nor the local authority. In some areas, the move to independence from county council support services led to tensions between the police authority and the county council. As we found in our case study areas, the fact that clerks and treasurers to police authorities were most likely to be employees of the county council gave rise to a conflict of interests, as they often had to adjudicate between police authority interests and those of the county council.

Number and length of meetings

In general, the new police authorities meet as full authorities more often and for longer periods than their predecessors. Most clerks reported that the full authority meets more often, though some continued with quarterly meetings. No police authority met less than quarterly and a few met every month. On average, the new police authorities are meeting about six times a year. They are also meeting for slightly longer periods, if anything, though most reported little change in the length of meetings. Clerks reported that the average length of police authority meetings is now about two-and-a-half hours. However, given that the nature of the authorities' work has changed so much, this is perhaps less significant than it first seems. Under the old police authorities, much of the work was undertaken in committees; new police authorities have a more slimmed down committee structure and therefore deal with a lot of work in full authority. Clerks in the new authorities generally felt that the move towards conducting business in meetings of the full authority was a positive development.

The nature of meetings

Changes in the nature of the meetings were the focus of some interest. Many clerks reported important changes in the nature of the debate. As we saw above, police authorities were no longer being dominated by one political party. The business of the meeting could no longer be decided beforehand in party caucus meetings, and this had opened up the debate. In such authorities, some clerks reported that councillors of all parties were now prepared to contribute to the debate as individuals rather than taking a 'party line'. Furthermore, they argued, the small size of the new authorities has made it possible for all members to make a more active contribution. On a large authority, it is difficult to catch the chairperson's eye if a member wants to make a contribution and easy to hide if the member wants to avoid contributing. This has changed on the new authorities.

The majority of clerks, or clerks' assistants, reported that there was now much more debate about the business of policing, rather than discussions of national party-political issues. A number of clerks said that meetings had become more focused and businesslike. It is important to note that 'businesslike' in this context was usually taken to mean a focus on performance objectives, targets and indicators. For example, the clerk of a shire police authority said that 'we have more questions and comments on the police authority report than we did on the old police committee report', but added that these questions often concerned detailed matters of statistical performance. Another clerk gave the following account of the changing nature of meetings: 'The majority of the time is taken up by the chief constable presenting an operational report and then it's open for any member of the authority to ask questions . . .It's becoming a bit more obviously performance-oriented, there's more statistical information about, whereas previously with a larger police authority . . . the questions tended to be fairly parochial.'

One clerk of a shire police authority put this change down to independence from the county council structure: 'Because for at least some of them it is their public service contribution – it's not diluted with concern for education, social services etc – it's therefore obviously more focused'. There were two general views expressed on the separation of police authorities from the day-to-day business of local authorities. On the one hand, there were those who felt that the increased distance from concern with other public services was deleterious and affected the quality of debate and decision-making within police authorities. On the other hand, the majority of respondents felt that the change was positive, in that it both reduced party-political squabbling, and tended to promote a stronger focus on 'police business'.

Not all interviewees felt that this change towards more 'businesslike' meetings was necessarily a good thing. For example, the following quotation from a clerk of a combined police authority came into this category: 'It is a more business-like way of working. I do detect among members sometimes a feeling that they lack a true role. So meetings are short, business-like, to the point, because there isn't much meat to get stuck into once the policing plan and the budget have been agreed.' Another clerk, from a metropolitan police authority, also felt that the new police authority's concerns with the 'business' of policing diverted the meetings from a consideration of important issues such as the overall style of policing in the force, or the force's approach to particularly difficult areas of policing such as racial attacks and domestic violence. Because much of the discussion at meetings now concerns overall performance targets, and statistical reports about objectives, indicators and financial performance, these wider 'political' issues rarely appeared on the agenda.

INDEPENDENT MEMBERS

The selection process

As outlined in earlier chapters, the government's original intention had been for the Home Secretary to appoint independent members, as well as the chairpersons, directly to the police authorities. This part of the proposed reforms underwent important amendments during its passage through parliament, and the final result was a rather complex compromise, which combined elements of local and national control. The process was for a local selection panel to be convened, which consisted of three people. One was to be put forward by the Home Secretary, another by the local police authority (in practice it was usually the chairperson of the police authority who went forward), and the third to be chosen by these two. This selection panel could shortlist up to 20 names (24 in the three larger police authorities) from applications for the position of independent member. This list would be forwarded to the Home Office, which would reduce the shortlist by half, and usually meant ten names being returned to the local selection panel. They would then choose the final five candidates from this list.

Table 4.3. Numbers of applications received for 'independent member' places on police authorities

Number of applications	Number of police authorities
Fewer than 50	5
51–100	16
101–150	9
151–200	4
Don't know	7

The survey collected information on the process of advertising for and selecting independent members, on the number of applications received, on the occupational/professional backgrounds of the members who were selected, and on their emerging effect on the operation of the new police authorities.

Just over half (22) of the clerks reported that some action (supplementary to the Home Office advertisements in the national press) was taken to encourage applications locally. Most placed advertisements in the local press, some targeted local companies and community groups by sending them application forms, some issued local press releases, or visited the section 106 committees to try to encourage applicants. Not all police authorities were able to provide the exact number of applications, but Table 4.3 illustrates the distribution in broad bands. For those authorities who had information on this question, the average number of applications was 97. The average number of applications was somewhat lower in the former single county police authorities.

As we outlined in Chapter 2, during 1995 a number of reports suggested that there had been political interference from the Home Office in the selection of independents. One report stated that Conservative Central Office was investigating the likely political allegiances of some candidates, and that this was affecting the selection process (see 'Labour buffeted by police chair losses', *Local Government Chronicle*, 17 February 1995, p. 17). Our survey confirmed that suspicions about the effects of undue political interference arose in a number of police authorities, but suggested that in reality these were relatively few in number. Indeed, in two authorities, clerks reported that the main political interference had occurred locally, with Labour members targeting known Labour supporters. For example, in one police authority situated in a Labour stronghold, the clerk reported that Labour councillors had seen to it that a good number of Labour supporters were selected as independents: 'I think it was politically influenced, there's no doubt about that.' Another representative of a police authority secretariat in a Labour-dominated shire authority also reported that local Labour councillors had tried to pre-empt expected Home Office political interference by specifically targeting likely Labour supporters.

A minority of clerks reported that there had been disquiet among elected members that the Home Office had exercised its responsibilities inappropriately. In a small number of cases this was explicitly linked to party-political considerations, as the following quotes from shire police authority clerks illustrate:

> A large number of our members felt that it had been politically motivated and said so, and in fact instructed me to write to the Home Secretary which I did, and I got an answer that the whole matter was being dealt with very objectively.

> I would be very surprised, first time round, whether they [the Home Office] didn't fix it politically, certainly in —shire; those they had allowed us to choose from were more likely to be Conservative voters.

> Whether it is apocryphal or not, there were certainly suggestions that local MPs, and local Conservative doers, movers and shakers were perhaps unofficially talked to, and I can't confirm that or t'otherwise.

In a metropolitan area, it was reported that a local Conservative MP wrote a letter of complaint to the selection panel about one of the people on the confidential shortlist sent to the Home Secretary, which meant that this MP had been given access to the list. This convinced local Labour councillors that Conservative Party Central Office had been 'vetting' shortlists of candidates. A clerk of a shire police authority with a tradition of Labour control also reported that local Labour councillors felt that the shortlist coming back from the Home Office had been influenced by party-political considerations.

In a few other police authority areas, clerks saw local suggestions of Home Office 'interference' in the selection process not in party-political terms, but as the actions of a control-minded central government department intervening to 'show who is boss':

> As the result of our interviews, we put forward the 20 names to the Home Secretary, and starred ten names and said having seen them, these ten names seemed to be the best ... We got 8 of the 10 preferred ones back, the Home Secretary took two off. The selection panel instructed me to write to the Home Secretary to protest that we had seen the people, he hadn't, how could he possibly over-ride the judgement of the selection panel. And I got a letter back from Michael Howard which could be paraphrased 'Look mate, you've done your job, I'm doing mine, these are the names I'm prepared to approve, now get on with it and choose the five you want' (shire police authority).

> The independents selection panel ... used specific criteria; the types of people they thought would assist and enhance the abilities of the police authority ... when we had the 10 (names) back from the Home Secretary those criteria were absolutely destroyed. I think ... the process is too heavily influenced by the Home Secretary and not enough is left for local determination (combined police authority).

However, the majority of clerks made no complaints about central government interference in the selection of independent members, party-political or otherwise. Many felt that the process of selection was bizarre and rather tortuous, but that this was precisely to *limit* the opportunity for central political determination of the selection, and that it worked. A number pointed out that the Home Office has little scope for, or little to gain from, political interference in the selection process in the ways that have been suggested. For example, 'almost any of the 10, and we would argue any of the 20 otherwise we wouldn't have put them forward ... had a broad enough experience' (shire police authority). Then, 'there's also the obvious position that if you're "prescribed" 20 to bring down to 10 the element of choice (for the Home Office) is clearly very limited' (shire police authority).

A few other clerks reported their authority's concern that the shortlist of ten that came back from the Home Office did not contain enough women or ethnic minority people, or did not provide a sufficient geographical representation of the force area, but again saw this as an unintended consequence of a rather complicated and drawn-out selection procedure, and a lack of applications from certain groups. For example, the clerk of one shire police authority reported that 'there were one or two surprises. . . . One or two who we thought were rather good didn't come back from the Home Office.' There was no suggestion that this was due to undue party-political interference.

The majority of interviewees reported that elected members were reasonably satisfied with the Home Office shortlist of ten (selected from their original 20). Although most elected members were still opposed in principle to the appointment of non-elected people to police authorities, given that it was now law, they accepted that the process had been undertaken in a satisfactory manner. From these findings, it seems reasonable to conclude that suspicions of political interference by the Home Office in the process of selecting independent members were not widespread.

Background of independent members

As outlined in Chapter 2, Kenneth Clarke argued that police authorities would benefit from the experience of local businessmen. His successor as Home Secretary, Michael Howard, stated that the selection of independents would provide for a greater representation of teachers, farmers and shopkeepers than had been the case before. Since the Act became operational, a number of criticisms have emerged that the selection of independents has shown a bias towards people with business management experience, as well as retired senior officers from the armed services (Loveday, 1995). This survey collected some general information about the occupational and professional backgrounds of the independent members who were finally selected to serve on the new police authorities. Our findings confirm a strong representation of businesspeople among independent members, but there is also a range of other experience.

When examining Table 4.4 the reader should note that only *broad* background data about independent members were gathered by the survey. The table includes a significant number of retired people, in which case they are categorised by their former profession or occupation. The category 'businessman' or 'businesswoman' was often used, which is very wide-ranging, and covers a variety of industry sectors and occupations. Nevertheless, it is useful to give a broad indication of the background of the independents. Almost half the independent members have a background in private sector business or commerce. When these are added to the accountants, solicitors and doctors, it can be seen that well over half the independent members are from the professions or business. The next largest single representation, 15 per cent, comes from the field of education, with a number of retired or currently serving headteachers, other schoolteachers, academics and college lecturers. People who were categorised as having military (or emergency services) experience constituted 7 per cent of the total. A further 6 per cent had experience as civil servants or local government officers. About 16 per cent were categorised in a broad 'other' category, a heterogeneous group covering trade unionists, clergy, voluntary sector, housewives, and other people who could not be fitted into any of the main categories.

Table 4.4 *Occupational/professional backgrounds of independent members*

Occupational/Professional Background	Number of independent members (percentages in brackets)
Management, business, commerce	91 (45)
Academics, teachers, lecturers	30 (15)
Professions (accountants, solicitors, doctors, vets, architects)	21 (10)
Armed and emergency services	15 (7)
Civil service, local government	12 (6)
Other	33 (16)
Total	202[1]

The findings in Table 4.4 partly bear out the predictions that businesspeople will be over-represented on the new police authorities, even though about half the independent members come from other backgrounds. A number of clerks reported that the selection panels in their areas had wanted to achieve a good balance of different backgrounds and experiences. For example, the clerk of one shire police authority said: 'When it came to shortlisting, we were looking to target under-represented groups and backgrounds.' Most reported that the police authority was satisfied with the independent people appointed, despite early teething troubles in one or two police authorities where some independent members resigned and new ones had to be selected by the same complex process. In terms of the distribution of members by background on particular authorities, nine police authorities had three independent members from the same category or background, five had four, and in four cases all the independent members in the authorities in question had a management/business or commercial background.[2] In addition, on one police authority, all the independent members bar one come from a military (or emergency services) background.

Despite what appears on the surface to be an absence of variety among the independents in some authorities, it is important to remember that even in these cases, the broad categorisations hide a diversity of experience (for example between a retail manager and a specialist management consultant). Overall, we

---

1. This total excludes independent members from one police authority, where the information was unavailable.
2. Note that the broad 'other' category was not used in this analysis of concentration.

would argue that our figures suggest that most police authorities have obtained a greater balance of occupational/professional backgrounds than some of the critics, and some of the early appraisals of the independents, have suggested.

The impact of independent members

Clerks were asked for their general perceptions about the contributions of independent members to the running of police authorities. On the whole, according to them, independent members seem to have blended in well with the new police authorities and in only a minority of areas do any significant tensions exist. It should be noted that the question involved a broad generalisation and that many clerks stressed that the independents could not be regarded as a homogenous group. Overall, the majority of clerks reported that the independents were making active contributions to the police authority, but neither more nor less than other members. The clerks in a minority of police authorities (seven) reported that independent members were taking the lead, and were more active and influential than other members. In the same number of authorities, the clerks felt that the independents were still finding their feet and learning about their role on the new police authorities.

In the majority of police authorities then, clerks reported that independent members have made active and positive contributions, but stressed that this did not distinguish them from other police authority members. This view from the clerk to a shire police authority was rather typical, when he said that the independents had 'made quite a considerable impact', but added, 'I wouldn't say they're any different to the councillors really.' The following quotation came from the clerk of another shire police authority, and was again fairly typical of this kind of response: 'I wouldn't say that on balance the independent members stand out from the rest of the membership as being particularly more keen, although I think generally the authority as a group of 17 people probably works more cohesively and shall I say with a higher degree of interest than the former police committee.'

In a significant minority of police authorities the clerks clearly felt that the independent members were the new authorities' leading lights. For example, this quote came from the clerk of a combined police authority who felt that independent members were making more of a contribution than councillors: 'Officers have been impressed by the calibre of the independent members and their willingness to get involved with business ... they are probably a bit more proactive than some of the councillors ... perhaps they feel, as a new ingredient in police authorities, that they have to prove their role.'

Another clerk (from a combined police authority) reported that independent members' business backgrounds had been a key factor in their greater levels of influence: 'the independently-appointed members that we have, have certainly been quite searching in the business-type questions that they've come along with.' Another shire police authority clerk was quite clear that the independent members were, on the whole, more active than the old police authority members:

The introduction of independent members has had an effect though. They've been quite influential on the authority. To put it bluntly, I think the local authority members perhaps in the past took it for granted that they were in the majority and because of the make-up politically (one party dominant) . . . there was maybe a tendency to not spend as much time on some issues and debate them, whereas the independents have brought more of a questioning role into business.

Another clerk said that the independents had brought significant improvement: 'The level of debate has increased significantly, there's no question about that, and I think that's due to the independent members . . . they have injected a different sort of level of debate' (shire police authority). In most police authorities where the clerk reported that the introduction of independents had improved the police authority, this was explained in terms of adding a business perspective. One clerk reported that the meetings of the police authority had been improved by the introduction of independent members: 'There's a lot more debate and discussion of an informed nature.' In a shire police authority the clerk reported that:

> I think that things have quickly settled down and they have made a valuable contribution. . . . Insofar as members are needed for working groups or if replies to correspondence are needed or any contributions are needed the independent members nearly always seem to be the first to get their replies back and first to volunteer, and I think their thirst for knowledge and learning has been quite great and they've been keen to take on board any duties which come their way.

Some clerks specifically identified the independent members as the driving force behind what they saw as a more effective and influential police authority. As the following shire police authority clerk put it: 'Definitely, yes, it's becoming more active and influential. The Labour members wouldn't agree with that. I think they're feeling vulnerable at the moment because of the introduction of these new members who are ruffling things a little bit . . . on balance it's promoting a wider debate on issues within the authority.'

In some police authorities, of course, clerks felt that independent members had experienced difficulties in settling in to the police authority business an‚d as a result, had made little impact. The following quotation from a shire police authority illustrates this view:

> They haven't felt easy in adapting to the formal committee which they have come into in the authority. They have not felt there is a way for them to put forward individual items for consideration and they are very reluctant to question what they are being told by the chief constable in the authority meetings with the press and public present. We've been disappointed with their ability to influence the work of the authority.

Depoliticisation

As noted above, an expressed aim of the reforms had been to remove party-political debates from local police authority business. Most clerks argued that the introduction of independent members had led directly to the dilution of party politics on the new authorities. In areas where the old police committee had been dominated by one political party, matters were often decided in a party caucus prior to police authority meetings. Now that no political party could rely on built-in majorities, the meetings were often effectively depoliticised. In a number of cases, clerks reported that this has improved the level of debate, and focused it on local policing matters rather than on national party politics. This kind of view is summarised by the clerk to one shire police authority: 'We do not engage in party politics, there's very little party-political discussion within them now, we talk about business matters relating to policing and the community.' Another shire police authority clerk reported the following effect of introducing independent members: 'It is much, much less political. The local authority members are barely in a majority even as a group, and because they are in different groups they rarely are together.' The clerk of a combined police authority made a similar point:

> The former police authority was very much a political animal. Clearly politics will always play a part in any debate, but there is no doubt that the influence of independent members has depoliticised meetings. Definitely the debate now is far more meaningful and professional, whereas a lot of the decisions which were taken by the former police authority were taken in group meetings outside.

The clerk of a shire police authority described the 'depoliticising effect' on members in the following terms:

> They are police authority members, they represent the whole authority, and they're not coming along representing their own particular niche. And that, of course, has been a welcome change from the previous set up, in which there was, I suppose inevitably, there was some politics involved ... There are people who come to the meeting and say 'oh, this is different to what I've been used to, no backbiting and in-fighting and having a go at each other' and so on.

In some authorities, the clerks reported that the usual state of affairs was that party politics did not come into things, but on particular occasions it would raise its head. The following shire police authority clerk was typical of this view: 'I think it's true to say that all the members of the authority see it as not being a political forum ... So obviously there are political groupings and they appear at budget times and things like that, more than they do in the year. But I think the general feeling is that politics takes a second place.' The clerk of another shire police authority made the following observation: 'Coming from a local government background ... I notice that it is a very apolitical committee. Politics don't come into it strongly. They recognise their job is to support the police force and to provide an effective service. I've never seen any political bickering.'

Not all the new police authorities demonstrated this 'depoliticisation effect'. There appeared to be two reasons for this. First, not all the police authorities were, or felt themselves to be, 'political' before the reforms. It is perhaps worth stressing that in a number of police authority areas, even prior to the changes, there was little party-political debate on the authority. For example, in one combined police authority the clerk reported that 'there is a long tradition of non-political alignment in this area and even though we have to select members now according to the political balance of the authority, that attitude hasn't changed.' Another shire police authority clerk reported that 'party politics have virtually never shown themselves in the forum of the police authority; it's a non-party-political organisation essentially, votes are very rare at a full authority meeting.'

Second, some authorities had continued to be just as 'political' after the reforms as they had been before. In a small number (three), clerks reported that independent members had become embroiled in the local party politics. For example, one clerk reported that: 'The party-political affiliations of the independent members come out, and they either join the lobby for the Conservative or they join the lobby for the Labour nominee.' The clerk from another police authority also described independent member involvement in party politicking at the local level: 'Without asking them, I would be surprised if they weren't all Conservatives. They therefore respond well to the chairman who is also a Conservative, and is a well-organised and efficient person. They have been influential in enabling him to get the chair and sustaining him in the chair.' Another police authority clerk reported that in his view the new police authority was much *more* political than the old one. He reported that independent members had become involved in the party-political debate, and that a number of issues had gone to a vote, which had given rise to what he described as 'some fairly deep-seated enmities'. All these three were shire police authorities, with no single party dominant locally, and no particular history of political tensions over policing. Thus, it was difficult to pinpoint from discussions with police authority clerks what factors had caused such political tensions to arise.

Group behaviour

In most police authorities, clerks reported that (partly as a result of this depoliticisation) independent members did not operate as a group. The following quotation from a shire police authority clerk was typical: 'Broadly speaking, no. They certainly don't meet regularly as a group. . . . In fact what has happened is that prior to each full meeting of the authority all members have met without officers, a sort of single group if you like.'

However, in a minority of police authorities, despite the lack of formal groupings, the independent members do appear to have formed informal groups, usually in response to the fact that elected members are formed into political groups, or because they are a new and identifiably different kind of police authority member. One example of this came from another shire police authority:

> They regard themselves as a group and whenever there is any business to be done where a one-off representative grouping is required, the authority now has a standing arrangement that there will be one magistrate, one independent, one Labour, one Lib Dem and one Conservative. There is a *de facto* separation of them into a group. . . . All three lots of political members do regard themselves as groups.

Some other clerks also suggested that independents did from time to time present a common front. One of these examples involved political involvement and was quoted above. Others included the following shire police authority: 'Loosely, I suppose, they operate as a group. . . . They tend to sit together, either consciously or unconsciously at meetings, they share camaraderie – the fact that they are independent members and they are appointed in the same way.' Another shire police authority clerk said that there was some marginal group behaviour by independents: 'In many ways the Conservatives, independents and magistrates have more of a common bonding than any other combination. They have been much more content, because there isn't the same dedicated support services, to let the chief constable run the organisation. They have let the chief run away with a lot of what was previously politically and officer-controlled.' A further example was the following:

> They [police authority members] don't like meeting in the Council Chamber in Shire Hall because automatically the council members sit in the seats that they would do for council meetings, so they sit in their political areas, leaving space in the middle as it were for magistrates and independents to find seats which, in effect, means independents are sitting as a group and magistrates are sitting as a group, albeit that magistrates and independents tend to mingle.

THE ANNUAL POLICING PLAN

The main reference year for questions about the production of published policing plans was 1996/7. These plans had been published in April/May 1996, some months before the interviews took place. However, most interviewees also made some reference to the experience of the first year of planning, 1995/6.

Police authority involvement in planning

Without exception, interviewees reported that the new police authorities had very limited involvement in the 1995/6 annual policing plans, the first to be produced following the Police and Magistrates' Courts Act 1994. Because of the short timescales, the new police authorities were still operating only in shadow form, and were largely preoccupied with the process of taking on their new duties and responsibilities and were unable to be involved in the detail of policing plans, which were left largely to the forces concerned. However, during the second year, most police authorities attempted to become more involved in the plans for 1996/7, though involvement in the process varied between force area.

The survey findings suggest that in the second year since the Act, policing plans remained largely police-driven, though with increasing levels of involvement of or consultation with police authorities. We asked clerks to describe the planning process for the reference year of the study (the 1996/7 plan), and at what point police authority officers and members became involved. This allowed the development of a broad typology of police authority involvement in planning, according to the clerks' viewpoint. It is again worth emphasising that the views of police authority chairpersons or chief constables may well have been very different.

Our typology consists of the following three categories of police authority: the 'rubber-stampers', the 'redrafters' and the 'junior partners'. The rubber-stampers were the minority of police authorities (eight) who, according to the clerks, appeared to have had little or no involvement in the planning process. The basic process in these areas involved the chief constable producing a draft plan quite late in the day, usually after Christmas, and the police authority briefly discussing the draft and making no more than minor cosmetic changes before the plan is published in April/May in a form largely similar to the chief's initial draft. The redrafters (23 of the police authorities came into this category) were the largest group, and had more of an input than the rubber-stampers. They saw the chief constable's draft earlier, between October and November, and were able to be involved in a more extensive consultation process. The final group was categorised as the junior partners, and had an earlier involvement in the planning process than the redrafters, and clerks perceived that chief constables went to some lengths to involve the police authority before the appearance of the first draft. In no force area did any clerk report that there were any major differences between the police authority and the force about local objectives or indicators, or anything else connected with the substantive content of the plan. Thus, this group was termed 'junior' partners, since the police force still clearly took the lead. A number of clerks indicated that police authority members were hoping to increase their level of involvement in the plan, and thus would move to a different category in future years.

The rubber-stampers
The clerk of one shire police authority reported that the police authorities' contribution to the plan was 'less than they would have liked to have made'. He went on to say that 'for last year it was very much a case of the chief constable saying here's my plan and the authority endorsing it. Over the year they've been pushing hard on involving [s.106 committees and other

consultative fora] and to get them to have a say in what should be the policing priorities.' The clerk of another shire police authority reported that 'so far it is very much the chief constable's policing plan'. Similarly, the clerk of yet another shire police authority described police authority involvement in planning in the following terms:

> Fairly disappointing experience in the first two years. In the first year everyone would have been hit by the timescale: operating from November and requiring a policing plan effectively by January/February and there wasn't much option but to accept what the chief constable put forward. The second year the authority still hadn't got themselves ready to make a greater input into the policing plan, and again the plan was very much chief constable dominated.

This clerk saw little influence of the police authority on the plans in the first two years: 'In the main that's been produced by the chief constable.' A similar picture was presented in another shire police authority, where the clerk said that 'the planning process so far has been largely, almost exclusively, police-driven.' The most clear example of relative lack of influence of police authority over the plan came from one metropolitan police authority. The clerk largely put this state of affairs down to the unwillingness of the chief constable to allow the police authority any leeway: 'The police authority has become involved very very late in the first two years, in so much as there has been a plan – a draft – presented by the chief constable almost as if it's the final thing, almost defying the authority to change it.' He added:

> I think inevitably, when the resources were taken from the authority and given to the chief constable, and he, as all chief constables did, became very protective of that ... I think it's more the police authority begging for things where it would have been given them before, I mean in terms of information or whatever. The example being like the plan, 'you're not having the plan until I give it you,' you know. Whereas I think under the previous authority we did have strategic plans, three-year plans and whatever, which were worked up and developed in cooperation. Because the Act said the chief constable produces the first draft, or the draft plan, it was taken as nobody else could do anything until he'd done that.

This led him to conclude that the police authorities' statutory responsibility for policing plans meant little in practice: 'It is a difficult concept, to have responsibility for a plan, where the police authority has no control over the resources that it needs to fulfil the objectives of the plan, and the chief constable only has to have regard to the idea, so it's a ridiculous idea really.'

The redrafters

In this kind of police authority, the consultation process starts earlier than is the case for the rubber-stampers. The usual process is for the police authority, PCCGs and sometimes other groups to be circulated with a report from the chief constable that outlines the draft objectives for the coming year. Following responses to this, the force puts together the full draft policing plan, which then goes before police authority to be ratified for full consultation. After some police authority discussion, this is sent out for the second level consultation, usually in the form of written comments from a range of bodies such as PCCGs, district and parish councils, community and voluntary groups, and the Crown Prosecution Service. A later draft is put together in response to these comments and, after some more discussion/amendment by the police authority, the final plan is ratified. Thus, the chief constable clearly makes an effort to involve the police authority, and gains its support for the force's objectives, but in the process the police authority still remains rather passive. One clerk from a shire police authority described this kind of police authority involvement as:

> certainly nothing major (came from the police authority). Matters of relative detail. We've got seven objectives, five of them set by the Home Secretary and we added a couple locally. The members changed the order (laughs). That's in a sense a relative detail, but it says something about their priorities. They put crime prevention and community safety first for instance . . . that began as a member view.

The clerk of a combined police authority reported that its influence over the plan was growing, though the late appearance of the draft still caused some problems:

> It is developing. We're not happy with the process. That's not because we haven't set it up right, it's because we've watched it develop and we think we can improve upon it. The chief of course produces the first draft. . . . In the first year it was all done in a hurry and we didn't say much about the draft before it hit the committee table. This year we've had a bit more input. . . . Once it gets to them at a formal meeting of the authority it's a bit too late to start thrashing around the concepts, the objectives. It is a fairly tight deadline for agreeing it and publishing it, and I think members feel constrained in what they can say at that later stage.

A number of police authority clerks expressed the need for a joint approach, that the police authority and chief needed to work together to develop the plan. The clerk of one metropolitan police authority underlined this saying: 'What we didn't want was a situation where he [the chief constable] just produced a plan, took it to an authority meeting and said "here's my plan" and then our members saying "well we don't like that, here's our plan".' Several clerks reported that police authorities were increasing their influence as they got used to their new role. The following shire police authority was one of these:

> The chief constable said last year, well there's the draft, and that's it, and the members changed it but not greatly. The second one, the 96/7 policing plan, I think they poked that around a fair bit really, slowly recognising that this is the

authority's plan. 'Thank you chief, for the draft, but, we're going to work on this now.'

Clerks were asked about differences the police authorities had brought to the chief constable's initial draft. Most reported that some differences were made, but nearly all described these as matters of presentation rather than substance. The following shire police authority clerk was typical of these, saying that the police authorities' amendments to the chief's draft were 'partly presentational and partly matters of emphasis, but they were pretty minor I have to say, they weren't things of any real consequence'. A metropolitan police authority clerk reported a similar level of influence: 'Minor comments and additions, rewordings and so on. But nothing substantial.'

The clerk of a shire police authority reported that the police authority had really tried to influence the plan in the second year:

> There was a very intelligent discussion there, I was very agreeably surprised. The thing did not go through on the nod as the first one did, when what the chief constable said was simply accepted and members confined their criticisms to the colour and this sort of thing. There was an intelligent discussion on the feasibility of these local objectives, whether the targets were realistic, where our particular difficulties were in the force ... and how these difficulties related to what we were setting out in the policing plan.

However, he added 'It still bears all the hallmarks of being a force plan, in many ways, which we'll get round to again next year.'

The junior partners

This group had the most involvement in the planning process. It has been called 'junior' partners because, though involved at an earlier stage and more active than other police authorities, it was still the police force that took the lead in producing the plan. In fact, there was little difference in emphasis between the police authority and the chief constable in any force. The most usual approach in these cases was for the members of the force command team, plus officers involved in planning, to form a working party to identify the key issues for the plan. Alternatively, the process begins with a force planning a seminar in the early autumn, attended by the chief constable and force command team, along with all heads of divisions and departments. Some members and officers of the police authority are invited to participate and to raise police authority concerns. Out of this comes the draft, which is put before the police authority and goes out for formal consultation in the same way as in the above category. A small number of clerks were very positive about the level of police authority influence over policing plans. For example, the clerk from one metropolitan police authority described discussions over the policing plan in the following terms: 'A lot depends on the chief's attitude, and he's taken a very open and constructive line on it. There's never the feeling that they've settled things within the force, even at officer level it's a genuine open discussion.'

A number of police authorities that fell into the category of rubber-stampers or redrafters indicated that the police authorities in their areas intended to move towards this final model of involvement in planning. For example, the clerk from the metropolitan authority that felt it had been given little opportunity to influence the chief's draft, reported that:

> The authority has grasped that nettle, and I think from now on will be involved in the planning process jointly with the police in writing the report. If not, I think the authority will take it upon itself to start preparing, by consulting on the objectives and targets in the plan, of its own volition. But I think the battle's been fought and I think there'll be joint working in future.

The clerk of a combined police authority, which we categorised above as a redrafter, said that:

> members here are anxious to have an informal involvement long before that first draft is put to them formally at a police authority meeting ... and we're now talking about for next year devising arrangements which allow members to sit down with the ACPO team and talk through the policy objectives that are going to go into the draft plan.

He added that this development arose naturally from the fact that police authority members viewed the production of the plan as central to their new role: 'I think our members see the policing plan as being their most important function, and therefore don't want to be a rubber stamp to a draft put in front of them at short notice.' One of the above shire police authority clerks also reported a desire among police authority members to become more involved in the plan in future years: 'This next year they have determined that they want if not to draft the plan, at least to have something ready to input into the chief constable's draft. They now have a working party of five to put their own thoughts in order in relation to what they want to see in the plan.'

Numbers of copies produced

There was great variation between police authorities in the number of copies of the full policing plan produced for 1996/7. The print run varied from a low of 150 to a high of 16,000. The average was about 2600. Many police authorities producing small numbers of plans (and some printing large numbers of plans) made efforts to disseminate the force objectives in other ways. Some did this by way of a shorter summary plan in the form of a booklet, others included a summary of the force objectives and targets for the coming year in local newspapers, or in the council tax leaflets, or both.

Primary audience

Clerks were asked to identify the primary audience for the plan. The biggest single group of clerks stated that the plan was primarily for 'the public'; some even described the plan as a 'PR document' and this was borne out by the glossy appearance and some of the phrasing in some plans, which highlighted the successes of the force over the previous year. A few clerks said that the police authority had not really considered who the plan was aimed at, but if pushed would probably say 'the public'. The public in this sense was a somewhat vague concept, taken to mean simply everybody in the force area. Table 4.5 illustrates the main audiences identified by clerks.

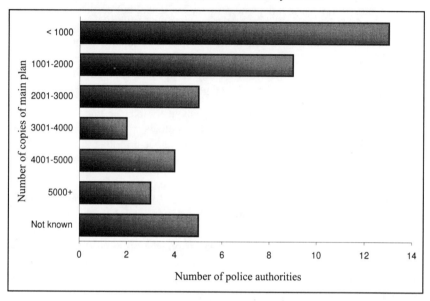

Figure 4.1 Numbers of copies of full policing plan produced

Table 4.5 Main audience for plan

Main audience for policing plan	Number of police authorities
The general public	16
Key organisations/individuals	13
The police force/police managers	4
Contract between chief and police authority members	1
Several/all of the above	7

Roughly one-third of clerks identified a more specific view of what is meant by public in this context. They meant bodies and organisations through which the public might be represented; a similar range of bodies were mentioned by clerks when asked in general terms where the plan was sent. The list included local authorities within the force area, community and voluntary groups, special interest groups, churches, local papers, libraries, chambers of commerce and trade, neighbourhood watch groups, and a range of other local bodies. One clerk described the main people to whomt they send the plans as the 'stakeholders'; another clerk gave a similar view by referring to the 'doers, movers and shakers' as the primary audience. Another clerk said there was a core target audience of about 200 such organisations locally.

Seven clerks did not identify one primary audience, but emphasised that the plan was for a range of different audiences. For example, one reported 'It [the policing plan] is seen as for quite a lot of different audiences, and part of the difficulty which we all struggle with is how to produce something which is read by and understood by, and in a sense appeals to, those different audiences.' Another clerk (from a combined police authority) reported that:

> I think one of the unsatisfactory things about the plan is that it has to have different audiences. I certainly see it as a contract after consultation between the chief constable and the police authority about priorities. . . . At the same time it has to serve as a PR document . . . and I think it also has some internal value within the force.

Several police authorities had directly addressed this issue of multiple audiences by producing different versions of the plan, as noted above. The detailed force plan would be directed at the police force itself, the Home Office and the police authority; a shorter version for easier consumption would be sent to a range of agencies and organisations (the narrower definition of 'the public' outlined above), and a council tax leaflet would be aimed at the wider public, meaning just about everybody.

A small number of clerks (four) explicitly identified the primary audience for the policing plan as the police themselves. For example, one (combined police authority clerk) said; 'It's very much a working document for the police themselves, I think that's where the main use probably is.' Another clerk (from a metropolitan police authority) highlighted the range of potential audiences, but in practical terms highlighted the police force as the main one within this:

> Certainly the plan, I think, is seen as a working document for the authority and the chief constable, and other public bodies like the district councils who may wish to monitor the activities of the police service, it's a useful document for other people to see but I don't really think it has a great deal of meaning for them. In fact, in future years we will produce a much more simplified pamphlet form with a wider distribution. So I think it's really an internal planning document.

One clerk stated that the plan was primarily for the chief constable and the police authority, as a contract of agreement as to what would be addressed in the coming year. Another clerk (from a shire police authority) gave a similar answer to the question about the main audience for the plan:

Good question. Well its done because it has to be done, that why it's done. That doesn't mean that it isn't useful to the authority. I assume it's useful to the Home Secretary, and I think it could be useful to the force, and I suppose at the moment it is correct to say that it is more for the police authority than anyone else. I can't say how much public input there was into it.

Consultation

Many clerks underlined the importance of consultation in the planning process. From our discussions, we were able to identify the primary method of consulting over the plan (for the 1996/7 one it is important to note that this is an evolving process, and many police authorities were attempting to improve and add to the process for the coming years). Table 4.6 illustrates the main methods of consultation about the policing plans, which were adopted within force areas. It is clear that in the second year of policing plans, PCCGs remained the primary mechanism for consulting over policing plans.

Table 4.6   Main method of consultation over policing plan

Main method of consultation on plan	Number of police authorities
Police community consultative groups (PCCGs)	32
Seminars for key organisations/public	5
Public attitude surveys	1
Mailshots of key agencies/people	1
Other	2

Although the PCCGs were by far the most commonly-identified primary mechanisms of consultation over the plan, few clerks regarded this state of affairs as satisfactory. The most often-quoted reason for this was that, being local fora, PCCGs have become rather parochial bodies concerned mainly with local issues and problems, and are not well-suited to discussing the strategic force-wide issues the plan must address.

Developments in consultation since the Act

The Police and Magistrates' Courts Act 1994 makes specific reference to the importance of local consultation in formulating local policing objectives. When the Act came into operation, we suggested that police authorities might be encouraged to develop their consultation mechanisms further, with a specific reference to the need to publish local policing plans (Jones and Newburn, 1995). We asked clerks for broad details about the framework for local consultation in the police authority area, and what, if any, developments had resulted from the Act.

The majority of clerks reported that the new police authorities had responded to their new powers and responsibilities by reviewing their systems for consultation. In a number of police authority areas, this review was underway at the time of our survey. Police authority working groups or special panels had been convened to consider the efficacy of the current arrangements, and recommendations for improvement. In a number of police authority areas, significant reforms to the consultative system had already been undertaken. Section 106 of the Police and Criminal Evidence Act 1984 placed a statutory duty on police authorities to consult the views of local people about policing. Although the Act did not specify what form these consultations should take, most force areas envisaged them taking place in geographically-based committees with varying degrees of police authority and force involvement.

Our survey confirmed that most forces had such committees, though their structure and membership varied within and between force areas. They have a variety of names – section 106 committees, police-community fora, police liaison committees, CAP (community and police) groups, police fora, core groups, PCCGs, local fora, community fora and PLACs (police liaison advisory committees). They take various forms. Some operate with a core committee-style membership, others simply take the form of open public meetings, and they receive varying levels of support from the police authority and force. The police authority administers and supports this network of consultation in the majority of areas, although in a minority of areas this is done by the police force. In all forces, clerks reported that the police force itself had its own, sometimes quite extensive, networks of consultation, independently of anything organised by the police authority. This involved police attendance at various kinds of meeting, district and parish council, victim support groups, neighbourhood watch schemes, crime prevention panels and a range of other bodies. In addition, nearly every police force now undertakes customer satisfaction surveys of some form or other. In most cases, this is undertaken in-house by the force research department. However, in a few forces, general customer attitude surveys are commissioned to be undertaken by independent bodies, such as local universities, or market research companies.

Of those clerks who reported that the consultative framework had been, or was currently being, reviewed, most said it had involved or would involve a reinvigoration of section 106 groups. The kinds of development that were mentioned included attempts to improve attendance by targeting various organisations and individuals, by leafleting local people and by advertising in local newspapers and radio. In one police authority, the meetings were to become open to the general public for the first time. In two force areas, the police authority was taking over the administration of PCCGs from the force. Several clerks from shire police authorities reported that the new 'independent' police authorities were attempting to build stronger links with both PCCGs and with local councils in the area. Most police authorities now operate a system where police authority members either chair, or at least attend, local consultative committee meetings. In two force areas, the former police authorities had not set up formalised section 106 committees, but one effect of the Act was to lead the new police authorities to set up a network of such committees. Only one force area did not yet have a framework of consultative committees. In other force areas, police authorities have set up new committees. For example, in one metropolitan area the police authority has decided to target special interest groups, rather than rely purely on area-based committees.

Only a minority of police authorities appear to be commissioning public attitude surveys of policing (independently of those carried out by their respective police forces), or indeed any other forms of market research. As noted above, this was usually seen as the preserve of the police force, or was considered to be too expensive.[3] However, a minority of police authorities were becoming involved in such activity. One clerk from a shire police authority reported that the local county council undertakes a bi-annual public satisfaction survey across council services. The police authority was putting resources to 'buying' some extra questions for analysis on policing. One metropolitan police authority reported commissioning a major customer satisfaction survey of policing, to be undertaken by a leading market research company. A small number of clerks reported that their police authorities were either currently, or planning to, develop other market research methods to feed into consultation processes, such as focus groups or consumer panels.

OTHER ASPECTS OF THE ACT
Section 24 funding

Section 24 of the Act allows for supplementary grants by local authorities within a force area to be made to the police authority to support policing in that area. The Act lays down that grants under this section may be made unconditionally or, with the agreement of the chief constable, subject to conditions. During 1995/6, a number of press reports focused on local authorities purchasing 'extra' police officers to police their areas (see, for example, 'Police to put officers out for hire', *Independent*, 25 February 1995).

We asked interviewees whether supplementary grants of this kind had been paid to the police authority. We found that only three police authorities had made use of section 24 funding. One of these involved a district council in the force area paying the shire police authority £100,000 a year for four extra police constables to work in their area. A contract was not drawn up for this, but instead a memorandum of agreement between the chief constable and the district council. One problem senior police officers have raised about section 24 funding is that, because police establishments are not flexible, recruiting more officers is a long-term investment. Many chief officers are unwilling to

---

3. Indeed, most police authorities have no budget whatsoever for research.

recruit extra officers in response to a short-term funding promise, which may disappear should political priorities change. This example perhaps illustrated the problem well, for the priorities of this particular district council changed and it decided that, after a year, the money would be better spent on CCTV and other community safety initiatives. Thus, the funding was discontinued.

In another shire police authority, the clerk reported that the 'holiday industry' had agreed to fund some extra police officers to work in a particular holiday area. The chief constable was reported to be keen to encourage new ways of funding like this. In the third example of section 24 funding, a combined police authority received £60,000 a year from an NHS hospital trust, which paid for two constables to work on trust property. This replaced a £90,000 annual private security contract. At the time of the survey, a district council within the same force area was considering whether it should pay a supplementary grant to the police authority for extra constables to patrol its area.

Few other clerks reported that the issue of section 24 funding had even arisen. In one shire police authority, the clerk said that one local authority had expressed interest in such a development, but that the chief constable was strongly opposed to the idea. Another shire police authority clerk reported that one council had considered section 24 funding in some detail, but concerns both from the police authority and the force about equity, with poorer areas potentially losing out, and about operational flexibility, meant that the idea was shelved for the time being. Four clerks said that it had not happened yet, but that there was no strong opposition locally. The fact that it had not occurred reflected the financial difficulties of councils in the area; they could not afford to spend more on policing. One clerk said that local authorities were not interested in paying extra grants, because they felt that they already paid once for policing via the council tax, and why should they pay again? A few clerks reported that no section 24 funding had happened in their areas, and such was the opposition to it on the police authority that it would be unlikely ever to happen.

Fixed term contracts (FTCs) and performance related pay (PRP)

A minority of police authority clerks (eight) reported that no FTCs had been introduced for serving ACPO rank officers in their areas, though they realised that new appointments would have to be made with an FTC. The clerks in most of these areas reported that this was because of a strong objection in principle to FTCs, either by the police authority, by the chief, or by both. One clerk reported that the police authority took an 'all or none' approach to FTCs and, since one ACPO rank officer refused to move to an FTC, they decided to avoid them for all serving ACPO officers. In four other police authorities, the clerks reported that some serving ACPO officers had opted to go for FTCs whereas others had not. In the rest of the surveyed police authorities, all serving ACPO ranks had moved to FTCs. The majority of these FTCs took the officers in question past possible retirement dates, so in many ways (and as a number of clerks wryly pointed out), the police authority had little to gain by offering such contracts.

The story was different for PRP, which was widely perceived as having been put on the 'back burner' nationally.[4] Only one clerk reported that the police authority was planning to introduce a performance element into the chief constable's pay for the coming year, which had prompted a detailed discussion about local performance targets between the chief and the authority. The clerk of this (shire) police authority reported that the chief was 'keen' on the notion of PRP. Two other clerks reported that their police authorities had considered PRP, but decided to await further developments at the national level. One of these had considered relating pay to personal objectives for ACPO rank officers, but decided against making charges of this sort. A number of clerks reported that their authorities were strongly against PRP in principle. One said that his police authority regarded it as 'dangerous', another reported that his police authority (and the chief) were 'totally against' PRP, and a third said that the concept was regarded with 'deep suspicion' locally.

CHANGES IN OVERALL POLICE AUTHORITY INFLUENCE AND EFFECTIVENESS

As noted earlier, a large body of research over a number of years has documented the growing centralisation of control over policing, and the relative lack of influence of police authorities within the tripartite structure. Our own research in the early 1990s found a number of factors behind this relative lack of effectiveness (Jones et al. , 1994). Though many critics saw the PMCA as further centralising control over policing, we argued that, in theory at least, the reforms had the potential to enhance the influence of police authorities. This section considers a range of factors behind the apparent lack of influence of police authorities under the pre-1995 structure, and considers the emerging effects of the changes based on discussions with police authority clerks.

Changes in influence and effectiveness

Clerks were asked broadly to compare levels of influence and effectiveness of the new police authorities with their predecessors, and almost half reported that the new arrangements had seen an increase in influence and effectiveness. As Table 4.7 shows, clerks of seven police authorities felt that the new police authorities were as active and influential as the old ones; a further 13 thought that it was too early to tell, or that the old and new police authorities were too different to compare (this group includes a number of clerks who had no experience of the previous police authority and therefore were unable to draw any comparison).

---

4. In fact the ACPO pay settlement in early 1997 effectively 'bought out' PRP, which is arguably now a dead issue.

It is important to note that this comparison with previous authorities is very general and highly dependent on the subjective views of one person. Chief constables and police authority chairpersons (depending on whether or not they had served on the former police authority), might have provided very different accounts. In particular, the question depended on what view the clerk took of effectiveness and influence. Some saw an effective police authority as one that concentrated on policing performance, was businesslike and focused in its meetings, and streamlined in its overall size and committee structure. A number of clerks spontaneously referred to the police authority's role as being to support the chief constable and police force. In contrast, other clerks referred to the importance of the police authority's independence from the chief, and its ability to oversee critically, if constructively, the development of policing in their areas.

Table 4.7   Influence and effectiveness compared with old police authority

Comparison with old police authority	All	Met PAs	Shire PAs	Combined PAs
More influential and effective	20	0	15	5
As influential and effective	7	1	4	2
Less influential and effective	1	2	0	0
Don't know, too early to say	13	3	8	1

The section below outlines the various factors mentioned by clerks to explain changes in the levels of police authority activity and influence. It is likely that all the following factors are significant in some way or another, as suggested by the following quotation:

> It's a combination of a whole range of factors. One is the fact that the police authority is independent, it is no longer tied into the county council in the direct way that it was before, and that's meant that we, including me, have been able to do things differently. The second one is the smaller number of members, and I think the third is the involvement of the independents (shire police authority).

Size and structure

Our earlier research (Jones et al., 1994) suggested that one reason for the relative lack of influence of police authorities was their size and structure. Police authorities tended to be too large to be effective decision-making bodies and they covered large areas with a range of local communities within them. Restricting the size of police authorities was thus a vital component of the 1994 reforms. Though they still clearly cover large areas and, as noted above, their smaller size creates problems for political representation in certain areas, it seems clear that the new police authorities are now more effective discussion and decision-making bodies because of their smaller size. A number of clerks who reported that the new police authority was more influential mentioned the size factor. One clerk from a combined police authority reported that the new police authority was a 'far more professional and active body, and that's probably because its more streamlined'. Another put the favourable description down to the increased involvement of all members of the police authority: 'The members have got more involvement than they had before, I think there was a fear before that they would lose out but I don't think that's actually happened, and I think the members get more involved in all aspects of policing'. A third also put the improvements in effectiveness down to the smaller police authority size: 'It is a smaller body, therefore you've got the situation of a small, single purpose body which is certainly more interested, more active in its own function' (shire police authority).

Statutory powers

We have argued (Jones et al., 1994) that, among other factors, the pre-1994 police authorities were constrained by their limited statutory powers. Where they did hold statutory powers it was clear that the police authority could have more influence. In this sense, we suggested that making the police authority responsible for publishing the local policing plan was a significant shift in statutory powers (Jones and Newburn, 1995). As outlined above, the influence over policing plans varied between police authorities, but no police authorities could be said to be actively taking the lead in setting objectives, or taking on the chief constable's draft and developing it themselves. Most clerks felt that the police authorities' influence would grow, but few saw this extending much further than it has already. Nevertheless, some clerks saw the change in statutory powers as an important addition to the police authorities' influence. A shire police authority clerk felt that the new authority was more influential and active because of its new statutory powers and responsibilities:

> I think it's a more positive and constructive organisation, largely because it's got certain statutory duties to perform, which certainly the chairman and other members have grasped and gone about doing something in an active way to carry out, whereas in the previous regime I think it was not really appreciated what it could or should do, and it certainly didn't have any statutory duty to do it in quite such precise terms that it does have now

The following clerk from a shire police authority saw the change in terms of enhanced strategic responsibilities making the police authority more proactive:

> It's certainly been more able to focus, or begin to focus on its role and ask questions about what is the role etc, and its certainly looking to develop and have some real input ... and not necessarily be driven almost by dictat.... They're not in there to sit on the chief's shoulders, they're there to look at strategy and objectives, and if necessary give him a hard time or praise him

depending on what's happened . . . It's certainly far more proactive than the old authority was.

Clerks in some other police authorities, however, perceived a decline in the authority's statutory powers. One, in a combined authority, reported that the new police authority had few powers relative to the chief constable: 'Another factor now is the limited role of the police authority. There is nothing of an operational nature, and very little of an executive nature. So there aren't the issues there to get too worked up about.' Another clerk from a combined police authority observed that the new police authority and its members were still searching for a role:

> Those who are from local authorities and perhaps haven't been on a police authority before find it hard to recognise that the chief constable is autonomous in operational terms. They are used to chief officers who have to accept the decisions of the committee. . . . I think they wonder sometimes what they're there for. They hear a lot about the policing service, they get a lot of update reports, they're there to monitor performance, but they can't affect the way in which things are done. It is a curious role for people to play. . . . It is hard to see how a police authority insists on improvements being made in order to fulfil their role, their duty to ensure an effective and efficient force. They are little more than spectators it seems to me, with no more than the power of influence.

Police authority type

We have previously argued that metropolitan police authorities may have a more active approach. This may partly explain why the clerks perceived the changes in influence and effectiveness differently in different types of police authority. Although the overall majority of clerks felt that their respective authorities were more influential and effective than those that had existed previously, none of those in a metropolitan police authority reported that the new authority was more effective and influential than the old. By comparison, the clerks from the majority of shire police authorities (15 out of 27) and of combined police authorities (five out of eight) viewed the new police authorities as more effective. No clerks from combined or shire police authorities reported that the new police authority was less effective. The following clerk from a shire authority clearly felt that such authorities had not on the whole been particularly effective or influential.

> The old police authority here was an extremely soporific beast. It was actually run by the chief constable, and people came in and nodded from time to time. We used to spend a long time talking about sickness in the force, and we always used to have a question about ethnic minority recruitment, and there'd always be a discussion about drink-driving. It was a very traditional shire county organisation, very friendly.

Metropolitan areas, on the other hand, have traditionally seen themselves as far more active and influential, so are perhaps more inclined to view the reforms as a disadvantage to be overcome rather than an enhancement of their powers. One metropolitan police authority clerk in particular personified this view when he argued that the high levels of influence and effectiveness of the old police authority had, through hard work locally, largely survived the reforms. He stated that the old and new police authorities were 'more or less the same ... the reforms presented the risk of losing things, of a deterioration and fragmentation of things. That's not our experience because we recognised that danger with the chief and worked very hard to stop it. So it hasn't done any damage, because we made sure it didn't.'

Two metropolitan clerks felt that their authority's effectiveness and influence had declined. One did not explain this development in terms of a lack of activity on the part of the police authority. On the contrary, he felt that the members had been more active, and this had partly resulted in the chief being less open to influence: 'It's certainly more active, and I think it's certainly more constructive in its criticism. I doubt whether it's more influential, I think it had more influence when it had more local politicians around' (metropolitan police authority). Another metropolitan police authority clerk was clearly opposed to the reforms, feeling that many of the statutory powers held by the old police authority, and the wider representation which was possible on a much larger body, had been lost by the new police authority, which as a consequence was struggling to find a role.

A number of shire police authority clerks reported that independence from the county council had helped the police authority increase its effectiveness. The following clerk from a shire authority thought that the increased independence from the county council was the primary factor behind the improvement in effectiveness:

> We might get an hour out of the old police committee. ... They saw their role perhaps somewhat differently in the sense that the chief was the operational man, and still is, but their contribution ... would be very much a reactive contribution, and they might raise certain problems in specific areas on a parochial basis, but the whole view of sort of adding value was in the context of a committee of the county council. And they didn't see themselves as the authority is beginning to see itself quite positively, as a separate body, and even including the councillor members and the magistrate members see themselves as that body corporate and begin to think, sometimes by specialising in certain areas. ... I think their perspective is different, and that's evolved fairly quickly.

This view was supported by another shire county police authority clerk:

> Previously of course the police committee was a committee of the county council, and I think it suffered for that really, because of the politics. ... It's independent, it's got its own budget, it's broken away from the county council ... surprisingly some would say (probably one or two of the elected members) ...

there is an acceptance that it's better and that it does work; they are doing a good job.

However, not all shire police authority clerks reported that independence from the county council had enhanced the activity and influence of the police authority, including the following.

I think it does lose influence to some extent by not being part of a larger whole [that is part of the county council] but, having said that, the fact that there are councillors, elected people, on it who do maintain that public accountability approach – it is different from a quango, no doubt about it. It is publicly accountable and certainly the authority want to make sure that it stays publicly accountable so the public know what's going on.

Self-limitation

A number of studies found that an important source of the lack of influence of pre-1994 police authorities was that police authority members and officers took a very limited view of the police authority role, and did not use the limited statutory powers available to them (Morgan, 1992). The lack of motivation and awareness among police authority members was a major target of the 1994 reforms, although clearly the government wished to encourage a particular kind of activism, focused on performance review and increasing effectiveness and efficiency. Our survey suggested that this is beginning to occur in many, though not all, police authorities. As we describe below, a number of police authority clerks felt that the former police authorities were already sufficiently active and influential. However, the majority mentioned that changes in the police authority membership were an important factor behind increased activity and influence. As we saw earlier, this was often related to the new independent members joining the police authorities. However, the majority of clerks qualified their positive views about the impact of independents by stating that other police authority members had made equally useful contributions.

Thus, it was a common view that police authority memberships *as a whole* were now taking a more ambitious view of their role. For example, the following shire clerk described the improved contribution of all police authority members as 'more active and more influential. There is no doubt that the chief constable has seen a lot more of his members, and they are showing a greater degree of interest in what goes on and where it goes on, and that's cascading down through the divisional structure.' Other clerks, such as the following from a shire police authority, detected a greater activism and interest among the membership as a whole, including magistrates and elected members: 'Much more (influential than its predecessor). I always thought the last one was tame. The chief constable turned up, told them a few stories and that was it. This one is asking some difficult questions, causing a bit of tension, but that's inevitable really.' A clerk from a combined police authority said: 'I was very much opposed to the changes. However, I think it is a more focused and more active authority than we had in the past. Everyone is very much tuned into policing and what it's all about, and very anxious to get to grips with it. They're very enthusiastic so, yes, it's good news.' And, a clerk from a shire police authority felt that:

> The police committee as such was a bit of a *laissez-faire* reporting organisation. These members are definitely now making decisions and addressing matters to the Nth degree in fact. Very much more active. I think it is probably doing what the Home Office hoped the parties would do now. The Committee tended to be a bit of a rubber-stamp to the chief constable. This is certainly different.

A small number of clerks observed that potential improvements in effectiveness and influence had so far failed to materialise. For example, some clerks felt that the self-limitation of the old police authorities was continuing to an extent under the new arrangements. The following quote came from the clerk of a shire police authority, who wanted to encourage the police authority to be more independent of the chief constable:

> I think potentially we have a stronger set of members of the police authority in terms of the contribution they are able to bring to it. My observation is that we still suffer from the 'compliance culture' among councillors or members of the police authority which I think will be difficult to break until the Home Office pay equivalent attention to police authorities as they do to falling over ACPO.

Another shire police authority clerk stated that he was trying to encourage a more assertive approach on the part of the police authority:

> I've made several attempts in the last year to try and gee the members up, to actually get the bit between their teeth and actually do something, you know, produce some local objectives that the chief constable hasn't suggested, to actually enlarge the consultation machinery, do something different, you know, do some advertising. And they don't really want to do it, I've not got sort of driving forces on the police authority that are prepared to take up the issues and run with them.

Relationship with the chief constable

Previous research has shown that most chief constables go to some lengths to develop good working relationships with their police authorities. However, it has been argued that 'when push comes to shove' the chief constable will always prevail (Reiner, 1992). The first two years following the PMCA saw a gradual bedding down of the new arrangements, and few clear examples of tensions between chief constables and police authorities. The police authorities have generally taken an informed but passive role in the production of policing plans; the police forces have in practice set the local objectives and targets, albeit with much effort put into consultation. Our 1994 study found that the relationship with the chief constable was an important element of the police

authority's power. Most clerks in our survey reported a good relationship with
the chief locally, though a minority referred to 'traditional-minded' chief
constables being less open to police authority influence. As the clerks from
two shire police authorities put it: 'So we are still in the situation where we
have a fairly dominant chief constable, and a behind-the-back, moaning
whinging authority (on occasions) if they don't like what he's done, but who
are not prepared to stand up to him and tell him they won't stomach it, which I
suspect is about par for the course.' And, 'We have certainly a difference of
view between the chairman of the police authority, and the chief constable . . .
it is about the chairman of the police authority seeing a more intrusive role in
relation to operational policing, and the chief constable being unable to move
from his fixed view.'

A small number of other police authority clerks reported some tensions
arising from the new arrangements. In a metropolitan police authority, the new
arrangements had led to some tensions between the force and police authority
over support services, and who does what for whom. The clerk described these
in the following terms:

> That to me has been the big change over the last 18 months. Before 1994 we
> sort of got on with the job between the staff here and the people for the police,
> and never really thought who was working for who. There's far more con-
> sciousness now, from the police in particular, about, well, 'what is it costing
> the budget?' and 'why can't *we* do this?', and there's a lot of uneasiness from
> my staff here; to say 'well look, the police are muscling in on that area, are they
> undermining us?'

A shire police authority clerk reported, in similar terms to Reiner's 'push
comes to shove' scenario, that 'at the end of the day, if the chief constable
feels strongly about something, the members I don't think are going to upset
his apple cart'.

More typical, though, were the majority of clerks who reported the good
relations and lack of tension between chief and police authority. The clerk of
another shire police authority emphasised that the constructive relationship
predated the reforms:

> Over the years, there has been a considerable degree of mutual trust, and noth-
> ing has happened to destroy or affect that mutual trust, and I suppose you could
> say the police authority are happy with the information they receive from the
> chief constable and they don't challenge it particularly. They do ask questions
> about it which are readily answered, but those questions tend to be more about
> seeking clarification rather than a direct challenge to the accuracy of the infor-
> mation, because they have no independent means of checking the reliability of
> the statistics that are given them. They pay a chief constable and rely on him.

Some police authorities felt the legislation had strengthened the relationship
between the police authority and chief, and many talked about partnerships

with the chief constable and working with him to deliver the best policing service. For example, the clerk of a combined police authority reported that:

> There's no doubt about it that one of the other advantages that has come out of the PMCA is this genuine forging of partnership between the police authority and the chief constable . . . the chief constable is now far more open with the police authority, and will ask for their views before actually implementing something which was not the case before.

The clerk of another combined police authority felt that the chief was now keener than before to communicate with police authority members: 'I'd say that independence (of the chief) is still pretty strongly preserved, but I think there's a realisation that you have actually to communicate rather better. Not over the heads of the police authority to the Great British Public, but you've actually got to communicate with members.' One clerk of a shire authority also felt the relationship with the chief was becoming closer: he mentioned that the chief constable had become 'much more conscious that he's got to think about his policies and how he delivers things'. Again, the theme was building on the previous strong relationship with the chief, which had always been a 'discursive and involved relationship. . . . It's a brave chief constable nowadays who says "I am the chief constable and I will do as I want".'

Another shire police authority clerk felt that the police authority had more control over the chief than under the previous arrangements: 'I think there was a myth going around at the time of the Act, that this was all about the chief constable becoming independent, he could do anything he wanted, he was holding his own land. In fact, the power to hold the chief constable to account has increased, and we find we are making him more accountable.'

Yet another reported that the new police authority was more assertive with the chief constable than the old one had been, and that this was due in large part to the influence of the new chairman:

> We have had some excellent and exceedingly subtle chief constables who knew how to manage their chairmen. . . . The chairman of the [new] police authority had been intended I assume to be a counterbalance to the chief constable in a way that the previous chair of the police committee hadn't been, and I think that is in the process of developing. I'm not implying that there is hostility on either side, but I think there probably is a move toward the police authority asserting itself *a little bit more.*

One shire police authority clerk spoke of the new police authority's desire to develop its own identity: 'I think there is a keenness, principally inspired by the chairman, to make this new regime work, and to be seen to be separate and independent from the constabulary, without necessarily creating any unnecessary barriers or divisions between the two bodies.'

Information and expertise

A number of previous studies of police authorities have identified a lack of information and expertise as an important factor behind the limited ability of police authorities effectively to fulfil their role. For example, Lustgarten (1986) argued that police authorities were dependent on the police force for the information upon which they were required to base their informed criticisms, and hold the chief constable to account. Given the new statutory requirements of the police authority, it is clear that there has been a major development in the quantity and quality of information available to police authority members. However, it is important to note that this information is by and large of a particular type, focused upon statistical performance targets and financial information. Our earlier research identified the need for police authorities to have a properly-resourced secretariat, independent of the police force, which would provide the informational and technical support to help police authority members undertake their functions more effectively.

As shown earlier, widespread changes in the level and type of police authority support have not yet occurred. Although a small number of clerks reported that the police authority had slightly increased the resources for its own support services, a number indicated that such a development would meet opposition from the chief constable, who would argue that money spent on police authority support should really be spent on operational policing. In general, metropolitan police authorities appeared to have a greater support base than police authorities in other areas. It was clerks from these areas who identified the independence of information as an important consideration for the future. One clerk (from a metropolitan police authority) reported that the information problem was still active for police authority members: 'I think it's fair to say that they [the police authority] would like more information, and more explanation of the information, than they're getting at the moment.' Another mentioned the problem of independence of information in connection with the possible introduction of PRP. He felt it inappropriate for chief constables to set performance targets that would be related to an element of senior officers' pay and then hold all the information that could indicate whether those targets had been achieved, and thus whether senior officers would received the performance bonus.

Political complexion

Our previous research provided only limited support for the idea that political complexion may have some effect on the levels of influence and effectiveness achieved by police authorities. In this study, the most deferential and ineffective police authority was a Conservative-dominated one. However, a Labour-dominated police authority from the North also limited its own role, and another Labour-run authority tried to be more assertive but was thwarted by a rather dominant chief constable. The influence of party-political complexion has clearly fallen significantly in most police authorities, given what was outlined earlier about the depoliticising effects of the reduction in authority size coupled with the addition of independent members. There was no clear effect of political complexion on the clerks' perspective on whether the police authority had grown or declined in influence. Police authorities chaired by Conservative councillors had a relatively high likelihood of clerks reporting an increase in influence (seven out of nine). However, of 16 Labour-chaired authorities, only two perceived a decline in police authority influence.

CONCLUSIONS

What conclusions can we draw from the telephone survey of police authority clerks? First, in general terms, despite all the concerns voiced about the likely impact of the 1994 Act, the reforms are bedding down and do not appear to have led to any significant conflict or tensions on police authorities, or between police authorities and chief constables. A minority of clerks reported resentment at what they felt was party-political interference by the Home Office in the selection of independent members. Although there were also complaints about the tortuousness of the appointments process, most clerks were fairly content with what had taken place, and reported that independent members were settling down on the new police authorities.

The introduction of independent members – one of the most controversial of the reforms – was, by the time of the survey, presented by clerks in generally positive terms. A minority of clerks felt that the independents were the leading lights on the police authority, and the key factor behind an improvement in influence and effectiveness. More generally, however, the majority of clerks felt that the independent members were not particularly distinguishable from other police authority members, and in just the same way as their peers, were making active and useful contributions to authority business.

There is little evidence in support of Kenneth Clarke's proposition that independent members would bring a range of experience to police authorities that had not previously been available to them. Most clerks suggested that the contribution being made by the new members was largely in line with what would have been expected from the elected and magistrate members already in place. In terms of broad occupational and professional categories, the largest group appears to be composed of people from commercial or professional backgrounds. However, a significant minority of independent members have other backgrounds. The main impact upon police authority business has been framed in terms of a new perspective, usually from business or commerce, and a removal of party politics from police authority business, which has emerged partly because of the presence of non-councillor police authority members, but also in part because of the reduced size of the police authority. The majority of clerks have again welcomed this depoliticisation, but a few pointed out that police authorities are now focused purely on the 'business' of policing, and fail to comment on relevant developments in the wider political context of policing, which should be part of their role. To this extent, 'managerialism' appears to have tightened its grip on police authority business.

The statutory responsibility of police authorities to publish a local policing plan was seen as highly significant in some quarters. In general, police authorities seem to take a rather passive role in producing the policing plan, which is primarily written by the police force in all force areas, although chief constables vary in the lengths to which they will go to involve police authority members and officers in the process. A number of clerks have indicated that police authorities will try to increase their levels of involvement in future, which may become a source of tension between chiefs and police authorities. Some police authorities are clearly unhappy at the minimal role they have played so far in drafting *their own* policing plan. It is becoming increasingly evident, however, that to increase their role police authority members would need to become involved in the process at a very early stage. This requires some reinterpretation of the formulation in the PMCA which states that 'a draft of the local policing plan *shall be prepared by the chief constable for the area and submitted by him for the authority to consider*' (emphasis added). Some police authorities clearly wish to become the 'drafters' – rather than simply the 'redrafters' of the policing plan.

In the first two years of planning, there has been little, if any, overt tension between forces and police authority over what should go into the plans, and most clerks reported a broad measure of agreement. In part, no doubt, this is a product of what one clerk called the continuing 'compliance culture', which exists in many authorities, where members find it difficult, or simply do not wish to, challenge the chief constable or other senior officers. That PCCGs or other similar groups seem to have so little input into local policing plans is a reflection not only of the forces' dominance in drafting plans, but of the difficulties associated with using local consultative mechanisms for such a purpose. Partly as a result of this, and partly because of the emphasis on consultation within the legislation, most police authorities have reviewed their arrangements for local consultation. It remains the case, however, that PCCGs are generally regarded as an inappropriate vehicle for consultation about strategic issues. A minority of police authorities are taking the lead in setting up new forms of consultation such as focus groups and specially-designed public attitude surveys, independently of those now routinely undertaken by most police forces. In general terms, most clerks appear to feel that the new police authorities have increased their levels of influence and effectiveness compared with their predecessors. However, this feeling is mainly restricted to the shire areas, and metropolitan police authority clerks were less likely to view the changes in these terms. This may well reflect our previous research, which suggested that metropolitan police authorities tended to be more active and 'hands-on' in their involvement in the making of local policing policy.

Chapter 5

Case Study A: The Metropolitan Force

THE POLICE AUTHORITY AND FORCE

In 1995/6, the force had a total revenue budget of over £360 million, and a staff of over 10,000 (of which nearly 7000 were police officers). The force had 11 territorial divisions, each of which was divided into a number of subdivisions. Senior officers reported that by 1995/6 about 11 per cent of the total force budget was devolved under local financial management (LFM). Although the Audit Commission and HMIC have criticised the force for its rather limited LFM (compared with other forces), the force command team argued that the corporate control needs of such a large organisation were such that further substantial devolvement of budgets should await the development of detailed financial control systems within the force.

The police authority had successfully applied to the Home Office for an increase in membership, and consequently had 19 members. The chairman was the same Labour councillor who chaired the pre-1995 authority. The new police authority was substantially smaller than its predecessor, which, with 45 members, was one of the largest in England and Wales. The new police authority inherited the large secretariat support system of the old one, based in the offices of the lead authority. The authority considered itself to be the leading authority in England and Wales in the field of community consultation. It had a large department employing over 20 full-time police authority staff working on community consultation, called the Police and Community Team (PACT). In addition, the lead authority employed a number of other staff to provide various services to the police authority. The chief executive and treasurer of the lead authority acted as clerk and treasurer to the police authority respectively. The police authority also had the services of an organisation and management unit (employed by the lead authority) of five people undertaking management services work, who worked alongside the chief constable and the treasurer (with a dual service-level agreement or SLA). The lead authority also employed people under an SLA to undertake some personnel and estates management services for both the police authority and the force.

THE CHANGING ROLE OF THE POLICE AUTHORITY

Interviewees had strongly contrasting views about the overall effects of the new arrangements. There was a range of opinion about the role and operation of the new police authority, not only among different police authority members, but also among senior officers and civilian staff of the force, and among police authority officers. There were also important differences between the perceptions of people who had served on the old police authority and those who had not, between councillors of different political parties, between independent members and elected members and, finally, between senior staff of the force and the officers of the authority.

On the police authority side, the clerk and Labour members held very different views from non-Labour members, and police authority officers from the clerk's office held very different views from those of other officers. The former clearly felt that the old police authority had been extremely effective and influential, and had been weakened by the changes of the PMCA. The latter were more sceptical about the effectiveness of old arrangements and thought the reforms brought about a distinct improvement. The view from the police force was also mixed. Senior officers clearly saw the potential benefits of the Act, and felt that the spirit of the Act was moving things in the right direction. However, they noted that in practice, the Act contained many grey areas of overlap and duplication of role, and in some cases they felt that roles were more confused after the Act than before.

It is important to note two historical aspects of the relationship between the police authority and the force in this area. First, during the early to mid-1980s, the police authority was one of the metropolitan police committees that had a tense and at times conflictual relationship with its chief constable. Following the abolition of the metropolitan counties in 1985, a joint board authority replaced the police committee. A number of longer-serving members reported a marked improvement in relations between the police authority and force during the late 1980s. Second, the pre-1994 police authority was generally considered to be very active and involved. This was reported by senior officers of the force, who complained that the former police authority had been very involved in the 'nitty-gritty' aspects of non-strategic decisions, such as the occupation of police houses, and matters of detail concerning the regrading of civilian staff and the capital programme. In the words of one senior officer, 'they were very intrusive, very time-consuming.' From a different perspective, senior members of the police authority saw these activities as a central part of their role in holding the force to account, as discussed below.

Size and structure

The 19 member authority consisted of ten elected councillors (from the ten metropolitan districts which made up the force area), six independent members and three magistrates. The elected component consisted of one Conservative, two Liberal Democrats and seven Labour councillors. The police authority met every six weeks, with meetings of the full authority lasting about three hours. It was reported that this was considerably longer than the meetings of the full authority prior to 1995. It was difficult to assess the significance of this development, however, for much of the business under the old system was carried out in committee, whereas under the new arrangements the full authority meetings deal with more items themselves. At the time of the study, there were three main committees. These were the Community Relations Committee, which dealt with PCCG-related issues, lay visitors' schemes, the media and public relations; the Management Committee, which dealt with audit, employment and complaints against the police; and the Emergency Committee, which dealt with urgent matters arising between police authority meetings. A number of other *ad hoc* working parties and project boards were also established to oversee particular matters, including the policing plan.

Police authority officers in community consultation units, senior police force staff and non-Labour members of the police authority saw the new arrangements very differently. One source in the police authority support unit, for example, described the old police authority as 'incredibly frustrating' because of its large unwieldy size, its tendency to get bogged down in party-political infighting, and its lack of assertiveness towards the chief constable. One feature of the new smaller police authority was that the metropolitan boroughs could each have only one councillor representing their local area on the police authority, which some members and officers saw as leading to a 'democratic deficit'. The chairman and clerk argued that the people of the respective areas were no longer being 'properly represented'. They clearly saw part of the elected members' role as representing the views of their local constituents to the police authority. The other members, however, explicitly distanced themselves from this view.

According to these other members (mostly non-Labour members), this view was based on a fundamental misconception of the role of a member on the new police authority. One (elected) member argued strongly that *all* members of the new police authority – including magistrates, elected and independent members – were there on behalf of the public across the force area. In his view, it was not their role to try to represent the particular interests of one borough of the force area. The member supported this point by noting that in many years' service both on pre- and post-1995 police authorities, a local constituent raised a concern about policing matters with him on only one occasion. In this sense, he clearly felt that he represented the people of his area in a symbolic rather than a practical sense, though this may simply have reflected the nature of his area, as much as the efficacy of local democracy. A number of members said they preferred a smaller authority because it gave members opportunities to contribute to debates, which added to the effect of the removal of explicit party politics from the authority's proceedings (see below). Some members felt that the outcome of debates being no longer predetermined by the pre-meeting caucus groups meant that the debate was more open and useful. Some of the force's senior command officers supported this view, with one ACC stating that 'it's a smaller authority, and it's noticeably more focused, there's no doubt about it.'

Powers and responsibilities

In Chapters 1 and 2, we outlined the various changes in statutory powers and responsibilities of the respective parties of the tripartite structure. We consider here some of the general shifts in powers and responsibilities, although the crucial issue of the responsibility for publishing a local policing plan is considered in more detail in a later section. Here we are concerned at a more general level with the emerging role of the police authority and its relationship with the force. The new police authority operates under Standing Orders (SOs), drafted by a joint working party of senior officers of the force and police authority, and then approved by authority members. Senior officers of the force reported that the transition was brought about relatively smoothly, and no major differences of substance emerged between the force and the police authority at this stage. Two major changes in the relative powers and responsibilities of the police authority and chief constable concern financial matters and personnel. Some members and officers of the police authority saw these as significant areas of loss of influence for the police authority, as discussed below. Given this, it is perhaps worth outlining briefly some of the more important parts of the SOs.

Much attention has been focused on the shift of financial management from the police authority to the chief constable. The SOs were prepared in accordance with the requirements of the Home Office code of practice on financial management, which were issued under Section 15 of the Police and Magistrates' Courts Act 1994. The SOs outline that the chief constable and the police authority treasurer shall agree the detailed form and timetables of the capital and revenue budgets, and the chief constable will have responsibility for drafting the budgets. These are submitted to the police authority for approval, but after such approval is given 'the chief constable may spend the budget monies without the further approval of the police authority'. Furthermore, the SOs make clear that the chief constable has virement powers (without police authority approval) between budget heads as long as such virement does not significantly change policing policy, or does not introduce significant future cost. The SOs lay down that virement may not occur from a capital to a revenue budget, and that the chief constable and his staff will 'manage and control budgets under the delegated budget scheme'. The treasurer retains a number of powers of audit and control. For example, he has right of access to records, documents or correspondence relating to financial transactions of the force or police authority. The chief constable is required to bring any serious financial irregularity to the attention of the treasurer and the police authority. Under the new SOs, the police authority remains responsible for appointing the chief officers of the police force. However, with regard to civilian personnel, the chief constable is now responsible for appointing civilian personnel, except in the case of posts that are not under the 'direction and control' of the chief constable. However, although some police authority members saw this as a major change, the SOs actually refer to this power being given to chiefs by Section 10 of the 1964 Police Act.

Some members and officers of the police authority saw the delegation of much of the detailed financial and personnel management as a clear loss of influence compared with the pre-1995 police authority. The chairman and clerk expressed this most strongly. In their view, the pre-1995 police authority had been an active authority, and a central part of its influence was exerted via 'hands-on' involvement in the detailed issues of staffing (recruitment and grading) via the old personnel subcommittee, and in financial matters such as the sale of police houses. It was argued that via these powers the police authority exercised a good degree of control over the chief constable. As the chairman put it:

> Chief constables will tell you it was a problem. Chief constables will tell you that administratively they had to do a lot of work that they didn't feel they needed to do. But what chief constables won't tell you is that because they were doing that work they were actually being brought to account all the time. They were being watched on everything they did, they were being controlled.

The chairman's views were supported by the clerk, who felt that there had been a significant loss of influence due to the Act. Not surprisingly, both identified to a degree with the old police authority, which they felt had been very effective. They thought that their police authority had suffered from reforms introduced to improve inactive and uninfluential shire police authorities. As we discuss in a later section, the new responsibility for publishing the annual policing plan was not considered to be a significant compensatory shift in powers towards the new police authority. In fact, it was considered to be rather a superficial 'power' in practice, given the influence of national objectives within the plan, and the fact that the chief constable is the driving force behind its substantive content. It is important to note that even some of the non-Labour elected members who were extremely positive about the reforms, when pressed, appeared to share some of the chairman's concerns about loss of police authority influence. They particularly regretted losing police authority responsibility for personnel and finance, which they felt had given the chief constable and force too much influence.

Depoliticisation

There was general agreement that party politics now played a much smaller part in the operation of the new police authority than under the pre-1995 arrangements. Under the pre-1994 system, councillor members of the various parties met in political caucus groups, and the magistrates also met together as a group prior to the authority meeting, to agree their 'line' for the coming meeting. Under the new structure such meetings no longer took place. Again, there was a range of views about the relative benefits and drawbacks of this development. On the one hand, the chairman and clerk emphasised the advantages that caucus meetings had provided, such as enabling issues to be discussed in detail prior to the meeting, without the constraining presence of either senior police officers or the press. In their view, this meant that all authority members were well-briefed prior to the full meeting, and the police authority (being dominated by one political party) would have the opportunity to develop a clear 'line' on matters of importance, and thus be able to question the chief constable more effectively. It was therefore argued that the 'depoliticisation' of the new police authority had increased the relative power of the chief constable over a less well-briefed and less coherent authority. A related point concerned the effect of depoliticisation on the kinds of issues the authority discussed. Although the removal, or at least reduction, of party politics from the police authority was often presented as an advantage, the clerk made the point that 'party-political' discussions were often about the significant wider issues of the day about policing. Much of this had been lost in largely technical debates about performance and finance.

Not surprisingly, non-Labour elected members, unelected magistrates and independents took a different view of depoliticisation and the cessation of pre-meeting caucus groups. A number of respondents described the depoliticisation of the new arrangements in positive terms. One member felt that under the previous arrangements, the Labour members were able to 'railroad' proposals through, and other members had little opportunity to have a meaningful input. Another member described the 'yah-boo' debates that had occasionally diverted the authority as revolving around members making party-political points about national issues instead of concentrating on the policing of the local area. Another member described the new authority as 'happier' for the absence of party-political 'backbiting'. Even members who praised the less 'political' nature of the new arrangements, however, reported that relations between members of different political parties on the pre-1995 police authority had generally been constructive. One long-serving member reported that the pre-1995 police authority had been a substantial improvement on the one that had existed prior to 1986, which was characterised by a high degree of political tension. A number of members mentioned the chairman playing an important part in smoothing over some of the political tensions of the past.

Party politics had certainly not disappeared from the police authority altogether. A member of the force command team said it still remained in the background, and would come to the surface on occasion. Another (non-Labour) police authority member felt that, although it had been less in evidence during the first year of the new police authority, it was beginning to resurface. In the meeting attended by a researcher, there were a number of interventions that could be described as 'party political'. For example, one item on the agenda consisted of a presentation on the government's Private Finance Initiative (PFI), and its possible implications for the force. Some authority members made a number of critical points about the ideology underlying PFI, to the extent that the presenter responded that he was not there to speak for the government. Similarly, the then Home Secretary's record on crime figures was criticised in party-political terms.

A number of members felt that the new police authority operated in a more 'businesslike' manner because of the decline in party-political debates. This meant that the police authority discussed the details of both major capital investments in the force and of technical matters of performance. In the police authority meeting that one of us attended, a central part of the discussion was about the previous year's performance. However, one ACC felt that what he described as 'political' considerations still constrained 'business' decisions. The particular example he gave was competitive tendering, when he felt that the police authority had ensured that some support services were retained in-house rather than put out to tender.

The police authority's relationship with the chief constable
All police authority members and officers stressed that the chief constable had developed a close working relationship with the pre-1995 police authority, which the move to a new structure had not fundamentally affected. Similarly, the force's senior officers and civilian staff reported that the good relations that had existed between the police authority and the force since the late 1980s continued under the new arrangements. However, a number of respondents – in the police authority and the force – detected sources of tension in the new arrangements, which could in the future put the good relationships under strain. Most of these related to perceived 'grey areas' of overlap in the responsibilities of the chief and of the police authority, particularly over the chief's delegated budgetary and personnel responsibilities, and their respective roles in producing the policing plan (considered in more detail below).

A senior member of the force reported that over 90 per cent of matters formerly requiring police authority approval were now delegated to the chief constable. The police authority is, however, still required to monitor the force's overall financial strategy and to hold the chief constable accountable for the exercise of these delegated powers. This remains a source of consider-able confusion. There were both senior members of the force, and police authority members, who saw a lack of logic in the new arrangements. The police authority treasurer employed an audit team to monitor the force's finan-cial management and to detect likely over-runs or even frauds. However, the treasurer still relied on the force finance team to uncover such developments and, without the force's cooperation, would be unlikely to detect any serious financial irregularities. On the other hand, in that senior officers of the force are not statutorily required to report financial discrepancies to members, and yet are more likely to come across such discrepancies, they have all the power but no responsibility. A senior officer at the force argued convincingly that the roles of the treasurer and of the force finance officer could be combined under one person, who would be made the Section 151 officer (so that he or she was statutorily required to report to members when things went astray), but be based within the force structure to allow both real management freedom and full access to the financial information.

One senior force officer felt that, despite considerable financial delegation to the force, the police authority still ultimately retained a high degree of power over financial matters. He pointed out that under the 'exceptional circumstances' rule (in the code of practice issued with the PMCA) they could refuse to delegate any financial management to the force: 'If really push came to shove and you got a really bloody minded police authority then they could stop us doing anything. I think that is what it says.' It seems that a crucial aim of the Act was to keep police authority influence over the force's broad financial strategy but to delegate day-to-day management matters. From the perspective of senior staff in the force, however, the police authority had yet to grasp the full implication of this new role. This meant that police authority members were continuing to ask questions about matters of financial detail. One ACC summed up this position as follows:

> There is still an awful confusion of roles for the authority and the chief, which has not been helped by the new legislation. ... They still find great difficulty in understanding a strategic role, they have delegated responsibilities to the chief for the first time here, whereas in other authorities they had these delegated powers to the chief constable going back years and years, but here it was a big change. So for those members of the police authority who were on the old police authority, they feel they have been robbed of their hands-on power, and haven't really got to grips with their strategic role. ... They're wanting to question detail, get into things which, frankly, aren't any of their business anymore.

Although the chief constable was widely commended for his good relationship with the police authority, some members still viewed the chief constable's position as rather dominant. One member, for example, reported that the chief constable was on occasions too dominant and rather unwilling to give enough weight to the police authority's view. However, another elected member commended the chief constable for his 'liberal' approach on a number of issues, which had resulted in criticism from some other police authority members. For example, the chief constable had supported improved consultative links between the police and the lesbian and gay community in the force area. Another example concerned the policing of travellers. A number of police authority members had criticised the police for failing to take firm action against travellers who had set up camps on land in their local areas. The chief constable made it clear on a number of occasions, including the police authority meeting attended by a PSI researcher, that he did not feel that the criminal law in general and 'hard' policing in particular were an appropriate response.

A number of police authority members and officers argued that the police service had experienced a net gain in influence relative to local police authorities due to the latter being so radically restructured over such a short time period. The reduction in size, the delegation of financial and personnel matters to the force, the requirement to publish a policing plan, and the need to recruit and incorporate independent members, had taken up much of the authority members' and officers' time and energy. Thus, the immediate effect of the changed structure was a perceived shift in the local balance of power towards the chief constable and force, although police authority members were hopeful that this might be redressed over future years, and that their influence would increase.

THE CONTRIBUTION OF INDEPENDENT MEMBERS

Because the Home Office had given the police authority special dispensation to extend its membership to a total of 19, it included six independent members rather than the usual five. By the time of the study, one of the independent members had been replaced because one of those originally selected had resigned.

There was no local advertisement for the six independent members. Just over 100 applications were received for the six places in the original round of appointments. The appointment panel followed the procedure of selecting a shortlist of 24 names submitted to the Home Office. The Home Office then pared this list down to 12, and the appointments board selected the final six names. The candidates were not called for interview, and were thus selected on the basis of their application forms alone. However, when a vacancy for an independent member later emerged, applicants were interviewed for the post, and this was subsequently adopted as part of the police authority policy for selecting independent members. The national survey of clerks' offices described in Chapter 4 showed that a minority of police authorities, including this one, perceived there to have been some party-political interference on the part of the Home Office in the selection procedure for independent members. The chairman described this as follows:

> There was a letter of complaint sent out from a local Tory MP who was complaining about an individual on the list of candidates that had been sent to the Home Secretary. But that list was confidential, so how did the Tory MP know who was on it? The Home Office must have vetted the lists via Central Office. In actual fact, the MP was right, the individual was a serving councillor which was not made clear on his application form. But the list should have remained confidential. . . . So that is proof that they were consulted about who was on the list. And MPs have played a part in selecting those individuals, and that should never have happened.

The professional backgrounds of the people eventually selected were varied, though they had a management or business slant. Two had senior management experience in large companies, one had been a school bursar, one a headteacher, one was a computer analyst, and one a self-employed driving instructor. Four of the independents were retired and two currently working. They included two women, and one ethnic minority person.

Although Labour members of the old police authority had been particularly opposed to this part of the Act, there was no evidence of it having created personal tensions between independent and other members on the police authority. Indeed, all police authority members – councillors of different parties as well as independents and magistrates – stressed that they worked well with each other and did not operate in distinct groups. Discussions under the new police authority had rarely led to formal votes, which by the time of the study had happened only once or twice since the new arrangements came into operation. Though independent members reported that they discussed issues between themselves prior to meetings, this was not formalised. In fact, one independent member described it as a 'chat over a cup of tea' or an occasional telephone call.

The only evidence of a perceived (minor) difference between independent and elected members appeared during a police authority meeting when a Labour councillor expressed concern about police authority representation at a national conference. The councillor complained that neither of the two police authority members who attended the conference were elected members, one being an independent and one being a magistrate. Overall, it seems that some councillors and police authority officers still disagree with the principle of appointing independent members to police authorities, and this occasionally manifests itself in irritation at the position adopted by individual independent members at police authority meetings. In general, though, there appears to be little tension between different types of members.

Clearly, the independents were not a homogenous group. They had different skills and backgrounds and, from discussions with councillor and magistrate members, it appears they made varying contributions to the authority business. This perception was confirmed by observation of a police authority meeting, when few differences in the quantity or quality of the interjections were apparent. There were important differences of view about the contribution of the independents among other authority members and officers, and senior police staff. Although Labour members were still clearly unhappy with the principle of 'quango-ising' police authorities, they accepted that some of the independent members had brought useful skills to the authority. One councillor reported that, although they had been regarded with some suspicion at first, it was now generally accepted they did a 'good job'. Non-Labour elected members and magistrate members were more enthusiastic about the independents, one describing the 'incredibly helpful' management experience of some and their ability to comment usefully on balance sheets and matters of finance. One independent member had had considerable experience as the chief executive of a construction company and was thus able to provide detailed contributions to discussions about new capital projects and the building programme. The clerk felt that although the independents had settled in well, their contributions were no better or worse than those of local authority members.

Some of the independents clearly felt that being outside the party-political machinery was a major advantage. For example, one said: 'As independent members we have no preconceived or ingrained notions of policing matters. We don't always have to look over our shoulders, we can say what we genuinely believe that the public want.' Some members pointed out another advantage of having independent members, who by definition did not serve on a number of other local government committees. This gave them, particularly those who were retired, more time to devote to police authority matters than most of the elected members. Interestingly, even those members who were most enthusiastic about the positive impact of independent members still described them as 'Home Office-appointed'.

As they did not have a local authority background, independent members were unfamiliar with police authority traditions. Consequently, some members thought, in authority meetings they were less deferential to the chief constable and other senior police officers. One member said that some of the independents 'seem less afraid to argue with the chief', and another reported that one independent in particular was extremely forthright in dealing with senior police officers. This was viewed with slight nervousness by some members, who made reference to 'loose cannons' and were concerned that good relationships between the police authority and the chief might be threatened by a more combative approach. Some independents recognised that their more direct approach to questioning the chief constable made some members uncomfortable. As one reported: 'You find that a lot of the political members will tend to pussy-foot a bit with the chief constable rather than be, for want of a better expression, blunt with him.' Another independent member expressed disappointment that the police authority was not more proactive in questioning the chief constable and trying to influence policy. This member explained that the new police authority was still bedding down, and that independent members in particular needed to develop a 'feel' for their new role. Occasionally, unfamiliarity with the niceties of dealing with chief constables could lead to tensions. The same member, who found this 'disturbing', felt that criticising the police organisation was like approaching a 'large unpredictable animal'. All independent members who were interviewed stressed the importance of supporting and working with the chief constable, but also the need for a critical and independent approach.

Senior police staff tended to view the independents' contribution in a positive light, though again there were important differences of emphasis between officers. It was generally accepted that the management and business expertise of some independent members had been helpful, but there was also a view that, along with other police authority members, the independents had yet to grasp their strategic role. One senior member of the force felt that the independents tended to want to be involved in the detailed management of the force, which was not their role. According to this person, some independent members could not resist trying to involve themselves in the 'nitty-gritty' of financial and staffing decisions. In fact, one senior officer of the force saw the independents as more of a problem than other members in this regard. Although this source agreed that independent members tend to ask more challenging questions of the force, he argued that these questions are aimed at the wrong target: 'independent members are asking difficult questions, which as you know the Home Secretary wanted, but difficult low-level questions.' It was reported that there was still a tendency for the police authority to concentrate on the matters of detail, over particular service-level agreements, over particular spending projects, and other 'nitty-gritty' issues, and less of a strategic discussion about how to set and address the longer-term objectives of the force. One of the ACCs made a similar point about the focus of some of the independent members' attention:

> It's the independent members who I think see themselves as a board of directors, which they're not. Particularly on financial matters, matters of detail, they clearly feel uncomfortable working at a strategic level, and want to get involved in the detail, even though it isn't their function, they're not equipped to do it, and basically, it takes quite a lot of officer time, trying to explain to them and trying to coach them in areas they don't have any great familiarity with. So the independent members, I think, if anything find it more difficult than the local authority members to understand the strategic role and function.

It should be emphasised that this view was not shared by all senior officers of the force. Several of the command team referred to the positive inputs of independent members with expertise in business and finance, one made particular reference to the 'searching' nature of the questions they asked, and another explicitly said that one of the advantages of involving people with senior private sector management experience is that they are able to grasp the strategic view in a way that local authority members find difficult.

The independent members themselves appeared to have different views about the proper role of the police authority. One clearly felt that the 'nitty-gritty' questions of detail were legitimate areas for their concern, relating his experience as a private sector manager to the kind of questions he wanted to ask the chief constable. Another, who appeared to take a different view, had expected the new police authority to be more involved in discussing wider questions about styles of policing, overall aims and objectives, and other such matters, rather than reacting to management reports from the police side and becoming involved in detailed comments on finance and buildings reports.

Observation of the police authority meeting showed that some independent members were certainly prepared to become involved and ask quite detailed questions. The members, as they had reported, did not sit according to party, magistrate and independent blocks, but mixed and matched in a large round-table format, with the chief constable, chairman and officers of the police authority at one end. There was no distinguishable independents' 'view' on any of the issues raised. Indeed, had the researcher not met police authority members, it would have been extremely difficult to distinguish between independents, magistrates and councillors based on the quantity or quality of their contributions.

LOCAL CONSULTATION

The police authority and the force each devote considerable time and resources to 'consultation' of various forms. The authority is the only one in the country to have a large unit devoted entirely to consultation with the community. The existence of this unit, and the amount of resources it takes up, has at times been a source of friction with the force. The community relations unit is called the Police and Community Team (PACT). It is large and employs 19 full-time staff responsible for administering the PCCGs, the youth fora, special con-sultative groups such as the Lesbian and Gay Police Liaison Group, various ethnic minority liaison groups and the lay visiting scheme. They service all the main committees, taking and keeping minutes, and analyse the main issues discussed at meetings. They provided the minutes to the meetings of the PCCGs in the two divisions that were visited as part of the study.

Police community consultative groups (PCCGs)
Currently, there are 31 area-based PCCGs across the force area, which are loosely based on the subdivisional structure, though some subdivisions have more than one PCCG because force restructuring has left the force and PCCG structure out of sink. About half the PCCGs meet monthly, slightly fewer than half every two months and the remaining three every three months. The PCCGs used to be organised according to guidelines that laid down the typical framework. They consisted of committees of invited representatives of the usual organisations – victim support schemes, residents and tenants groups, citizens' advice bureaux, chambers of commerce and trade, ethnic minority groups and other community organisations. More recently, the police authority has changed the PCCGs' structure, and they now operate as open public meet-ings. All the same organisations are invited, but the meetings are intended to be more inclusive. There has also been an attempt to move away from 'formal' places such as police stations or town halls, to wider social venues such as schools or community centres.

Members and officers see consultation as a crucial part of the police authority's remaining responsibilities, especially in the light of the generally perceived loss of influence in detailed areas of finance and personnel policy as outlined above. One PACT officer explicitly said there was little left for new police authorities to do other than set the budget and produce the policing plan. Thus, consultation was a key area in which the police authority could take a lead. The PCCGs were not established to examine strategic issues, as we discuss below. It was accepted that they were useful fora for discussing local problems, but that much of this revolved around quality of life issues.

We were unable to attend PCCG meetings in either of the subdivisions visited during the study, but the minutes of the meetings over the previous year were made available. They suggested that the average attendance was rather low (15 in one, 20 in the other), though occasionally a large attendance was recorded (40 at one meeting in September 1995). They were attended by the local subdivisional commander, usually another officer (a sergeant or inspector) and a police authority officer. The kinds of issues raised were familiar ones for PCCGs, including complaints about numbers of police officers, turnover of local officers, response times, youths causing annoyance, people riding bicycles without lights and, on one estate in particular, intimidation of witnesses. The minutes recorded that the police presented rough breakdowns of local crime problems to the meetings. Both the subdivisional commanders we interviewed were asked about their PCCGs and both said they were useful channels of communication with a relatively small number of interested local people and organisations. Divisional commanders were required to produce business plans outlining local objectives, and the planned use of resources in addressing these objectives, in the coming year. Both subdivisional commanders presented the intended 'divisional objectives' to their PCCGs, and had some feedback, though there was no evidence of the PCCGs changing local priorities proactively. However, they were given the opportunity to have their voices heard and one subdivisional commander undertook some crude analysis of the PCCG's and his staff's main concerns for incorporation into the divisional business plan. As mechanisms for setting local objectives or discussing the strategic direction of the force, however, it was generally accepted that the groups would play a limited role. They did not have the information, expertise, resources or, crucially, the inclination to undertake such a role.

Specialist consultation: young people, the gay community and ethnic minorities
PACT officers reported that youth forums were established because young people were noticeably absent from PCCGs, and that much of the discussion in PCCGs involved complaints about young people. The PACT approach was to target a 'captive audience' in schools, and it piloted a scheme involving youth consultation forums based in secondary schools. At the time of the study, there were youth fora in 100 secondary schools in the force area, as well as a few in special schools and sixth form colleges. The team was also attempting to establish similar schemes in universities and colleges. Police authority officers reported that the youth fora had raised a number of issues, including a focus on young people as victims (as well as perpetrators) of crime. The meetings were not chaired or led by the police, though police representatives were invited. PACT officers contrasted this with the more traditional 'schools liaison' approach, whereby designated police officers visit schools and deliver lectures to pupils, often focusing on anti-drugs and anti-crime messages. In the view of the PACT officers, the youth fora have informed and open discussions that allow young people to have a real input.

The PACT team organised two ethnic minority consultation groups in particular parts of the force area, and attended a community forum in the area of highest ethnic minority concentration. Though police authority officers underlined the cautious approach of the police to consultation, they accepted that important changes had occurred in the policing of these particular communities. For example, in one area of the force with a large ethnic minority population, it was reported that the local PCCG successfully campaigned for a more sensitive approach to the use of stop and search by local police officers. In the view of PACT officers, this had positive effects on local police–community relations. The lesbian and gay group considered a broad range of issues, including policing. The PACT officers viewed this as an example of a community-led initiative that asks the police to respond, rather than a police-led exercise (by way of contrast with the way they saw many PCCGs).

Public satisfaction surveys

The force, rather than the police authority, undertook a range of public satisfaction surveys. Its Development and Inspectorate Department was responsible for these, as well as for collating and analysing the suite of performance indicators monitored by the force. Department staff reported that more than 200 PIs were being monitored in the force at the time of the study. Initially stemming from the need to monitor the ACPO Quality of Service PIs, three elements to the programme of satisfaction surveys had been developed: (a) exit interviews for visitors to police stations (sample size 100 customers per station); (b) a telephone survey of satisfaction with the police (sample size 2500) contracted to an outside agency; and (c) a postal survey testing public satisfaction. Staff accepted that although small sample sizes and low response rates limited the reliability of these findings, it was still felt that they provide useful indicators of public satisfaction with various aspects of policing.

Different views on consultation

There was a difference in emphasis between the approaches to consultation advocated by senior police officers and by senior police authority members and officers. Senior police sources had reservations about placing too much emphasis on PCCGs and stressed their limitations as a mechanism for discussing force objectives. They pointed to the low average attendance, the predominance of localised 'quality of life' issues in the discussions and the 'unrepresentative' nature of PCCG meetings. A senior officer of the force stressed that the police are involved in a range of 'consultative' fora, in addition to the PCCG, which the police authority do not recognise as consultation. He cited the large number of homewatch schemes, which the police in the force area service, the annual conference of homewatch coordinators, *ad hoc* events such as parents' evenings arranged by the police in a particular area to discuss the drugs problem, as well as the in-house customer surveys. He stressed that he was not suggesting that PCCGs should be disbanded, or that they were useless, but that they had their limitations and that consultation should be considered in a broader sense.

Senior police staff generally accepted that taking the lead on community consultation was an important role for the police authority, and one senior officer said that the force would be hoping to 'use the authority more' for this in the future. However, there was some concern expressed that, by trying to become involved more directly in community safety matters with local authorities in the force area the police authority was beginning to stray into 'operational' territory. In the words of one senior officer:

> They see a role for themselves in liaising with local authorities, with victim support groups, with drugs advisory councils, you name it. They see themselves as having a role in communicating with these groups on behalf of the public. We keep making the point, the police force is about delivering policing to the county, we do that by partnerships and talking to these people. We can't talk to these people through the police authority and its officers. . . . There is a danger that if the police authority start to see more of a role for themselves as intermediaries, it starts again to muddy the waters, would be expensive, and in the end would cause confusion in the minds of the public about what they expect the police force to deliver and what they expect from elsewhere.

In contrast, the PACT officers seemed to think that the police had a rather one-dimensional view of consultation, which required the police always to be present. They reported that the police had been upset by a consultative meeting they held for Asian youths in one area, where it was perceived that there was a poor relationship with the police. The police were not invited to the meeting because, according to PACT officers, the youths asked that they should not be there. They also stressed the need for involvement in fora that are not just focused upon policing, such as the lesbian and gay project, but which have important implications for policing matters.

Despite some important differences about consultation, there was general agreement that it was extremely difficult to consult in practice. The lack of interest and involvement of the wider public makes it almost inevitable that attendance at meetings is unrepresentative, unless the circumstances are highly unusual. This suggests that a greater stress will be laid on obtaining in-depth qualitative data via focus groups to supplement the quantitative information of customer satisfaction surveys. One senior officer strongly supported the need to consult, but saw this in symbolic rather than substantive terms. Given the large amount of time and resources that go into various mechanisms of consultation, he questioned whether the final outputs provided value for money. This was related to the fact that as far as policing is concerned there are many 'publics', which leads to conflicting demands upon the police.

THE ANNUAL POLICING PLAN

The 1996/7 policing plan

The 1996/7 plan is slightly longer than the previous year's, has more local objectives and, for the first time, sets hard performance targets. Its overall appearance and presentation – glossy cover in A4 format – are similar to the 1995/6 plan. It is 22 pages in length. The inclusion of both the force's and the police authority's crest suggest joint ownership, though the title clearly states that it is the plan of the police authority. The authority's chairman and chief constable both signed the foreword and an opening section outlines the authority's responsibilities and structure. The names and telephone numbers of police authority members are listed in the plan. There are some brief details about the consultation framework within the force, describing the PCCGs and youth fora. The plan incorporates all the national key objectives (KOs), which are clearly identified as such, and eight local objectives (LOs). These are actually force-wide objectives and are presented in the same subject sections as the KOs. Some LOs are in the same general subject area as KOs, but with a different emphasis (for example on prevention rather than detection). All the KOs have the given key performance indicators (KPIs), and all the LOs have their own set PIs as well. Specific performance targets are set for all PIs. A section outlines the nature of targets and explains that they have been set with reference to past performance and expected future demand. The plan emphasises that PIs should be seen as only one element in checking police performance. It includes some broad details about planned actions in support of objectives, though not for all of them. A financial section includes a breakdown of funding sources and presents the revenue budget divisions between broad budget heads. The distribution of revenue budget between different policing functions is illustrated and there is a general description of the force's capital programme.

Objectives and performance indicators

As noted above, the 1996/7 plan includes all the national key objectives (with the corresponding KPIs), as laid down in the Home Secretary's letter of December 1995. In the plan, KOs are incorporated along with LOs into four core service areas: call management, crime management, traffic management and public reassurance. The KOs appear in a different order from that of the Home Secretary's letter, though it is unclear whether the Home Office was suggesting a prioritisation. Senior police officers made it clear that they saw no prioritisation either within the KOs, or between KOs and LOs, because they were all mixed in together, although they are identified separately. They reported that it was a deliberate decision not to number them in order to avoid giving the false impression of an order of priority. The service area of call management contained one objective, the KO 'to respond promptly to calls from the public'. Crime management included the KO about maintaining/

increasing violent crime detections, and KO3 (targeting and preventing crimes that are a particular local problem). The plan also included the objective to target repeat victimisation under this KO. The PIs for this objective were drugs enforcement ones, arrests and disposals under the Misuse of Drugs Act. The crime management theme also included the KO about increasing domestic burglary detections, along with a number of local (i.e. force-wide) objectives. LOs were quoted as being complementary to the KOs, but had a different slant in some cases. For example, the aim to increase detections and reduce the total incidence of burglary may ultimately conflict (and did appear to conflict given the figures in the annual report). Discussions with senior police officers suggested that this objective was added as a deliberate counterbalance to the KO on burglary. For example, one ACC reported that 'we would rather reduce total burglary than detect more burglaries, which is why we added a force objective about reducing the total number of burglaries.' The plan included relatively few 'quality of service' type indicators in the plan, and no reference to standards of service.

In total, the 1996/7 plan set out eight local objectives. These were:

- to target the illegal supply of controlled drugs (PI: the number of detections for drug trafficking);
- to encourage those who misuse drugs to seek treatment and support and to promote initiatives to prevent the misuse of drugs (PI: number of drug prevention initiatives);
- to reduce the number of offences of burglary in a dwelling (PIs: number of domestic burglaries as a percentage of total crime/number of offences per 1000 households/burglary dwelling detection rate);
- to reduce the number of burglaries other than dwelling (PIs: number as a percentage of recorded crime/number of offences per 100 officers/ number of primary detections per 100 officers/total detection rate);
- to reduce the number of thefts of motor vehicles (PIs: number of thefts as percentage of total crime/per 100 officers/primary detections per 100 officers/total detection rate);
- to reduce the number of thefts from motor vehicles (PIs: as above, except theft *from* motor vehicles);
- to promote and support greater safety for all road users (PIs: number of fatal casualties/number of other injuries); and
- to cooperate with young people, schools, parents and residents to promote community harmony (PI: the number of complaints of youths causing annoyance per 1000 population).

It is interesting to note the broad range of PIs which the plan includes. For example, some objectives have three or four PIs. This appears to relate to the point made in the plan about the partial view PIs give of police performance. It contrasts with force B's approach, which is to reduce the number of objectives and PIs for the sake of clarity and understanding.

The planning process

As with almost all other police authorities, the planning process had developed greatly since 1995/6, the first year of published policing plans. During that year, it was widely accepted that, because of the timing of the birth of the new police authorities and the appearance of key national objectives, the plan had been almost entirely police led. For the second year of planning, the reference year of the study, the planning process was somewhat more developed.

In early September 1995, a report was submitted to the police authority which had been jointly written by the chief constable and clerk to the police authority. This outlined the proposed planning process and the broad principles in producing the policing plan. Members' views were sought about how best to consult over the plan. In early December, the chief constable reported that drafting of the plan was underway. However, it was not until the Home Secretary's key objectives were announced late in the month that the draft plan could be finalised and circulated for discussion by special seminars in each division of the force. The full police authority discussed the draft plan at the end of January. A number of drafting suggestions were made, including the need to refer to both the chief constable and the police authority when mentioning priorities for the coming year, and the importance of referring to the public meetings that had been held to discuss the plan. On 16 February, the police authority discussed the final version of the plan and suggested a number of minor amendments. The plan was finally published in April.

Within the force, the plan was drafted in the Development and Inspectorate Department by a planning team of three people, one of whom wrote the document. Although it is the police authority's plan, a member of the planning team reported that the department had limited contact with the police authority. There was no direct contact with police authority members, but there were a few informal meetings with the officers of the police authority. One officer thought that the police authority's influence was over the plan's appearance rather than its substantive content. Local objectives were set to complement KOs – with consultation through the PCCGs. The actual staff on division were also asked for their views about the main policing problems affecting their area, usually via multi-rank teams or staff meetings.

The planning cycle for the policing plan of 1997/8 had just begun at the time of the study. This consisted of a first round of local consultation occurring in September, and intended to give rise to the main issues to be incorporated into the annual policing plan. The divisions were at that time undertaking consultation (both with police staff, and with local organisations and PCCGs) after which they were required to send a report to Development and Inspectorate detailing the main local policing problems. The planning team would then collate and analyse the reports from all divisions and departments, and still from this analysis a series of force-wide themes. In addition, a memo had been sent to all divisions and departments during August, which asked for suggestions for inclusion in the annual plan. These were also to be analysed by the planning team at headquarters. The aim was to set the local objectives in November and have the draft plan sent to the police authority for discussion and review by early December.

Officers from the planning team reported that during discussions about the 1996/7 plan, members appeared particularly concerned about presentational features when the aim had been for them to concentrate more on matters of substance. To encourage them to concentrate on content rather than presentation, it was decided that the draft of the 1997/8 plan would be submitted to the police authority in a plain word-processed document format. Another problem the planning team identified was that the budget information is not usually available until February/March, which means having to put together the annual plan before the final budget decisions have been made. The force was working to bring the planning and budgetary cycles into line.

Following adoption by the police authority, the plan goes to the design and print stage. In 1996/7 4778 copies were printed, of which over 3000 went to the police authority, and about 1500 were kept for distribution by the force.

Consultation over the policing plan

Representatives of both the police authority and the force accepted the need for strategic consultation at a different level from the PCCGs, which were not really designed to consult over a force-wide annual policing plan. PACT officers argued that it is extremely difficult for people who have been used to coming to PCCG meetings and discussing local policing issues and quality of life matters, then to think about the broader strategic issues that need to be fed into the consultation over the plan.

The police authority developed a number of methods for consulting about the policing plan. In the first year (1995/6), the authority had written to individuals and organisations asking them to comment on or express their concerns about the chief constable's draft plan, but this had not worked very well because so few responded. In addition, the draft plan had been discussed at PCCG meetings, though again the meetings tended to raise parochial issues rather than discuss strategic priorities. In the second year (1996/7), the draft policing plan was discussed at public seminars (one in each division of the force area), to which the general public and key organisations and individuals were invited. These seminars occurred after the chief's draft plan had appeared in December, so there was little time to introduce changes and the process was again perceived as unsuccessful, though an improvement on the first year.

At the time of the study, work was underway on preparing the plan for 1997/8, and further developments in consultation had been established. First, a postal survey of the public had been undertaken, with the help of the force research department. This was a basic questionnaire in which people were asked to tick boxes alongside objectives about which they had concerns and given space to add some of their own. Second, the police authority was aiming to use focus groups of particular sections of the population to feed in to the planning process. Third, the consultation process was started earlier, before the appearance of the chief constable's draft plan. A policing plan working party was established, consisting of some members of the police authority, who were to liaise with the force planning team. This fed into the force's own consultation processes and affected the shape of the draft plan itself. This was then discussed by the police authority working party and, eventually, by the full authority. In general, the PACT officers were very positive about the impact of the new planning requirements on police authorities, one even stating that 18 months or so into the new authority they had achieved more in terms of consultation than the old police authority did in nine years.

Three clear themes emerged as matters of concern from the plan's 1996/7 consultation exercise: domestic violence, witness intimidation and racial harassment. The three themes were subsumed under a rather broad 'community harmony' local objective. Police authority members supported this wording. They did not want a local objective about 'youths causing annoyance', for this was felt to stigmatise all young people as 'problems'. This actually seemed to suggest that the three themes were overlooked, for youths causing annoyance is totally different from all three. There was a feeling within the PACT team that this language was confusing and that the plan needed to be framed in a way people could understand. In the police authority survey about the policing plan objectives, few people appeared to understand what the 'community harmony' objective actually meant.

Police authority influence over the plan

The policing plan is another area of potential overlap between the chief and police authority. In general terms, a command-level officer summed up the view that the policing plan 'leaves again much room for confusion between the strategic role of the authority and the executive powers of the chief constable'. This officer summed up the 'force view' on the division of responsibilities over the plan, but clearly accepted that a degree of confusion remained:

> We're trying to hold the line on policing plans that the policing plan is about what must be done. The how to deliver it is a matter for the chief constable. That starts a very simple, easy distinction which I think is the right distinction, but of course like all such matters, as you start getting down into the drafting, then it becomes rather more difficult, and there are rather grey areas which start to fade together.[1]

---

1. This follows the distinction outlined by Butler (1996) and discussed in Chapter 3.

Those police authority members who expressed the view that the new police authority had less influence, perhaps not surprisingly appeared to place less weight on the policing plan. It was not that they felt they had been prevented from having an influence, or that it was dominated by the police, simply that the plan was not a particularly powerful form of control. The chief constable's draft plan seems to have been widely accepted within both the force and the police authority. There was no strong opposition to the content, and the local objectives set in the draft were not changed significantly for the final version.

Thus, although some leading police authority members and officers had no major complaints about either the substantive content of the plan or the planning process, they did not appear to see the plan as a significant new lever of accountability for the police authority to use. For example, the following statement by the chairman suggested that the policing plan was not a major change from what existed before:

> I have always believed that we've always had these powers, if you look at what we've got. Alright, so it's written into a policing plan, so they've brought in a new Act and told us that we have to write a policing plan. But we used to go out there and consult with the public before, we used to listen to what the public wanted, and we used to take on board their views and wishes, bring them back, sit down with the chief constable when we were doing the budget, and he would have his proposals there based on the divisional commanders' perceptions of the public's concerns in their areas, and he would bring a financial package to us in order to address those problems. Now all that we are doing now, is writing them in a booklet and saying we will address this area, and we will see that the chief will address this area, and now we are putting targets in, from the Audit Commission and the Home Secretary's targets, and then the police authority's targets are put into the report. But if you ask the public what they want, I would bet 95 per cent of them would say it is a complete waste of time writing all this up, what we want is more bobbies on the beat.

The chairman also noted that the chief constable need only 'have regard' to the plan, so that if the police authority insisted on putting an objective into the plan against the chief's wishes, it would not follow that resources would be devoted to that objective. In a similar vein, the clerk to the police authority felt that the policing plan had yet to take on the significance that some commentators had placed upon it. The police authority had yet to have a major influence over its policing plan. This was not because they were not allowed to have an influence. Indeed, the chief constable's draft was perceived as largely in tune with the main concerns that had arisen from attempts at local consultation. He said there had been little change from the original draft other than in the phrasing and some other relatively minor presentational matters. He reported that the police force had totally dominated target setting, in contrast to some other force areas where police authority members had made significant inputs into the actual performance targets set. The chairman and clerk hoped that the police authority would become more proactive in influencing the policing plan. Their main aim was to improve the consultative process and obtain a clearer view of public priorities early in the planning cycle. Despite the earlier comments about the first two years' policing plans, both the chairman and the clerk appeared to think that the plan could in future become an important mechanism of influence for the police authority.

Other members of the police authority were somewhat more positive about the amount of influence the police authority had exerted over the plan. The general view was that, under the circumstances, a reasonable amount of influence had been exerted over the objectives. It was generally accepted that the chief constable would take the lead in deciding the plan's substantive content, and that developing strategic consultation mechanisms was difficult. It was suggested that the police authority's influence would grow in the future, but this depended on it being able to tap into a meaningful public 'view' on matters. The clerk expressed a wish to move to a position in which the police authority consulted prior to setting objectives rather than consulting over objectives already drafted. In general, members of all types perceived the plan as a joint venture between the chief and the police authority and did not appear to have ambitious plans for taking the lead in deciding objectives. However, a minority of members had more ambitious hopes for the police authority role. For example, one expressed doubts about how far the plan should be seen as jointly owned: 'I think he [the chief constable] genuinely wants it to be perceived as a joint plan, whereas we would prefer it to be an absolute authority plan, because that is what we are there to do.'

Even the more ambitious members felt it was inevitable that the force would take the lead in drafting the plan and setting local objectives. No members envisaged a situation in which the police authority took the chief constable's draft and then itself produced the second draft. It was generally accepted that the police were the professional service providers, and that such decisions should largely be taken by them. One non-Labour member speculated whether a more radical element among the Labour councillor membership might wish for the police authority to be more proactive over the plan, but admitted that, as yet, there was no real evidence of any such developments. There were no specific examples of members of the police authority disagreeing over local objectives or other aspects of the plan, or of disagreements between the police authority and chief constable. When asked about their opinion of the local objectives, authority members appeared to be broadly satisfied with those in the plan, but accepted that they had not taken the lead on selecting any of them. It thus appeared that there was a good deal of consensus between those local concerns highlighted by the force consultation exercise and those that came from the police authority-led approach.

The independent members we interviewed generally expressed a more positive view of policing plans than other authority members. They clearly felt that this was the central plank of the new police authority's strategic role, though, as outlined above, some difficulties were being experienced in fulfilling such a role. Although they agreed that at present the plan remained rather uncontentious, they appeared to have ambitions to make it a much more effective lever for police authority influence over the police force. Senior police force staff clearly felt that the police authority had been an important influence on the plan but that the timing of the Home Secretary's KOs had disrupted the planning cycle. In general, the plan was not seen as a source of tension between the chief and police authority, though the potential for future conflict was recognised. This was based on a traditional reluctance to see the police authority interfering in 'operational matters'. A command level officer made a clear distinction between the police authority's and the force's respective roles regarding the plan. In his view, the police authority was to be concerned with the overall objectives of the force (the 'what'), whereas the force's role was in the operational approach to delivering this (the 'how'): 'I have no difficulty whatsoever with them saying "OK chief, this is what we want you to deliver, and this is how you'll be held accountable" because that's how we manage the force, that's how we talk to divisional commanders.'

This view clearly accepts that it is the police authority's role to set the force objectives and to hold the chief constable accountable for performance against them. Yet, it does not address the case of a police authority setting objectives with which a chief disagrees. The balance of power clearly remains with the chief, in that he or she only has to 'have regard' for the objectives. The ACC quoted above clearly recognised this point in the discussion about the hypothetical case of a police authority imposing an objective on an unwilling chief constable. Should such a situation occur under the new police authorities, the officer argued that 'the chief can say, "I hear what you are saying, I am statutorily bound to take notice, and I have taken notice, that's it".' Thus, according to this view, the objective could appear in the plan, but no significant resources need be put towards addressing it.

Costed policing plans

Senior officers and civilian staff of the force argued that until the force had developed more sophisticated financial information and activity recording systems, it would be impossible to put together a fully costed policing plan. The costings contained in the plan were thus at a fairly basic level, with no attempt to link finance to the force's aims or cost specific objectives. The revenue budget appeared in the back of the plan, along with a pie chart showing how the total carved up between responsibilities of chief officers. The plan did not contain a functional or activity costing, nor any reference to the development of systems to address this. A senior officer of the force had been investigating developments in other forces, and reported that very few forces had taken real strides towards real activity costing. In his view, the only two forces actually to have made significant progress on costed policing plans were Thames Valley and Cleveland. He reported that Cleveland was approaching a full functional costing system, based on its command and control system, that could accurately measure the activities of all the force's members. He accepted that his force was still a long way behind this stage and that to cost functions accurately, the force would have to develop a significantly upgraded command and control system, a management information system capable of dealing with these data and provide all staff with personal data terminals. This officer was working on a joint report with the police authority treasurer about fully costed policing plans, but did not envisage them being developed in force A for some years yet.

IMPLEMENTATION AT THE LOCAL LEVEL

The development of policing plans into an effective mechanism of external accountability is dependent on two key conditions. First, that the police authority (and other external bodies) are able to exert a significant influence over the plan. Second, that the plan actually effects what happens at the operational level. Much of the above discussion has concerned the degree to which the police authority was able to influence the plan in the first two years of planning. The subsequent sections examine the emerging effects of planning at the local level within the force.

Divisional autonomy and local policing plans

We visited two subdivisions in the force area to examine policy-making at the local level. The picture of a relatively centralised force was confirmed by both subdivisional commanders, who reported a limited amount of subdivisional and policy-making autonomy. There were examples from both subdivisions where local officers' wishes had been circumvented by central pressures in the force. In one subdivision, the shift system was changed after pressure from headquarters, even though the subdivisional command team regarded the existing system as more effective. In the other, an initiative by two constables involving the organisation of five-a-side football matches for local young people was stopped because it was no longer part of force policy to put resources into activities that were not perceived as important 'policing' functions. This caused considerable annoyance on the part of local officers, who had perceived the initiative as a success. Aside from these particular examples, we heard the complaints common to many police forces about too many demands on limited resources, and the lack of understanding at the centre (HQ) level about the realities of policing at the sharp end. Subdivisional commanders also confirmed the limited extent to which the force had adopted local financial management.

Despite these complaints, subdivisional commanders expressed general support for the principle of policing plans, the introduction of objectives and performance measurement. As one subdivisional commander put it:

> There are hundreds of things that a bobby can do when he goes out there, there
> are lots of absolutely whacky laws on the statute book. There are a million and
> one laws he could enforce, in a million and one ways and in a million and one
> places. So it is quite right and proper, given that we are paid by the public, and
> we are public servants, that there is a planning structure which makes us
> prioritise, direct, measure and make us accountable for what we do, and I'm
> glad that structure is there.

They also reported that the subdivisions had been consulted about the contents
of the force plan, and the local (as in force-wide) objectives. Subdivisional
commanders described the in-force consultation process much as it had been
presented by officers from the HQ department with responsibility for planning
(see above), and appeared to be satisfied that they had an opportunity to
influence the force objectives. They had put out a memo to their inspectors
which detailed the suggested force and national objectives, and requested
comments and information about other local problems and concerns. A
number of inspectors reported that these memos had been discussed at shift
briefings by lower ranking officers. Much of what was in the policing plan
was perceived as predetermined by the Home Office and by national issues.
This was not considered to be problematic, for there was a general consensus
about the relevance and importance of the national objectives.

The subdivisional commanders were not required to write plans for the
subdivisional areas, but did contribute to wider divisional 'business plans',
which had been introduced force-wide for the year 1996/7. The business plans
were not public documents, though we were allowed to read them for background information. Business plans were required from all departments and
divisions within the force, and HQ staff described these as the 'working
documents' through which the force policing plan is addressed. Business plans
were to include details of resources, national and force-wide objectives,
divisional objectives, details of various action plans and projects, and timescales for completion. Divisional review boards would meet every three
months to assess the progress towards objectives outlined in the business
plans. The plans were structured according to a planning guide issued by the
HQ Development and Inspectorate Department, and in the first year of
business plans there was little variation between different divisions.

The two divisional plans for the respective subdivisions we visited were
quite similar in length and appearance. Each included some background details
about the division (population profile, main crime problems, divisional structure and staffing), followed by some SWOT (strengths, weaknesses, opportunities, threats) or STEEL (social, technological, economic, environmental,
legislative) analyses. There then followed some details of particular projects,
to be led by named officers and 'project teams'. In both plans, these were
directed at what were termed 'strategic' areas and involved subjects such as
value-for-money improvements, the improvement of administration in the
division and increased quality of judicial services. There was some more detail

about local action plans, for example below each of the objectives listed in the plan there was a series of action points. The appendices to the business plans each included national and local (force-wide) objectives from the policing plan, with sections on 'action and timescales' for each, detailing a number of possible actions in support of the objective. At present, these remain at a rather general level, and there is no attempt to link specific resources to particular objectives. The business plans may also detail 'divisional' objectives additional to those in the annual policing plan. One divisional plan we examined identified two divisional objectives, 'To respond promptly, efficiently and courteously to all calls from the general public' and 'To enhance relations with the community by recognising and where appropriate rewarding good citizenship'. The second divisional plan we looked at did not identify any purely divisional objectives.

Relevance of objectives

In general, the national and force-wide objectives included in the policing plan were seen as relatively uncontroversial. Both subdivisional commanders interviewed accepted they were relevant and useful objectives. One said: 'I've no qualms about them.' However, they also noted that local consultation about the force-wide objectives did not always raise the national and force objectives as the areas of greatest local concern. For example, one subdivisional commander reported that:

> By and large, the majority of problems that people raise are not really mirrored in the objectives of the policing plan. The biggest problems which came out of the last meeting, and probably every one that I've been to, were cars speeding, parking on grass verges, that sort of thing. The things that effect the general quality of life in a particular area, they're the things that people complain most about. Not everyone is affected by burglary, not everyone is affected by drug abuse, not everyone has their car stolen. Whilst those are our main key crimes, burglaries and car thefts, the majority of people aren't really affected by them.

The other subdivisional commander stated that the national and local objectives contained in the plan were largely relevant to the policing of his area. However, the main problem, which restricted the relevance of the objectives, was the sheer number of objectives and PIs coming down from the centre and causing total confusion at the local level. Having defended the principle of planning with reference to the need to prioritise, the officer noted that additional objectives and different levels of plan made it difficult for police officers and the public to prioritise:

> Unfortunately, a process which should make things clearer to people is itself far too complex, and instead of imposing order, prioritisation and direction, it's confusing people. In summary, we've too many plans. We've got national objectives, we've local objectives which should be called force objectives, and we've the opportunity to set local objectives as well. We've a five-year plan,

we've a business plan, we've traffic strategies, we've a hundred and one of these things, and while I can understand that the world is a complex place, if we're trying to simplify it for the public and for the operational officer, we've a long way to go.

In summary, his view was: 'if you've too many priorities, they're not priorities.'

One strong theme coming up from local consultation was concern about youths causing annoyance, and the need for the police to take action to solve this problem. One subdivisional commander highlighted an interesting aspect of this, reporting that a considerable amount of police time was now being taken up, and in his view wasted, by responding to calls from the public about youths causing disturbance. This was because of the emphasis placed on the objective, which arose from local consultation. In his view, pushing police into a 'measurable' enforcement-based activity was an ineffective use of resources. In most cases, the young people accused of 'causing annoyance' were usually committing no criminal offence and were simply 'hanging around' in groups. The commander felt there was too much intolerance of young people by adults, which led to a tendency automatically to perceive young people as a threat. Simply sending a patrol car out to disperse crowds of bored young people did not help. However, an attempt to apply a more problem-solving approach by two officers on the subdivision met with resistance from force HQ. When they tried to extend their five-a-side tournament, they were told that this was not part of force policy. Thus, in his view, the local objective was leading to an inappropriate and ultimately ineffective police response.

A common theme in both subdivisions was that the excessive demands placed on limited police resources severely constrained the amount of pre-planned proactive work the police could undertake. This was seen as an inevitable feature of policing that limited the usefulness of planning. These problems were particularly severe in one of the subdivisions we visited, which was one of the busiest in the force area. At the time of the visit, three murder investigations were under way and all detective staffing was tied up with these, even though, as the subdivisional commander pointed out, this would mean a maximum of three extra detections under violent crime. However, as noted above, there was general support at the subdivisional command level for the principle of planning, objective-setting and performance measurement.

Goal displacement

There was evidence that objective-led policing, particularly the publication of performance indicators, was having some effects on policing. However, discussions with lower-ranking officers suggested that the monthly 'subdivisional performance indicators' (which had been introduced force-wide in 1993) were having more effect than the 'policing plan performance indicators'. This problem was identified quite clearly on by one subdivisional commander who argued that there was a surfeit of plans.

Both subdivisional commanders cautiously attributed some change in practice to published objectives, though emphasised this was difficult to distinguish from general changes brought about by recent developments, such as the Audit Commission's report on crime management, and economy and efficiency developments in general. Neither commander could identify any major changes in resource allocation resulting from the introduction of performance objectives and targets. The differences were perceived to occur at the margins, for example during 'cross-over time' between shifts, when officers were encouraged to be more proactive in pursuing the set objectives. There were also officers whose usual duties did not include response policing, the area constables, who were given proactive roles and tasked with responsibility for particular elements of the objectives. There was no evidence of officers being taken from uniform patrol duties and placed in specialist squads with a view to particular objectives, such as drugs or burglary squads. However, both subdivisions had what were called 'support units' – a squad of officers taken from the uniformed shifts and detailed to carry out proactive operations in connection with drugs. These had been given a wider remit, since the introduction of policing plans, to address the policing plan's other local objectives.

Taking one subdivision, officers of inspector level and above generally took a pragmatic view of the performance objectives and measurement. Both uniform relief and CID inspectors reported that the requirements of demand-led policing restricted opportunities for proactive policing addressing the plan's objectives, but nevertheless argued that, when possible, the objectives were addressed. Again, little concrete evidence was provided for this and it was framed more generally in terms of 'focusing minds' on certain aspects of policing. The main examples given of action in support of objectives were crime pattern analysis, proactive work during the cross-over period of shifts and the expanded roles of the subdivisional support unit. Officers at inspector level again emphasised that, though objectives and PIs were considered important, they were not 'rammed down people's throats', and they were managed flexibly and realistically. One described the discussion of monthly performance information with the shifts as more like a 'chat over a cup of tea' than a 'grilling'. Officers at this level generally felt that the primary shapers of policing were the burgeoning demands on the police service and that there was little evidence of a shift to more enforcement-oriented activity. Again, this discussion focused more on the 'subdivisional PIs', which were broken down by shift, than the policing plan PIs attached to the national and local objectives.

A very similar picture emerged on the second subdivision – general, if sometimes begrudging support for the concept of planning and proactive policing. One senior detective officer on a subdivision was highly dubious about what he saw as the 'wasted' resources that go into largely 'public relations' documents. While he credited the system of objectives and performance measurement with having given police work an increased focus, he felt that the published objectives largely reflected what the police were doing

already. He noted a more general trend towards policing becoming performance oriented, with growing concern about effective use of resources. Senior
officers, he argued, would think twice now before starting a complex fraud
enquiry, which is highly resource intensive. He reported that he was reluctant
to put resources into investigating a spate of indecent exposures in the area
because it would not get him a 'tick' (in terms of national or local objectives).
Two section constables confirmed the view from the other division that,
despite management's protests, they felt they should justify themselves more
in terms of concrete PIs. They said there were over 40 PIs, but identified a few
they saw as crucial. These were all enforcement oriented ones, such as fixed
penalties, breathalyser tests, stops and searches, and numbers of arrests. These,
they said, were perceived as the PIs officers 'could do something about'. They
mentioned an increased awareness of PIs between shifts and, as a result, a
spirit of competitiveness. This was generally regarded as healthy, though they
feared it could be taken too far.

Skewed policing?

Some commentators argued that the introduction of systematic performance
measurement systems would skew policing towards the more easily measured
areas of enforcement. For example, they might encourage police officers to
make arrests rather than defuse situations, issue fixed penalty tickets rather
than give warnings, enforce rather than prevent. It was beyond the scope of the
present study to measure systematically the degree to which significant shifts
of this sort are emerging. However, anecdotal evidence suggested that changes
of this kind were rather limited and certainly not related to the policing plan
objectives. Neither subdivisional commander reported that the plan's objectives had skewed policing towards more measurable areas in any major way.
On the contrary, they both emphasised the eclectic nature of the policing
objectives, which they felt covered many different aspects of police work.
Neither commander perceived any priority within the national objectives, or
even between national and local objectives. One pointed out that the presentation of national and local objectives in the policing plan was a deliberate
reflection of this, with national and local objectives mixed together (though
identified separately) and with bullet points rather than numbers. This was
meant to suggest that all should be given equal priority.

Commanders considered the monthly performance information a useful
management tool. It could give the subdivisional command team a broad
indication of what was going on and of what shifts were productive in what
areas. However, a number of anomalies limited the utility of this information.
First, linked to the point made earlier about there being too many plans, there
was more than one set of performance information. Though monthly information on policing plan indicators was provided for subdivisional commanders,
it was not broken down between shift. More detailed subdivisional PIs had
been produced for several years, which were more use to commanders for

looking at differences in work between shifts and departments. Although there were areas of overlap, the subdivisional indicators covered more detailed things such as traffic processes. These paper-based systems that came down from HQ were considered very time consuming. Neither subdivisional commander claimed that measured performance was pushed to such an extent that officers were encouraged to rush out and issue as many fixed penalties as possible, though junior officers provided a slightly different perspective.

Officers below the level of inspector were, perhaps unsurprisingly, more dubious about the merits of plans, objectives and PIs. All the lower-ranking officers interviewed were aware of the plans and the force objectives, and some remarked that the policing plan objectives were fixed to many walls in police stations. However, some described the plans as 'management documents', and a few were dubious about the amount of resources devoted to producing plans and monitoring PIs. Two section constables said that the introduction of subdivisional performance indicators had 'definitely' affected the way in which they police. These were different from the policing plan indicators, and had been introduced some years previously. They argued that the main effect was to be seen in traffic process work, whereby officers would attempt to demonstrate productivity by issuing more parking tickets or fixed penalties. One constable said that since the introduction of PIs that measured different aspects of the traffic process, 'I have booked someone on many a time when I would have possibly given verbal advice.' Another constable reported that such effects lead to strains in community relations, and said that one evening a shift that had been grilled for being unproductive went out and placed a large number of parking tickets on illegally parked cars in a particular area, which enraged the local community. However, with regard to the policing plan objectives, there was little reported change. Officers reported that they were 'slaves to the radio' and, though they were aware of the objectives, there was little they could do to address them proactively. Some officers reported that PIs had led to shifts he had just given his relief a 'pat on the back' for their improved figures on the monthly PIs.

The area constables (permanent beat officers) denied there had been a major shift in resources. One such officer argued that the continued existence of his post illustrated how far senior officers were resistant to simply figure chasing. He said the role of area constable officers had little direct impact on PIs, yet they were still seen as an important contribution to the policing of the area.

Two points in particular arose from visits to subdivisions. First, despite some officers' insistence that PIs had led them to a more enforcement-oriented style of policing with regard to traffic process, there were also PIs that were not enforcement-oriented (for example, the number of Vehicle Defect Rectification Scheme reports, or number of verbal warnings). Second, it was the old PIs that were the real objects of interest, and not particularly those connected with the policing plan objectives. This could be because they had been around for longer, or, more likely, because they were broken down by shift so could be used for more detailed comparisons of 'performance' within the subdivision.

Changes in recording practices

Another concern raised by opponents of strict performance measurement systems was that police officers will find ingenious ways of 'fiddling the figures' to present the appearance of improved performance. The classic example given in the past is of secondary clear-ups (via such things as TICs), which improve detection rates. There was no evidence of recording practices changing in this way in force A. Indeed, the changes in policy that had occurred actually had the opposite effect. Detectives on one subdivision complained about the force having stopped the policy of making prison visits. Prior to this, each division had CID officers employed full time making visits to convicted prisoners to clear up unsolved crimes. Another justification for such a policy was that some officers saw it as a good source of intelligence. However, in 1996, the force announced it would no longer be undertaking routine prison visits in this way. The overall detection rate for certain offence categories immediately suffered, a fact that did not go unnoticed at the police authority level (though primary detection rates improved). Detectives on subdivision confirmed that their detection figures had immediately looked much worse, and complained that they had lost the good deal of criminal intelligence such visits provided.

One interesting recording matter came to light in relation to the force policy on domestic violence. In line with other police forces nationally, force A attempted to demonstrate that officers were currently taking domestic violence much more seriously. Thus, even though victims were often likely to retract, or refuse to press charges, police officers were encouraged to take full statements that would have led to a charge had the victim cooperated fully. This could count as 'detected, no further action', which was unavailable to officers who simply gave advice and left the scene. Some officers saw this as a way of 'cooking the books' so that CID could get another tick for violence detections.

OTHER ASPECTS OF THE ACT

By the time of the study, all command level officers in the force bar one were on fixed-term contracts (FTCs). A senior police authority officer described the introduction of FTCs as a 'farce' in which the command team officers all were put on contracts that took them beyond their possible retirement dates, and got them extra money for so doing. However, he felt that in the future FTCs might be a lever for increasing police authority influence, because when he was asked about the danger of police authorities exerting too much power over chief officers via FTCs, he replied with the question, 'Do you mean that they would be more accountable?'

Senior officers in the force expressed different views about FTCs. One ACC supported their introduction, arguing that in the past chief constables had been allowed to stay in post for too long. He felt a period of five to ten years should be the tenure for a chief because the position was so vital for the force, and 'even the best has weaknesses'. He referred to the example of the Metropolitan Police whose commissioner usually has a five-year period of office, though the current incumbent has been given a seven-year contract because of his relatively young age. He thought that the disadvantages of permanent tenure far outweighed any advantages and was not helpful either in terms of account-ability or in developing the police service. However, the ACC argued that the current methods of recruitment should be changed, and that police authorities should be actively headhunting for prospective candidates rather than 'doing the circuit' and having interviews by huge panels. He thought that police authorities needed to take the lead on this and not allow HMIC the influence it had in the past. He conceded that there was a danger of unconstitutional pressure being applied to chief officers, but felt the source of this was the lack of clarity in the division of powers and responsibilities within the Act: 'I think that is an unhealthy situation when the same police authority are also having the power to determine the financial rewards and career future of the indi-vidual concerned.' He felt that the root of the problem was the rushed 'fag packet mentality' of the legislation, which had not been properly thought through. Another ACC said he agreed with FTCs, and also thought that chief officers should serve for no more than ten years. He accepted that there was a danger of discouraging younger officers from seeking promotion to ACPO ranks. He accepted the theoretical dangers of unconstitutional pressures being brought to bear on chief officers nearing the end of FTCs, but thought that this would not happen in practice. He felt that, given sufficiently strong characters in the positions of chief officers and given the available recourse to the Home Secretary, such pressures would be ineffective. Another ACC expressed a very different view; he felt FTCs would have a negative effect on the service. He argued that career development for senior officers was restricted as a result and that a large number of potential ACPO rank candidates would be dis-couraged from applying for the senior command course: 'People who cannot get FTCs to take them beyond 25 years service have everything to lose by going for them.' However, granting FTCs that take an officer beyond 25 years' service gives no advantage to the police authority, so there is little point in having them at all.

CONCLUSIONS

A number of broad conclusions can be drawn from this case study. First, it is clear that although no major conflicts have arisen in the first two years after the Act, significantly different views are held about the effects and future implications of the reforms. One body of opinion sees the police authority as having clearly lost influence. It has lost its role in the detailed financial management of the force and plays a rather passive role in the process of planning and objective-setting. However, the police authority did have an opportunity to make amendments and put forward suggestions. This places it in our 're-drafter' category developed in Chapter 4. Even if it could exert a substantial influence over the plan, it is argued, the chief constable need in any case only 'have regard' to it. Some leading police authority members and officers thought that it should still have a role in some of the more detailed management aspects concerning personnel and finance. They argued that the dilution of party politics meant that the police authority did not discuss many important matters. On the other hand, non-Labour authority members and senior officers of the force welcomed depoliticisation, and subscribed, in their rhetoric at least, to the technical, performance-oriented model of a police authority.

Second, there seems to be general agreement that the new arrangements contained significant areas of overlap and confusion of roles. There appeared to be three main problematic areas, the first concerning consultation. Both the police authority and the force retained a role in this, and both appeared to want to take the lead. The second area of overlap was the production of the annual policing plan. It is clear that, although the official approach is a joint one, during the first two years of planning the police force dominated the process. There was no sign of dissent or conflict over the plan, although some senior officers thought that this might happen in the future. The final area of confusion was related to the delegation of much financial and personnel management to the force. The police authority treasurer's department, and the force finance department, each have responsibilities in this area and their roles are not clearly demarcated. Senior members of the force were irritated that the police authority continued to see a role for itself in financial management and asked detailed questions about finance at authority meetings, which the force felt was no longer part of its remit. The police authority certainly had the capacity to play a leading role in consultation with the public. It had a much larger support staff than any other police authority in England and Wales, and substantial resources were put to organising and servicing consultation mechanisms, and reporting their outcomes. In addition, the police authority invested resources in producing its own 'strategic plan' (distinct from the local policing plan).

Third, the case study illustrated how the introduction of policing plans with national and local objectives and PIs has expanded even further the already large body of performance information that is now produced about police forces. The research suggested that a rationalisation of performance information is required, with a range of suites of PIs with different bases being monitored and produced for different audiences and different reasons actually confusing rather than clarifying performance, and thus making it difficult to focus policing activity. This illustrates a key problem with the performance-oriented managerialist model of policing, which requires police forces to define their 'core business' areas, set clear goals and measure performance. There is a valuable emphasis in this approach upon finding out what citizens want from policing and effectively delivering it. However, as critics have repeatedly pointed out, it comes up against the accusation of overly simplifying policing. Thus, greater numbers of objectives and PIs are added to take into account the complex, multi-faceted nature of policing. The approach of force A places greater weight on the complexity argument than that of some other forces (such as force B, as will be shown in the next chapter). Thus, they included a much larger range of objectives and a vast suite of over 200 performance indicators. But although this arguably takes more account of the multiple goals of policing and the complexities of the concept of 'performance', it ultimately constrains effective prioritisation at subdivisional level, which is one of the main purposes of planning.

Finally, the case study gave rise to a number of interesting issues concerning the relationship of consultation and local policing objectives. There were a number of examples of either local consultation or police authority members sending a clear message to the police force to attend to a particular policing problem. In each of these cases though, it could be argued that had the force provided the 'response' being suggested to it, the resulting approach would have been illiberal and short sighted. One example concerned the issue of 'youths causing annoyance', which was a common complaint from PCCGs and other consultative fora. Whereas the PCCG members wanted the police to 'do something' about the problem, with the emphasis on an enforcement-oriented approach, at least one subdivisional commander disapproved of adult 'intolerance' of young people and supported the adoption of a preventive problem-solving approach. Another example concerned the issue of travellers, when democratically-elected local representatives criticised the chief constable for not dealing with travellers more effectively. The chief constable consistently refused to bow to demands to target travellers, arguing that this was not a matter for the police or the criminal law, but rather was a civil matter for local authorities. This brings into sharp focus the change in political circumstances that has occurred since the major debates over police accountability in the mid-1980s, not least in this force. Furthermore, force A is now recognised as a leading force in improving communication between the police and the gay community. However effective or otherwise this policy has been in practice, it provides an important illustration of how the notion of conservative-minded chief constables resisting the liberalising pressures of their police authorities became increasingly redundant during the 1990s.

Chapter 6

Case Study B: The Shire Force

THE POLICE AUTHORITY AND FORCE

Force B is a shire police force, which in 1996/7 employed 3336 staff including 2322 police officers. The total force budget for the financial year ending April 1997 was £115 million. At the time of the study, the force was divided into nine territorial divisions, which form the basic management units for the force. The previous subdivisional structure was removed by a force reorganisation in the early 1990s. The development of local financial management (LFM) in the force has been rather limited to date. Senior officers and civilian staff in the force management team held the view that the force's corporate control needs precluded extensive devolution of budgets, at least until more sophisticated financial monitoring and control systems were developed. Another important background factor was that the force had a relatively new command team. The chief constable and three ACCs were all relatively new appointments, although the chief and one ACC was promoted from within the force. They all took up post during or after the introduction of the Police and Magistrates' Courts Act.

Before the Act, force B was administered by a shire police authority which operated as a county council committee. The move to independence from the county council and the establishment of a freestanding police authority therefore constituted a greater change than for the authorities in the other two case study areas (which already had police authorities that were more independent of the local government structure). This force area was one of the case studies in our previous work on police governance (Jones et al., 1994). Prior to 1995, the police authority had 27 members, of whom 18 were elected councillors and the remaining nine were magistrates. The former police authority had a Labour majority, with ten of the seats held by Labour councillors, seven by Conservatives and one by the Liberal Democrats. Despite this Labour domination, leading members and officers of the old police authority had been keen to emphasise that the police authority was not characterised by party-political infighting, and promoted an image of bipartisan consensus. The same Labour councillor was chairman of both the pre- and post-1995 police authorities.[1]

---

1. Since the fieldwork was completed the police authority has elected a magistrate member to the chair.

When the PMCA became operational, the police authority did not apply to the Home Office for an increase in its post-1995 membership, for it was generally felt that such an application would be refused. The new 17-member police authority consisted of nine councillors (six Labour, two Conservative and one Liberal Democrat), five independent members and three magistrates. The county council continued to organise support arrangements for the new police authority. For example, the county council clerk and treasurer continued to act as the new police authority's clerk and treasurer respectively. The police authority employed a small number of staff, based at County Hall, to service the authority. These included the assistant clerk, a policy and research officer and some secretarial support. The assistant clerk, together with the policy and research officer played a leading role in servicing the network of police community liaison bodies the police authority had organised in the county.

THE CHANGING ROLE OF THE POLICE AUTHORITY

In general, there was greater consensus in the force B area about the overall effects of the changes than there had been in force A. There was widespread agreement that many of the changes the PMCA introduced had had a positive effect on the police authority, though there were some important exceptions to this view. A number of respondents compared the post-1995 police authority very favourably with its predecessor. A member who had served on the old police authority said that the new police authority asked much more challenging questions of the chief constable, and also received more information from the force. An independent member who had previously served as a county council officer reported that the old police authority's influence was mainly restricted to deciding how much money went into the overall police budget. The chief constable was reluctant to be critical of the old police authority, but compared the new one favourably with its predecessor. According to the chief constable, the new police authority was 'more proactive and more questioning'. 'I do think it's a better police authority than it was previously, even though it was not bad. It [the new police authority] has adopted a far more meaningful role.' Another senior officer was extremely positive about the changes, describing the police authority reforms in the following terms:

> I think it's actually been a huge bonus. . . . I didn't like the way the system worked before which I felt was just a rubber-stamping thing. The police authority tended to be almost deferential to the authority of the chief constable, wasn't questioning when I thought it should be questioning, and was in totally inappropriate cases. . . . It's a lot more questioning and a lot more influential than it ever was before.

The director of finance felt that the questioning of officers by members on financial issues was now far more rigorous, saying: 'You have to be totally on your toes now, they don't miss a trick, and that really is no bad thing at all.' However, she still felt that there was a huge variation in the overall level and quality of the debate, ranging from extremely rigorous and stimulating discussions on some papers, to pointing out spelling mistakes on others.

This view of a largely improved police authority was supported, though perhaps less enthusiastically, by discussions with members and officers of the old authority. The clerk, for example, stated that the new authority was 'talking about policing much more ... it is a different animal. Partly forced by the legislation they produce a policing plan and really get into it'. Not surprisingly, the chairman was loath to criticise the old police authority (which he had also chaired), but accepted that elements of the reforms had a positive effect, particularly the requirement to produce a policing plan (about which he was very enthusiastic). However, another police authority officer thought that the new police authority was 'no better and no worse' than the old one. It was felt that the level of authority input into policing policy remained fairly limited and would inevitably remain the preserve of senior police managers.

Size and structure

The new 17-member authority consisted of nine councillors, five independents and three magistrates. Its previous Labour dominance was reduced to two-thirds of the elected members (along with two Conservative and one Liberal Democrat). The police authority had a number of committees, the most important of which were the standing finance and audit committee and the quality of service committee. In addition, there was an appeals committee (deciding on appeals from police support staff), a staff liaison committee (for consultation between police authority members and the staff associations), and a local joint (APT & C) staff committee (to discuss civilian staffing matters). In addition, the 14 police liaison advisory committees (PLACs), which were the Section 106 committees for local consultation in the county, were each chaired by a police authority member.

One immediate change under the new structure was that meetings of the new police authority now took place in different parts of the county (the pre-1995 police authority had always met in County Hall, the county council headquarters). The full police authority generally met once a month, with some extra meetings to discuss the draft policing plan and the main budget. The clerk reported that full authority meetings under the new arrangements tend to last about three hours (although the meeting attended by a researcher lasted considerably longer than this).

The reduction in size of the police authority was less keenly felt than it had been in force A, perhaps because the magnitude of the change was less – from 27 to 17 members. Few people connected with the police authority complained about the reduction in size, apart from the chairman who felt that, along with the introduction of independent members (see below), it had caused a 'democratic deficit'. Other police authority members referred to the smaller size of the police authority positively, suggesting that a 17-member committee was more businesslike, and could deal better with matters of detail. In addition, it encouraged active involvement from members and most felt able to contribute to debates, which they had not always done before. One member said that the smaller size of the meeting was 'more conducive to discussion' and that the level of debate had improved significantly. This was particularly felt to apply to the magistrate members, whose involvement had been limited on the pre-1995 police authority; the three who remained had become actively involved in the business of the new police authority. This was related not only to the size of the police authority, but also to the lessening influence of party politics.

Depoliticisation

The change in the structure of the police authority considerably reduced the influence of party politics. A number of police authority members, as well as police authority officers, identified this as the biggest single change since 1995. Prior to meetings of the old police authority, there had been political caucus meetings and the police authority line was effectively decided in the majority party caucus. The full police authority meeting thus took on a rather symbolic role, although other members had the opportunity to discuss and comment on matters. These formal pre-meeting meetings had stopped with the introduction of the new police authority. Although a number of members referred to the diluted effect of party politics, it was interesting to note that certain aspects of party politics remained in the background. In particular, there was some evidence of political tension within the ruling Labour group, partly caused by members also belonging to the ruling group on the (now separate) county council (which is considered in more detail below). One Labour member felt that other Labour members found it difficult to criticise aspects of policy the chairman supported because they were reluctant to 'break ranks'. The clerk said that many Labour members had found it difficult to adapt to the new police authority when they had to win support for their proposals via argument and persuasion, rather than relying on their majority to get things through the full police authority. One independent member remarked on how rare it was for the police authority to go to a vote and that most things went through in consensus. However, senior police officers reported that under the pre-1995 arrangements, issues almost never went to a vote. Thus, although still rather infrequent, votes were actually more common on the new police authority. Another authority member reported that at first the members of different political parties, independents and magistrates had sat in different blocks at police authority meetings, now everybody 'mixed and matched'. Senior police officers also noted that party politics had been largely removed from police authority discussions. One police authority member described what he saw as the benefits of the 'dilution' of party politics on the police authority, but added that there had been losses as well, in that the wider political debates about policing were no longer considered:

In the new environment it is more difficult to actually engage in the political debate about policing. ... But the Home Secretary has made numerous proposals which impact upon police authorities directly, not to mention those coming from the Labour Party, but these don't get a mention at the police authority. I think it's not because ... we don't in conversation say what we think of some of these proposals, but we don't have formal debates about these areas of policing. It is partly because we get drawn into talking about the nuts and bolts, and partly because only half of us are interested openly in the political side ... I am not entirely persuaded that it's a good thing to depoliticise a police authority to that sort of extent.

An interesting addition to the discussion about 'politics' arose from a conversation with an independent member who repeatedly referred to himself as 'non-political' and having 'no political axe to grind'. In interview, however, he spontaneously made several statements that could easily be construed as 'political', supporting the then Home Secretary's proposals for 'boot-camps' for young offenders and generally arguing for a more punitive approach to criminal justice. For this member, the mere fact that he was not an elected councillor meant that he was not 'political'.

Powers and responsibilities

One independent member cogently summed up what he saw as the new police authority's three main responsibilities: to appoint command team officers, to consult over and publish an annual policing plan, and to hold the chief constable accountable for the performance of the force against this plan. From discussions with the force finance director, it was clear that some of the tensions and grey areas that were problematic in force A were also becoming visible in this force area.

The main changes introduced by the Act devolved much of the responsibility for managing staff and financial matters away from the county council and to the police force. This had meant a radical expansion of the roles and responsibilities of the force finance department. There was clearly a view that the police authority was still searching for a role for itself. A number of members reported that the focus of the police authority's interest was now on performance monitoring. Much of the police authority discussion concerned objectives, indicators and targets for different aspects of policing, and no longer examined the wider context of policing (as noted above).

Relationship of the police authority with the county council

Another important aspect of the reforms concerned the police authority's move to independence from the county council. This meant that whereas the local element of police funding in the past had been related to the standard spending assessment (SSA) for the county council, now the police authority was financially independent. Although relationships between the county council and police force had always been good, for a number of years the force had not received full funding of the SSA policing element, since policing had to compete with other services such as education for a share of local expenditure. When the Act became operational and police authorities became independent precepting bodies outside the local government structure, the amount of money available for policing in the county was no longer related first to the SSA and then to the political process to decide between competing demands, but was the outcome of a new complex formula. While some (mainly metropolitan) police forces were net losers under the new formula, force B was a net gainer; the financial settlement represented a generous expansion in expenditure. In the first year of operation of the new police authorities, the force received £2.6 million in extra funding. Police authority officers and senior staff in the force believed that this considerably smoothed the process of reform.

The move to independence caused some difficulties in relations between the police authority and the county council. In particular, the force developed its own finance and accounting systems because it was felt that the county council's accounting charges were too high. The consequent staff losses at the county council caused some conflict of interest for the clerk and treasurer to the police authority (who were of course also clerk and treasurer respectively to the county council), as well as for some police authority members who were county councillors. The police authority was very supportive of the force's move to independence from the county council's services, although apparently this led to particular difficulties for Labour police authority members who had to go against the wishes of their ruling group on the county council. At the time of the study, the force was still purchasing some architectural and other financial services from the county council. With a renewed emphasis on value for money within the force's approach to support services, the force's finance department no longer assumed that the county council would provide support services in-house, but considered a range of other options. An important example of this concerned the project design and contract letting services of major police building schemes. Under the previous arrangements, these had been provided by the county council. After the reforms, the Home Office gave approval for the replacement of a divisional headquarters building. The police authority agreed that the provision of architectural design and project work should be put out to competitive tender. The contract was won by the architectural department of a neighbouring county council, with significant savings to the police budget.

The telephone survey of police authorities described in Chapter 4 showed that a minority of shire police authorities have distanced themselves from their respective county councils to such an extent that they no longer use any support services from the council and operate from offices away from council buildings, some in police headquarters and some in other accommodation. This option was fleetingly considered in force B, but most police authority members accepted that at least for the initial years of the new police authority they should remain based at County Hall. It was more convenient for the councillor members of the police authority who had offices there. In addition, the two principal officers to the police authority were also based at County Hall. The county council also provided some other hidden support such as faxing and photocopying services. However, the chief constable clearly saw the county council in different terms under the new arrangements, and said it was simply another customer along with the district councils and other local bodies. The effects of the local government review was later to complicate matters further, when the main city council in the force area became a unitary authority entitled to two seats on the police authority.

While police authorities around the country have to different extents been distancing themselves from the local councils of which they were once a part, in this county it appears that the initiative for some of this distancing came from the county council's ruling group. Though the police authority chairman stressed the importance of continuing to base the police authority in County Hall and of keeping close contact with local government, other Labour members on the county council seem to have been distancing themselves from the new police authority. We heard that the chairman's office had been moved from the corridor containing the offices of the chairmen of other county council committees and a few Labour county councillors who were not members of the police authority had joked about the new 'quango'. A senior local authority officer contended that Conservative members were keen to distance the police authority from the county council, but we had no direct evidence to support this.

One Labour member who had served on the former police authority, described it as having been 'semi-detached' from the county council even before 1985. Since the PMCA, it had become even more detached and he felt that this might encourage local authorities to set up their own crime reduction groups, or police monitoring units, in order to have some influence over policing and crime prevention in their local areas.

The relationship between the police authority and the chief constable
It was widely agreed that relations between police authority and police force had been good under the old police authority, and this continued after the new one came into operation. Police authority members and officers all described relations as healthy, and remarked on the chief constable's open and inclusive style. The chairman partly ascribed the good relations to the force performing so well against national objectives and partly to the appearance of a totally new command team as the changes were coming into operation.

A senior police authority officer reported some minor tensions and problems in the relationship with the force, which he described as 'little pricklers'. These included different views about support to the police authority, which wanted to appoint a research and policy officer to service members' inform-ation needs. The chief constable apparently felt that such an appointment was unnecessary, arguing that the force research department could provide the police authority with whatever information it required. However, most members of the police authority wanted to appoint their own research officer in order to gain more independence from the force. The chief constable expressed disappointment at the police authority's insistence that the sponsorship policy be overseen by a working party of members. However, these were relatively minor disagreements and the chief constable decided not to make a stand against the police authority about them. He said in interview that the minor tensions or difficulties that had arisen had resulted more from members' over-enthusiasm than from any significant political hostility.

There was a difference between the force and the police authority over the level of balances. The force finance director wanted to keep balances at a certain level because since the police authority had become a stand-alone body it could no longer rely on the county council to bail it out in the event of an overspend. In her view, a healthy level of balances needed to be kept in case of overspend, or unforeseeable expenditure commitments. Some police authority members clearly thought the level of balances the force proposed was too high and argued that more money should be spent on operational policing. There was, however, agreement at the end of the day, and no acrimony existed on this point.

THE CONTRIBUTION OF INDEPENDENT MEMBERS

In addition to Home Office advertisements for independent members in the national press, the local selection board advertised the posts in the local press. This resulted in about 120 applications for the posts. The shortlisted candidates were informally interviewed in a process the clerk described as a 'bit of a beauty competition'. The backgrounds of the five independents chosen were quite varied. Two members had commercial business experience – a board director of a major pharmaceutical company and a board director of an airline company. A third independent member had been a senior local government officer (with the county council), another was a teacher, and the fifth worked for the Benefits Agency. Two of the independents were retired, and two were women. There were no ethnic minority people, though the clerk reported that the old police authority had been keen to encourage applications from minority ethnic communities. There were different views about 'political' interference in the selection process. The clerk clearly thought that the Home Office had interfered, saying 'there's no doubt that Howard asked the local constituency parties to put people forward and to comment, say if we sent 20 names Howard would ask the local Conservative constituency parties to give them ranking, and stuff like that.' Another police authority officer was of a different view and argued that the room for central political interference was limited, given the degree of local involvement in the selection process. He thought political interference was more likely to come from local politicians and argued that Labour members were keen to appoint at least two members whose backgrounds suggested that they might have more left-leaning views.

Although Labour members in particular still opposed the principle of appointing non-elected people to police authorities, it does not appear to have caused major tensions during the first years of the new police authority. The chairman reported that although he felt the introduction of independents had been unnecessary, it had provided an opportunity to involve people from a wider range of backgrounds in police authority business. It seems that things settled down quickly on the new police authority and that relations between members of different types were good. One councillor who had been a member of the old police authority said that the effect of independents was 'better than feared'. In his view, they were all committed and helpful, and included some 'very able people'. There was no evidence of the independents, or other kinds of member, acting as a group, though most councillors had opposed their appointment as a matter of principle. For example, this councillor said that 'like any other politician I quarrelled about the fact of lay members and their method of selection, and the potential for interference by the Home Secretary, but it has to be said in practice that it works.' A Labour member reported that any initial tensions quickly dispersed as the independent members began to make useful contributions. The commercial experience of some independent members was viewed as particularly beneficial. The chief constable referred to the 'business acumen' of some of the independent members and reported that they were prepared to ask very challenging questions of the force command team. Another senior officer saw the introduction of independent members as a crucial factor behind the improved input of the new police authority: 'The independent members I think have been a huge refreshing change because they challenge the received wisdom that "we've always done it that way". . . . They have been more questioning, they have started to say, well why don't we do this and why don't we do that, and challenge some of the assumptions that were made by previous members.'

Another ACC described the introduction of independents as 'a breath of fresh air', and also referred to their 'business skills'. Senior police staff felt that the independent members were perhaps less deferential than the members of old police authorities and that they were a key influence behind the authority becoming more active and more questioning. One ACC reported that the independent members had asked 'some very pertinent, searching, high-level, strategic questions in contrast to the traditional police authorities where people were very often given a question to ask and then went through a ritual of asking the question, but very often hadn't got a clue whether the answer was accurate, inaccurate, a good answer or a bad answer'. He clearly wanted the commercial influence of the independent members to be brought increasingly to bear on the police authority, which he thought still occasionally descended into party-political bickering.

Three of the five independent members were interviewed. These were probably the most active and interested members because of the self-selection for interview.[2] All three had seen national advertisements for the posts and some years previously one had been added to a Cabinet Office list of suitable people for service on quangos and other bodies. When the PCMA came into force, the Cabinet Office contacted him and sent him application forms for the police authority post. All three people interviewed were confident senior people and keen to make a contribution. One of the businessmen framed his interest in terms of improving police performance; he felt that the detection rates were not high enough, and saw it as part of the police authority's role to ensure that performance on such matters improved significantly. He added: 'I don't think it will be considered that we are providing an effective and efficient service until detection rates are substantially higher than they are now.'

LOCAL CONSULTATION

In the early 1980s, as a response to the Scarman Report, the police authority developed a network of police liaison advisory committees (PLACs). At the time of the research, there were 14, each chaired by a member of the police authority. Local councillors, magistrates and independent members were all involved in chairing PLACs. For a number of years, the police authority had funded a full-time secretary to administer the PLACs. After the 1995 Act, this person became a full-time committee clerk employed by the police authority, though he retained responsibility for servicing the PLACs. This officer saw their primary role as to inform the public about the nature of policing and resources. In his view, the main source of criticism of the police was the public's ignorance of policing problems and resources available. When the police authority first introduced the network of consultative committees it drew up a constitution and terms of reference for the committees. The constitution laid down that the committees were to be advisory, were to be organised on a subdivisional basis, were to be chaired by a member of the police authority and were to meet quarterly. The constitution lays down that the chairpersons can admit the public to meetings 'after appropriate consultations'. There was a maximum membership of 15 people, including a 'core' membership comprising the chairperson, one district councillor per district in the subdivision, one representative of parish councils, and one representative from the local trades council. The police representative was to be a local divisional commander. Each committee was to co-opt other members as appropriate and, in cases where representatives from the African-Caribbean or Asian communities were desired, they were to be nominated by the 'Afro-Caribbean and Asian Forum', a local organisation. Membership was to be reviewed annually by the core membership.

PLACs met quarterly, usually alternating between closed committee meet-

---

2. The chairman asked police authority members to volunteer themselves for interview rather than allow PSI to approach them individually.

ings and public meetings held in different areas of the police division. In 1995/6 the average attendance at open PLAC meetings was 54. Analyses of the subjects raised at these meetings have been carried out since PLACs were established in 1983. Since that time, the five most frequently raised topics have been traffic problems; community policing and requests for more police officers; vandalism and criminal damage; young people and the police, and public disorder and nuisance. These are fairly typical of the reports of consultative committees in many police force areas (see, for example, Stratta, 1990). Both divisional commanders interviewed said that discussions at their PLACs were dominated by 'quality of life' issues such as vandalism, noisy neighbours and youths causing annoyance. This was considered particularly relevant given that the PLACs were the main vehicle of consultation over the policing plan, which focused more on strategic issues. The police authority devoted substantial resources to servicing the PLAC network. All local residents were invited to the open meetings, which was likely to be costly in terms of postage and copying. The assistant clerk clearly felt that the PLACs played an important part in the police authority's role in consulting with the public, though he expressed frustration at what he saw as the general public's ignorance about policing. Another police authority officer felt that PLACs were rather unrepresentative, with insufficient numbers of young people, women and ethnic minorities. There had been some important developments at the local level since the Act. One independent member who chaired his local PLAC reported that he was dissatisfied with the attendance records of some of the core membership, and would write to these organisations asking them to ensure that a representative attended PLAC meetings. On another division, there was a restructuring of the PLAC on the initiative of the PLAC chairman (another independent member of the police authority) and the divisional commander. The aim was to make the PLAC more dynamic and to target influential people in key organisations in the community.

Public satisfaction surveys

For some years, the force has run a programme of public satisfaction surveys, aimed initially at targeting the satisfaction levels identified by the ACPO and Audit Commission PIs, but then adapted to include the service standards set in the annual policing plan. The force employed a civilian market research officer and two part-time research assistants to undertake the market research, for which the annual budget (not including in-house staff costs) came to £14,000. Over a three-year period, the aim was to cover all 420,000 households in the county in the public satisfaction surveys. The response rate to the main survey was 20 per cent. A 'quality network group', consisting of staff from the performance and planning department and divisional 'quality inspectors' (one appointed for each division), met monthly to discuss quality management. The department conducted internal surveys of force staff and external surveys of the public. Market researchers interviewed people leaving selected police stations about the quality of service they received for one of the PIs. They also undertook specific surveys, for example of racial incident victims, and an internal 'cultural audit' (which interviewed staff about their attitudes to the police organisation and management). The external quality assurance programme for 1996/7 included a number of surveys on specific aspects of policing – immediate response, burglary, assault, road traffic accidents and station front-counter services. There was also the ongoing police/ community relations survey based on a postal questionnaire distributed, with a reply-paid envelope, along with PLAC invitations to local residents (covering all households). The results, which were broken down by division, included a number of findings about how well the public think the police are performing, levels and types of contact with the police, perceptions of and satisfaction with levels of patrol, and views on what police priorities should be. A summary of the police/community relations survey findings was provided in the preread documents for the force planning seminar (see below).

Different views on consultation

The members and officers of the police authority were clearly enthusiastic about the concept of consultation and saw themselves as a leading police authority in this regard. They were certainly one of the few police authorities to take a systematic view of consultation, actually undertaking analysis of the frequency of issues raised and putting significant time and effort into servicing the PLACs. On the police side, however, there was some concern about what was actually coming out of the consultative process. It seemed as though a key role of consultation was symbolic, with the need to be *seen* to be consulting as important (if not more so) than the actual outputs of the consultation itself. This made it a rather expensive use of resources for little tangible return. Some senior police officers clearly felt that the kinds of topics raised at PLAC meetings were rather peripheral to the real business of policing, though one of the divisional commanders we interviewed was an important exception to this rule in that he felt the policing plan paid insufficient attention to these lower level concerns (see later).

THE ANNUAL POLICING PLAN

The 1996/7 policing plan

The 1996/7 policing plan differed in important ways from that of the previous year, particularly in having fewer specified objectives and performance indicators. Like policing plans in most other force areas, it was produced in A4 format and, at 38 pages, was longer than average. It included background details about the county, mentioning a number of developments with implications for policing. These were summarised under broad headings, such as 'political or legal', 'economic', 'social and cultural', and 'technological developments'. The section included a 'demand gap' graph, which showed trends in reported crime set against numbers of police officers in the county. The graph, which depicted spiralling crime rates against very limited growth in police resources, was a precursor to the focus upon crime that underpinned the entire plan. The presentation of the plan, with the police authority crest and name on the front cover and a joint foreword by the chief constable and the authority chairman, suggested joint ownership between the constabulary and the police authority. This foreword placed 'tackling crime' at the centre of the coming year's priorities. A section outlined the police authority's roles and responsibilities, followed by a list of police authority members. A small section outlined the structure of consultation, explaining that there were 14 PLACs and also giving broad details of the constabulary's market research programme. As discussed below, the plan was framed around the key national objectives, but including a single 'local' objective, which was identified as the Department of Transport's national objective to reduce road traffic accident casualties. However, senior officers of the force stressed that local problems raised through the consultation process would be addressed by departmental and divisional plans. In common with most other policing plans, the force B one contained only limited financial information in the form of a breakdown of the projected budget, and broad details of sources of funding. The capital programme was also described in broad terms. The financial information was not explicitly linked to any objectives and there was certainly no attempt to cost specific ones. The plan also included broad details of proposed developments in personnel and training, in value-for-money approaches and in performance review. A summary booklet accompanied the main policing plan.

Objectives and performance indicators

The 1996/7 policing plan was much more focused around key national objectives than the previous year's plan had been. It was among the most focused of all plans in England and Wales. The national objectives were quoted as given in the Home Secretary's letter and all came with nationally-set KPIs. The single local objective related to road traffic casualties: 'In collaboration with other agencies, to reduce the number of road traffic accident casualties by one-third of the 1981–85 average by the year 2000'. The plan explicitly identified this as another national objective. Specific targets were set for all KPIs, each in the context of last year's performance. Policing plan objectives were framed within three broad 'service areas', each including a range of 'service standards' framed in terms of public/victim satisfaction. There was a brief discussion of methods and tactics to be used to address these objectives.

Discussions with the force command team confirmed that they had wanted the policing plan to be highly focused around the 'core business' areas of policing. The KOs appeared to be the driving force behind the plan, for they were the only objectives quoted. A statement in the plan that the overall aim for the force and authority in the coming year was 'working together to make —shire safer' confirmed the impression of a strong crime orientation. Within it, the main priority was to 'tackle crime in all its forms more effectively'.

Senior officers argued that the emphasis on crime 'in all its forms' was a deliberate attempt to avoid an over-concentration on Home Office classifications of crime, at the expense of 'quality of life' issues. The aim was to encourage divisional commanders to address problems such as anti-social behaviour in their local (divisional) objectives. One ACC stated explicitly that the plan was built around the Home Secretary's national objectives. The response in force B was to develop a focus on three core business areas: crime, 24-hour response and traffic, within which the force objectives were framed. This officer argued that 'one of the weaknesses in policing has been trying to do everything for everybody, and we're now beginning to become focused in the same way as a commercial organisation has got to remain focused.' He said that the KOs were 'emphatically' making the force do things it otherwise would not have been doing. The explicit focus on crime was apparent in the following quotation from the same ACC: 'Crime is the major issue, therefore of the core businesses crime takes precedence. And then within that, violence is the thing that people are most concerned about, then comes burglary, now we will go away and concentrate resources into those areas.' He later qualified this, stressing that other areas of policing remained important too: 'I'm not saying that policing is about crime, I'm actually saying that we now have greater clarity about trying to maintain the balance between the three elements.' However, he felt that crime was the priority within the three elements. This provided an interesting contrast with the views of divisional commanders, as we discuss later.

The planning process

Within the police force, the Policy and Planning Department at force headquarters had primary responsibility for producing the draft annual policing plan. The department had put together a strategic five-year plan for the force in 1993, and this process was influential in what was to follow. Prior to 1993, planning processes within the force were very much driven by the budgetary cycle. The annual process consisted of a system of bidding for a share of the total budget. The command team and other senior staff then considered these bids before the total was divided up. The 1993 strategic plan was intended to introduce a sense of corporate vision and strategy to what was perceived as a rather disjointed and *ad hoc* process. However, in the views of staff in the Policy and Planning Department, this failed because the linkage between the budgetary cycle and planning was so highly ingrained that few people thought further than 18 months ahead. This resulted in what was supposed to be a strategic plan looking rather like a 'huge wish list'.

When the PMCA became operational, it led to changes in the planning process by introducing an annual policing plan the chief constable drafted, but which the police authority published and owned. Planning department staff felt this helped reinforce the view of an annual planning process being distinct from bidding for a share of the budget and based it around the need to consult widely about organisational objectives. A senior civilian member of staff was given the full-time job of managing the planning process, but other members of staff were to be involved as and when required. The first plan following the Act, that for 1995/6, was developed very rapidly because the reforms had only just been implemented. The following year provided more opportunities to develop the planning process, and the Policy and Planning Department produced a timetable that outlined the stages up to the publication of the final document. The overall aim was to give all involved parties a stake in the plan, including the public, police authority members and police force staff.

Consultation for the 1996/7 plan began in June 1995 and involved a preliminary collation of information from PLACs and internal consultation to assess the main themes facing the force and the public. This provided the basis for the development of a 'pre-read' document, which outlined some broad areas for discussion by a 'force planning seminar'. This was a two-day seminar in September involving senior staff from the force and also five police authority members, who discussed the main priorities for the coming year. In 1995, the seminar included all divisional commanders and departmental heads, representatives of the staff associations and trade unions, along with five members of the police authority quality of service committee. The full police authority had arranged a special meeting the week before the seminar at which members (to whom the 'pre-read' planning document had been circulated) discussed priorities for the year and briefed the five police authority representatives who were to attend the seminar. Following the seminar, the Planning and Policy Department produced a draft plan in late October, which tried to incorporate the key issues and priorities raised at the seminar, as well as focusing the plan on the key national objectives. In 1996/7, for the first time divisions and departments had to produce their own local plans in support of the force-wide plan. These required local divisions and departments to demonstrate how they would help achieve force-wide objectives. They also provided an opportunity to identify local divisional or departmental objectives.

The first draft of the plan produced in October was discussed by the command team, and then by a meeting of divisional and departmental heads. Between October and December the draft was discussed and modified within the force. In January, it was forwarded to the police authority quality of service committee, which discussed it and suggested some modifications. After these had been introduced, the latest draft was sent to various organisations for comment (see below), which led to some further suggestions and changes. By the time the plan was approaching its final version, there had been ten or 11 drafts. The quality of service committee held at least two meetings to discuss the drafts, and during this time modified drafts were being passed back and forth to the command team for discussion. Amendments were agreed between the police authority and chief constable. Although the force clearly took the lead in the planning process, staff in the Policy and Planning Department still argued that the police authority owned the plan. In their view, while the amendments the police authority suggested were not substantial, this reflected the early involvement of police authority members in the force planning seminar at the start of the process, before any actual drafts appeared. The fact that differences could be resolved at this early stage, along with the fact that police authority committees discussed and agreed all drafts and amendments, was sufficient to establish ownership. Police staff involved with planning said they saw the police authority as a kind of 'editorial board', and felt that members had significant opportunities to influence the plan's substantive content and presentation. The final draft was discussed at a full police authority meeting in early April 1996. Even at this late stage, further minor amendments were suggested and implemented (mostly minor grammatical and presentation features) before the final version was agreed.

Staff in the Policy and Planning Department decided that the plan should be presented in various formats for different audiences. The full version of the annual plan was mainly meant for the Home Office and for statutory and voluntary bodies, rather than for members of the general public. About 1200 copies of the full version were produced, plus 3000 summary booklets and 750,000 leaflets summarising the force objectives, which were sent out with council tax bills. The force also produced a pocket sized card for all members of staff, summarising the objectives, service standards, PIs and targets, and containing details of current performance. Posters listing the objectives and targets were produced for police station noticeboards.

At the time of the study, the annual planning process remained independent of the budgetary cycle. The force was attempting to integrate the two processes. There was still concern that the annual policing plan process, articulated around internal and external consultation and with little systematic linkage to the budgetary cycle, would end as an uncosted wish list. The director of finance would than have to translate this into a meaningful budget, after the budget settlement had been announced in January. At the time of the study, the annual planning process could only be informed by a budget prediction, the final settlement not becoming known until late December or early January. In an ideal world, priorities would be identified and options costed before the budget was settled. Thus, for the following year's planning seminar (1997/8) participants were specifically asked not to generate a 'wish list', but to outline some costed programmes.

Consultation over the policing plan

External consultation

It was difficult to assess the contributions of internal and external bodies to the development of the policing plan. One aim had been to obtain a copy of the initial draft plan, and compare this with the final document. However, this was not possible because the original draft was no longer available, having been modified and amended continuously during the planning process.

External consultation about the policing objectives was mainly addressed through PLACs, which discussed the objectives for the coming year at their meetings. As in other forces, it was clear that PLACs tended to focus on more local issues and were ill suited to strategic discussions. Furthermore, many of the concerns raised at PLAC meetings were about lower-level social disorder, rather than the policing objectives that went into the plan. Senior police officers had various interpretations of this. Some saw it as further evidence of the rather marginal and symbolic nature of this kind of consultation; the PLACs were viewed as small and rather unrepresentative local talking shops simply not suited to strategic objective setting. Alternatively, some divisional commanders argued that PLACs raised these matters because they were genuinely held local concerns, even though it was accepted wisdom that objectives surrounding burglary and violent crime received more emphasis within the police organisation. Nevertheless, despite what was seen as rather limited input, prior to the drafting of a full plan all PLACs did at least have an opportunity to comment on suggested objectives for the year and to suggest others.

The main drive to external consultation arguably came after the first drafts of the plan had been produced. In January 1996, after the command team and the quality of service committee had discussed the police authority's draft plan, it was sent out to local authorities, chambers of trade and commerce, branches of the Crown Prosecution Service (CPS) and some other organisations, which were given one month in which to reply with their comments. About 16 replies were received. Most were very supportive of the draft, but some suggested changes or additions. These replies were included in the minutes of the police authority meeting in late March 1996, which discussed the plan. The meeting concluded that the general theme from the comments was a need for more emphasis on crime prevention and partnership. A number of replies requested that more details about the sources of statistics on customer satisfaction be included in the plan, along with more detailed area comparisons within the force. One parish council complained that the indicators and targets within the plan put too much emphasis on recorded crime rates, which was (in the view of councillors) misleading. It also questioned the amount of local consultation that had occurred prior to the plan. Another parish council complained that the plan made no mention of car crime. A chamber of commerce commented that it failed to say what happens when targets are not met. The county council referred to the plan's emphasis on numbers of detections and argued that crime prevention should be given higher priority. It argued that anti-racist police objectives should not be confined to inner-city areas but extended across the whole force area, and raised concerns about the drugs education project (DARE), which had taken up significant police resources. It was argued that an objective evaluation of the effects of the DARE project should be required in order to decide whether this was a good use of resources. The CPS requested that the plan include some reference to its (the CPS's) work, and to the service-level agreement signed between police and the CPS during the past year.

The main response to these comments was the addition of a page on 'crime prevention and community safety', which reported that 'the commitment to tackle crime by increasing detections is matched by a determination to reduce crime by prevention and community safety initiatives'. However, detailed plans of forthcoming community safety partnerships were not included, nor were any detailed PIs or targets relating to this side of police work. The paragraph outlined the importance of multi-agency work, and the need for locally-designed partnerships, and gave four examples of partnerships in the county involving the police. This did not really change the whole tone of the plan, which remained very much crime-oriented and built around the national objectives. As one senior officer at headquarters noted: 'the effort and emphasis is on detection; the rhetoric is on prevention.'

Internal consultation
In addition to the external consultation, there was a process of internal consultation prior to the drafting of the plan. Different divisions and departments were asked to submit reports of the main problems and issues facing them, and which they felt needed to be included in the annual policing plan. Given the clear focus of the plan on crime, we explored whether this had caused debate or dissension from certain sections of the force. However, no evidence of any major differences appeared. A number of senior officers lamented the lack of a greater emphasis on crime prevention in the KOs, but a high degree of consensus appeared to exist about the plan. The head of community affairs reported that he had stressed the importance of prevention in the planning seminar, and this had met with wide agreement. His view was that his department could work within the KOs to produce community affairs-type objectives. After the force had decided to concentrate on the KOs, the community affairs department had a meeting to try to come up with departmental objectives in support of the KOs. It was felt that high visibility policing and call response were objectives that were relevant to this department. Furthermore, violent crime is very difficult to prevent, whereas domestic burglary has always been a major focus for crime prevention. The two departmental objectives thus included improved crime prevention for the elderly and the reduction of repeat burglary victimisation. Because of the emphasis in the KOs on detections, the department decided to introduce a scheme to encourage postcoding of property and to encourage CID to use ultraviolet lamps on recovered goods. The input into the drugs initiative was via the DARE scheme, in which 24 police officers have been seconded to teach drugs prevention full time in primary schools.

One ACC reported a good deal of consensus over the plan's overall focus on crime, certainly at the planning seminar. He speculated that this may have partly been due to the guiding hand of the force command team, who all had substantial CID backgrounds. This officer saw the argument about prevention versus detection in the KPIs as something of a red herring. He accepted that the KOs were badly drafted, but doubted that divisional commanders would turn away from opportunities to reduce the total numbers of burglaries on their divisions simply because the KPI is framed in terms of numbers of detections. He said that if the force did this, then 'we are incompetent buffoons and we should go, and I'm sure the police authority would probably tell us we should go'. As far as he was concerned, the objectives system was simply to focus the force on standard aims and measures, but the system should be introduced in a thoughtful and considered way. In his view, middle management (divisional commanders) would play a crucial role and needed to appreciate the full complexities of a performance management system.

Police authority influence over the policing plan

Police authority members and officers were very positive about the introduction of annual policing plans, and about the ability of the police authority to influence the final document. For example, the chairman described the plan as an 'amazingly successful' part of the PMCA, and a 'huge boost to the tripartite relationship'. He felt the authority was already exerting a good deal of influence over the plan, and clearly saw its production as a key part of their new role. Other police authority members were also enthusiastic about the policing plan, and felt the force had given the police authority a good opportunity to influence it through being involved in the force planning seminar. The quality of service committee had subsequently discussed drafts on several occasions, and the chief constable had agreed to a number of amendments in response to these. Most of these changes were concerned with matters of presentation rather than substance, but police authority members appreciated the chief's willingness to respond to suggestions.

Some members accepted that, in substance, the draft had changed little from that put forward by the force. One member said 'it was the chief's plan . . . we were looking at the style rather than the content of it.' Another elected member supported this point, saying, 'our arguments were mainly about presentation and detail, they weren't about substantive policy.' But these comments were phrased as descriptions of the authority's current role, rather than criticisms of the chief constable. Furthermore, the force saw this as evidence of the success of their approach of involving representatives of the police authority at the start of the planning process. This meant that the main themes could be agreed before the attempt at a first draft. Because involvement in planning was still a relatively new thing for police authorities, members argued that the authority was still learning and that it would gain more influence over the plan in future years. An independent member summarised the police authority's influence as follows:

> Yes, I think the police authority did have a good opportunity to participate in the process of deciding what the priorities and approaches should be. But it is still the force plan, they hold a conference with a few of us invited. They write

the plan, and it tends to come forward too late for the police authority to do much about it. Of course, you dot some 'i's and cross some 't's, you make the odd change or two, but nevertheless the sort of style and content are determined by the force.

Other independent members who were interviewed had a very positive view of the police authority's influence over the plan. One described it as 'very significant' and said that involvement in the planning seminar established a feeling of 'shared ownership' of the plan. Another independent member felt that the police authority had had an important influence over the plan, despite the 'strong guiding hand' of the force planning department. One independent member predicted that the police authority's influence would grow in the future, but added that it would necessarily be focused upon style rather than content. A number of police authority members remarked on the need for a cautious approach in the early years of planning, to retain a good working relationship with the chief constable and force. Members argued that, as professional police officers, the force would inevitably take the lead in planning. It could never get to the stage of taking the draft from the police and making it substantially different, or insisting on a local objective to which the chief constable was opposed, because the plan would then become a meaningless document. This implicitly recognised the fact that the chief could simply 'have regard' to the document, but largely ignore it if he came to see it as imposed upon him rather than something he and the force had helped shape.

Interviews with senior police staff generally confirmed this view of a limited but noticeable police authority influence over the plan. The chief constable reported deciding to involve police authority representatives at an earlier stage than did other forces. This had drawn some comment from ACPO colleagues, but the chief constable emphasised he wanted a joint approach, and wanted to avoid any substantial conflict over drafts of the plan. He said the five police authority members took a 'very active part' in the planning seminar and made a very positive input to the plans. However, he was clear that the power balance would not shift much more towards the police authority: 'I don't think it will go any further than it has done, not within my authority . . . I don't think it will because of the relationship we've got.' The chief did, however, allow the new arrangements to include at least the potential for conflict between chiefs and police authorities over the contents of annual policing plans. The chief constable was asked what he would do if the police authority insisted on including a local objective with which he disagreed, whether it arose from their own consultation or the beliefs of members. He responded that since the information upon which the members would be relying would probably in any case come from the force, such a situation would be highly improbable. In the unlikely event of the police authority absolutely insisting on an unpalatable objective, he said 'I suppose I'd have to "have regard" to it.'

One ACC said that the command team was the most important influence on the policing plan. The police authority 'informed' the plan via the seminar and by later comments and discussion, but the substantive content came from the force. This officer was surprised that the police authority had removed some details of costings, which the force had included in the draft. He found this bizarre, since he thought concern with the costings would be uppermost in the minds of police authority members. The force had accepted this because, at the end of the day, 'it was their (i.e. the police authority's) plan'. This officer clearly saw the policing plan as a management document to focus the organisation on its key aims and to outline the roles of each part of the force in achieving these aims. He thought that the overall crime-oriented approach and focus on KPIs might partly be related to the new command team all having had considerable CID experience. He did not think the police authority's influence over the plan would grow substantially in future years. Another ACC reported that the police authority 'signed up to' the plan drafted by the force, though it did make a few stylistic changes. Another ACC was disappointed with the police authority's input to the plan, which he felt was restricted to 'nitpicking' over minor details. He argued that the force would have welcomed proper informed criticism. As it was, the police authority was very supportive, but the force felt none the wiser about whether this was because they had got it right or whether the police authority would have been supportive whatever they had written. He reported that senior police officers had been much more ambitious than authority members in discussions about proposed levels of performance targets.

IMPLEMENTATION AT THE LOCAL LEVEL

Divisional autonomy and local policing plans

The force remained relatively centralised in budgetary terms. Divisional commanders reported that increased levels of budgetary autonomy would help their ability to respond and manage according to local needs, but in general felt they had enough freedom to manage within the force's overall framework.

The year 1996/7 was the first in which all divisions and departments were required to produce their own business plans. Divisions undertook internal and external consultation over these plans. Both the ones we visited consulted staff over the plan via multi-rank planning teams, and discussions at shift briefings. The multi-rank planning teams had been introduced on both divisions as part of the Investors in People (IIP) programme. In addition, both divisional commanders reported that they undertook extensive external consultation. One wrote to 40 local organisations with details of national objectives and some proposed local (divisional) objectives. He also presented them for discussion at a meeting of his local PLAC. The other division was located in a city centre, and community groups were rather scarce. The divisional commander discussed the draft objectives with a meeting of his local PLAC (which unanimously supported them), and with a body called the City Centre Steering

Group (which included representatives of the city council, businesses and voluntary bodies working in the city centre). This process led to the division adopting a number of local objectives and 'concerns'. The City Centre Steering Group wanted the police to address the problem of persistent beggars in the area, and also to try to reduce the operation of non-licensed cab drivers and levels of illegal parking in the city centre. Members of the PLAC wanted the police to deal more effectively with prostitution (the city's red light district was part of this division). The police staff on the division raised the problem of drink-related violence, which also became a local objective.

The two divisions we visited produced contrasting divisional policing plans, though both were clearly linked to the force-wide and national objectives. The city centre divisional plan began with a foreword from the divisional commander explaining how the divisional plan came out of the 'Force Plan' and was consistent with the force aim of 'Working Together to make —shire Safer' and 'Tackling crime in all its forms more effectively'. This was followed by a broad overview of the demographic and industrial structure of the division, and a brief summary of the crime and incident levels for the previous year. There followed a short list of 'partnerships' on the division, and an account of the objectives for the coming year. All the national objectives were listed, followed by two key LOs (to increase detections for commercial burglary and for car crimes), and then four 'local concerns' (prostitution, beggars, indiscriminate parking and contravention of taxi and private hire regulations). The plan included quite detailed accounts of each objective and provided specific divisional targets and standards of service for some of the objectives, but none of the 'local concerns'. For example, the national objectives KO3 and KO4 (targeting local crimes, and high visibility policing) were not given divisional targets. The plan also included four management objectives concerned with the building of a new custody suite, the Investors in People scheme on the division, the policing of the 1996 European football championships, and extending the availability of training and equipment in information technology. The plan concluded with a detailed breakdown of the division's resources and management structure.

The other divisional business plan was rather brief by contrast. It included the national policing objectives KO1–KO3, but did not mention KO4 or KO5. It identified three local policing objectives: to maintain/increase car crime detections, to increase detections for criminal damage, and to target and prevent incidents of antisocial behaviour. All these objectives came with given service standards, specific targets and a brief 'action plan' listing reactive, proactive and diversionary actions in support of the objective.

These plans suggested that there was a reasonable degree of local autonomy in setting objectives and targets, albeit within the framework of the national objectives. This view was supported by an interesting anecdote told by a senior officer at headquarters. The commander of a division with a high proportion of ethnic minority people included a divisional objective to increase the confidence of ethnic minority people in the police approach to racial harassment. The target for this objective was to obtain an *increase* in reported crimes of racial harassment. Apparently, this had caused some questioning from command level, and the suggestion that such an objective might divert resources away from addressing national objectives in general and burglary in particular. It was reported that the divisional commander insisted on keeping this local objective, and argued that racial incidents were a priority on his division. The target was achieved, with a significant increase in the number of racial incidents reported to the police, which was seen as a measure of the increase in confidence of ethnic minority people in the police approach. This anecdote supported the perception of a senior headquarters officer that the drive towards improving performance against the key objectives had led to some tension between the centre and divisions:

> There are tensions. They [divisional commanders] are trying to do things for local needs. The pressure is to get bottom line results – detections. So yes, they have to set up specialist teams, and have to put people onto making sure the paperwork is right, and making sure the results are right. It's human nature that what gets measured gets done.

However, we found no other specific examples of the plan leading to any significant tensions between divisions and headquarters, and senior officers in the force argued that the above anecdote described a rather untypical incident.

Relevance of objectives

Given the primacy of the national objectives in shaping the annual policing plan, we explored the degree to which divisional staff shared the command team view of the importance and relevance of these objectives. A number of points emerged from discussions on this issue. First, the initial reaction of most police staff – from all ranks and functions – was a strong endorsement of the key national objectives. This was most usually framed in terms of a statement about how they reflected what was already being done, rather than redirecting police activity. For example, one divisional commander said that 'the KOs are the things which the police tend to focus upon anyway.' The other divisional commander reported that in the absence of KOs and a requirement to produce a formal business plan, the division would probably have had largely the same priorities. Officers of lower ranks expressed this view more strongly. For example, a uniform inspector said of the KOs, 'they chose what we do'. A senior CID officer on one division said that the KOs were 'bread and butter stuff' for the police service. A section inspector said 'the national objectives are basically the things of major concern to the division anyway, and all it's made us do is put pen to paper, and produce more accountable returns of what we are doing.'

The second point is that although many officers claimed that the KOs were non-controversial in this sense, most went on to express views that appeared to question their relevance locally. For example, one divisional commander argued that public concerns focused on matters from which the police service traditionally tended to distance itself, such as vandalism, antisocial behaviour and other 'quality of life' problems:

> Now if we actually start talking to members of the public and asking them their concerns, and bearing in mind that if you don't give them any lead, they will probably come out with things like car-parking, dog-fouling on the pavement etc. But if you give them a focus in policing terms, and ask them what's important to them, you tend to find that what comes at the top is antisocial behaviour, quality of life issues.

The officer followed this up by questioning the apparent consensus over the relevance of the KOs:

> Now the question . . . that's got to be posed, and I don't think anybody has been brave enough to do it yet, is have we really tested public opinion in respect of the national objectives? And if we really asked them the question 'do you feel that these are important?' I know what the answer would be. I would suggest to you that the answer would be 'They're not' . . . what they would say is, 'there's nothing in there about these bloody people who keep upsetting me week in week out because of their stupidity and actions' ... why haven't we asked them?

Other officers put this less strongly and it was rare for CID officers to disapprove of KOs in this way. However, it was generally accepted that the main concerns members of the public raised in fora such as PLACs were different from those identified in the policing plan. One uniformed inspector argued that this simply showed the lack of public understanding about policing. He contrasted their concerns about vandalism and graffiti with what he called 'real core policing' issues, such as violence and burglary. A number of other officers (also from the uniformed branch) felt that problem solving and quality of life issues were actually more important than the KOs for the majority of people. For example, a shift constable on one division said that local people were not particularly worried about the number of recorded detections for burglary, but rather 'they want to know that this or that problem has been looked at and solved'. This kind of view was, unsurprisingly, common among permanent beat officers (PBOs). One such officer said: 'The general public and their day-to-day lives are not reflected in the key objectives ... Do we give them what they want, or do we give them what we think they want?'

A number of police staff expressed surprise that crime prevention or crime reduction did not receive more emphasis in the national objectives. As one divisional commander said: 'if you look at the way they are framed, apart from number three, there is no mention of crime reduction, and I find that strange. ... Now surely, if you look at the original definition of policing, prevention always came before detection.' A number of officers noted that the KPIs were framed in terms of numbers of detections, which could mean that successful crime prevention would make improvement of the KPI more difficult. One section inspector put it like this: 'now if I reduce the burglary rate, I have done a service to the community, and I have done my job which is the prevention and detection of crime. But poor old X [the divisional commander] will come to his burglary statistics which have actually dropped as far as the government is concerned, because he's not actually detected so many now.'

Skewed policing?

One of the aims of bringing in a performance measurement system with clear objectives is to skew activity and resources towards the priority areas. But a common criticism of such systems is that they might skew activity too far into overly-narrow areas. This was a point clearly recognised by the head of the CID who said:

> Whenever you set any objective, you are in danger of either overtly or covertly skewing performance, because what you automatically find is if people are being measured against a certain outcome then that will consume their whole thinking. And I think you have to be very careful that you don't skew your performance into two or three areas just because they are being measured, to the detriment of the whole myriad of tasks that policing actually represents.

Police staff on division did not report any major changes having resulted from the introduction of policing plans and policing objectives. Most officers referred to marginal changes, such as 'helping us to focus better', or 'nudging' officers to pay attention to certain problems. Officers reported an increase in supervisors' references to national and local objectives in briefing sessions. Proactive policing operations now tended to be justified in terms of a national or local objective. One officer reported that requests for overtime, which were framed in terms of dealing with one or other of the divisional or force-wide policing objectives, were looked upon more favourably. On the division that had chosen to target begging as one of its local concerns, a patrol constable referred to a 'surge' of activity against street beggars. Another constable reported that whereas drug dealing had been considered a rather low priority on his division, since the plan (in which KO3 concerns drugs), there had been a noticeable shift in attention towards this problem. One divisional commander speculated about some of the changes his division had brought in over the past year, and thought that particular objectives, both national and local, might have provided a 'nudge' to taking action. A number of officers stated that the biggest change they had seen since the introduction of the annual policing plan was the increased amount of paperwork and returns they had to fill in to account for how their time was spent. Some referred to the current approach being a natural progression from earlier initiatives such as 'Planned Policing' and 'Policing by Objectives', which were based on similar principles.

It was difficult to find evidence for any significant change in terms of resources being shifted to particular functions. Given the focus on crime at the force level, and the predominance of KOs in the annual policing plan, it was thought that divisions might be encouraged to put more resources in specialist squads to improve their crime statistics. Both divisions had specialist squads dealing with particular national and local objectives, but these predated the system of planning and the KOs. For example, both divisions had a section of CID officers forming a proactive burglary squad, and both had a section of officers taken from the uniformed reliefs who were able to work in plain clothes and undertake specialist operations. This latter squad had been developed from squads called 'the sixth section', which had been available for football crowd duty and other special projects. Although they had predated the objectives, their work had been redefined to focus upon national and local objectives after their introduction. The city centre division also established a small car crime squad in response to a local objective. One local officer noted that when resources were directed at drug-related crime, the car crime figures had gone up, and so pressure rose on the division to deal with that. Although most of these squads existed prior to the objectives coming in, some officers reported having been bolstered with extra staff following the introduction of the policing plan. However, both divisions actually increased their allocation of PBOs during the year, so there was no evidence of a general shift of patrol staff into proactive crime squads. A number of officers argued that many of the changes in CID had occurred as a response to recent reports by the Audit Commission, which had encouraged the establishment of crime desks and a more proactive, intelligence-led brand of policing. The introduction of the policing plan and national objectives had simply continued this process, rather than led to anything new in itself.

The growth in the number of PBOs, and special initiatives such as the 'summertime blues' (offering extra overtime for officers on summer evenings to deal with drink-related public order problems) were justified with reference to KO4 and 'high visibility policing'. On one division, patrol officers in the city centre had been issued with florescent yellow jackets, and directed to areas where they would be seen by larger numbers of people.

There was only very limited evidence of the performance system skewing behaviour towards enforcement-oriented activities, though a number of officers expressed concern that this might happen if the system was not managed with sensitivity. A CID officer noted that if performance was to be measured on numbers of detections, this might provide a disincentive to investigate more complex cases, such as commercial fraud. A PBO was concerned that police officers might feel more inclined to place fixed penalty tickets on large numbers of cars, and enforce laws against a variety of petty offences, simply to get a 'line in the book'. These, however, were all hypothetical examples of what might happen, rather than concrete examples of what was actually happening, and it was generally felt that the performance system was not yet being managed so as to encourage officers to raise 'productivity' in these kinds of ways. Nevertheless, one senior divisional officer saw the danger as a real one:

It's alright Michael Howard or the chief constable, or command saying, 'you will do everything else', but if it's not being measured at that level, how do they know we are not just concentrating on that? And it clearly is skewing us, if that's the right word, because you don't get any kudos, or any brownie points, or any ticks in the box for helping the old lady across the street. Now the fact that we don't get measured won't cause me a problem so long as at my level there is integrity, and people are strong enough to turn around and say; 'yes, we are down on burglary, we are down on this aspect, and the reason is because we're doing this' . . . I am not sure that all others are strong enough to do that.

Many of the uniformed shift officers made the point that their job was largely demand-led. Response policing left little time for proactive objective led work, which they saw as the role for specialist squads, the CID, and the PBOs. The main changes since the Act for these officers were increased mentions for specific objectives at shift briefings, and their occasional involvement in an operation to address one or other of the plan's objectives. This aside, they argued that the new plans and objectives had changed little in what kind of policing they did, or how they did it.

Changes in recording practices

A common problem with performance management systems geared towards improving performance against largely quantitative measures is that they may lead to changes in recording practices rather than 'real' improvements in performance (Rogerson, 1995). This force had placed a strong emphasis on improved statistical performance against the national objectives. It was therefore important to explore officers' perceptions of the degree to which this was reflected in changes in recording practices to improve the appearance of results. In general, officers were clearly reluctant to discuss actual examples of 'massaging the figures', but several raised concerns that a tightly-defined performance measurement system could ultimately lead to result manipulation.

There had been some changes in policy that many officers perceived as being led by the need to increase detections. The force had recently reintroduced a policy of routine prison visits, which allowed convicted people to 'write off' other offences when in jail, but not receive any further punishment. The ultimate result of such a policy was an increased number of secondary detections. This policy was strongly opposed by many officers on division, especially within the CID. Several CID officers felt that the policy was an unethical way of increasing total detections. They argued that word quickly spreads among offenders when a police force adopts such a policy, with the result that arrested people are not willing to have other offences taken into consideration (TICs). They simply say to the officer, 'come and see me in prison', for they know they will receive no extra sentence for admitted crimes. There is the added danger of people being encouraged to admit to crimes they did not commit, simply to improve the force statistics. Not one officer at divisional level spoke in favour of routine prison visits, although it was force policy to engage some divisional CID officers full time on such activities. One division had two CID officers in a prison visits squad. At command level, the argument in favour of a policy of routine prison visits was framed in terms of improving victim satisfaction and increasing sources of criminal intelligence, rather than in terms of better raw detection figures. Divisional officers were dubious about such claims. One CID officer complained that it was a poor use of resources, and could only be justified as a way of improving crime figures:

> Numbers-wise it's very productive, it's detections on the cheap. You pick the right prisoner and you'll get 30 or 40 jobs marked off, but in terms of man-hours, one visit is going to cost you seven man-days . . . Alright, they're getting detected numbers, it's a tick in the box, and at the end of the year on the chart, we will come up probably the highest detections rate per 100 officers.

On division, there was a perception that pressure to undertake routine prison visits came from the HMIC in the first instance, and was then taken on by the command team as part of force policy. A number of officers argued that primary detections should be the main focus of interest, and that performance in terms of overall detections was simply a 'fix'. Command level officers remarked that the force had previously been criticised by HMIC for having a low level of crime detections arising from prison visits relative to other comparable forces. It was stressed that, at the national level, prison visits are recognised as a legitimate method of detecting crime, and one which is provided for in the Home Office counting rules. Thus, despite the concerns of some operational officers about prison visits, the Home Office clearly expects chief officers to utilise this method of detection.

The visits to two divisions provided other examples of where changes in recording practices can give the appearance of different results. For instance, Home Office counting rules now allow recording as 'detected, no further action' cases of domestic violence in which an offender is arrested and statements taken, but the victim then withdraws the complaint or refuses to appear in court. This can improve overall detection figures quite considerably. The commander of the city centre division partly explained the lower level of detections on his division by reference to the smaller number of families living there, and therefore fewer opportunities for 'detected' cases of domestic violence. This recording practice also conformed to the force policy of taking domestic violence more seriously. According to two section constables, prior to this policy officers would often simply give advice and leave (in cases where it was thought that the victim would be likely to withdraw the complaint). The new recording practice encouraged more positive action from the police, in terms of taking full statements and arresting the assailant.

There were other examples of changes in recording practices, but most of these were examples from the past rather than current practice. These included 'word coming down from CID' that attempted burglaries were to be classed as criminal damage, in order to improve the divisional burglary figures. Of course, if an offender was caught in such a case, the charge would be the more serious one of attempted burglary, as this would also improve the figures. A senior officer on one division referred to past cases of 'lost property books full of stolen purses'. The main point was that none of these practices were new, and certainly not the result of policing plans and performance measurement. In fact, some officers who were quite explicit about examples of massaging the figures in the past, argued that such practices have become far less common in recent years, particularly since the introduction of computerised standard crime recording systems and since crime desks were established. However, one section constable did link a change in recording practices to the new objectives, reporting that a new crime number had been introduced for 'vehicle interference', and that this had led to a decrease in the number of recorded cases of attempted theft of motor vehicle. This followed the introduction of a local objective on car crime. It should be noted that 'vehicle interference' is, in fact, a criminal offence, although not embraced within the Home Office counting rules as being a recordable offence. A number of officers argued that there was a real danger that result manipulation would increase if the emphasis on statistical performance continued. One officer described his fears about developing a culture in which success is increasingly defined by quantitative measures: 'You will say to me, well surely there are measures in being to prevent this. Well yes there are, but you can always get round such things. And what I am saying is now I think there is a greater danger of this. I really believe that.' Another senior officer provided a number of examples of deliberately distorted statistics arising from the application of performance measurement to the National Health Service, and added; 'If you think that the Health Service has manipulated figures, you wait until it hits the police service – we are past masters at it!'

It should again be noted that, although controversial, the reintroduction of routine prison visits has received official encouragement, not least from HMIC, and should not be equated with some of the later examples of result manipulation. In general, HMIC has an important role in auditing the recording practices of divisions to check that nothing untoward is going on. One officer reported that there had, at one time, been a practice of recording multiple burglaries in one student residence under a single crime number. This led to quite a significant reduction in the reported burglary figures, because of the very large number of students who lived on the division in question. An HMIC inspection was extremely disapproving of this practice, and insisted that henceforth multiple burglaries of this kind were no longer recorded as a single crime.

OTHER ASPECTS OF THE ACT

Fixed-term contracts (FTCs) had been introduced for all command level officers in the force, but only in one case did the five-year contract not take the officer beyond 25 years' service. For the other officers, FTCs arguably meant little in practice because if the contracts were not renewed they would all be able to retire on full pension. One ACC felt that FTCs could potentially make senior police officers vulnerable to political manipulation and may discourage talented younger officers from seeking ACPO rank. He highlighted the danger that FTCs might encourage short-term thinking by making senior officer feel disinclined to build up reserves for the future, or invest in new systems with longer-term benefits, if they were unlikely to be around when the benefits started to accrue. Senior officers generally felt that performance-related pay (PRP) was rather irrelevant because, in their view, senior police officers are not greatly motivated by the financial aspects of their jobs. The main danger of PRP was felt to be as a potential threat to corporacy if it were related to individual rather than corporate objectives.

The chief constable was placed on a five-year contract, but this would take him beyond his 30 years' service and thus, arguable, the implications of it not being renewed would not be major (at least for him). The chief accepted that FTCs were a potential source of unconstitutional influence being exerted by police authorities, expressing this as follows: 'If you had a police authority that was wanting to be manipulative, and you wanted a renewal of your contract at the end of the period, and they were trying to influence you in operational matters, the person involved would have to decide whether his moral courage was such that no such influence would affect him.' He added that he could not see such a situation arising with his current police authority, but in other force areas with less supportive police authorities 'the danger is there without any doubt at all'. The police authority in this area had decided that all FTCs would be for five years with a given non-negotiable salary level. The chief constable thought that this 'would have to be looked at'. He was certain that PRP would be introduced for chief officers, with the police authority responsible for the chief constable's PRP element. The police authority and chief constable would be jointly responsible for the PRP element in the pay of ACCs. The police authority had set up a working party to consider the issue, and the chief constable admitted to some 'slight concerns' about this. He had asked to be involved in the consideration, but had no idea at this early stage of what the police authority approach would be.[3]

CONCLUSIONS

This case study provided some interesting contrasts with that in force A. First, there was a much greater consensus within this force about the perceived benefits of the changes brought about by the PMCA. One of the most controversial aspects of the Act, the introduction of independent members to police authorities, had led to few if any problems in this force area. Independent members appeared to have settled in well, and their contribution was

---

3. As noted in Chapter 4, PRP was effectively 'bought out' in the ACPO pay settlement in early 1997.

welcomed by senior staff of the force and also by other police authority members. Senior officers of the force were particularly keen to utilise the business management expertise of some independent members. This underlined how the force command team supported a managerial approach from the police authority. No significant examples of tension had appeared between the police authority and the force, and the good relations that were reported to have existed for some years appeared to have emerged unscathed by the reforms.

Second, the planning process in this force area displayed a comparatively high level of involvement of police authority members at an earlier stage than in many other force areas. The police authority fitted into the third category of our typology of authority involvement in planning, developed in Chapter 4, and could reasonably be described as 'junior partners' in the process. Police authority members were involved early in the planning process, having been invited to participate in the force planning seminar over seven months prior to the publication of the final document. This appeared to instil a feeling of joint ownership of the plan into police authority members. Leading members saw the requirement to publish a plan as a major boost for the authority within the tripartite structure, and a central focus for all their activities. Police authority members were positive about the amount of influence they had exerted over the plan. Having said this, the force's senior officers were clearly the driving force behind the plan. They framed a plan geared towards improving organisational performance as defined by the national objectives, and then sold it to the police authority members. The result was one of the most tightly-focused policing plans in England and Wales, at the centre of which was an explicit embrace of the national objectives. There was a striking consensus about priorities at command level within the force, and a general commitment to a crime-oriented, performance management policing model.

At divisional level, although the committed drive to improve performance against the key objectives was generally supported, it did create some tensions. Local commanders expressed concern about a perceived over-emphasis on quantitative crime-related measures and the relative lack of emphasis on crime prevention. They also noted that many of the social nuisance and quality of life issues they found to be the primary concern of most local residents, received little attention in the policing plan. Fears were also expressed about the danger of developing a narrowly-conceived 'performance culture' that gives too much weight to quantitative measures of performance.

Both the force and police authority made considerable efforts to consult the public over local policing priorities. However, it appeared that in practice this exercise played a rather minor role in affecting the actual shape of the final document, especially when compared to the national objectives. This was partly because, as in many other force areas, it was difficult to obtain a clear picture via established consultative mechanisms of what the public might want from policing. The PLACs were not considered the ideal mechanism for consultation over the kinds of strategic concerns that are found in the policing plan. It was the force rather than the police authority that was taking the lead in developing market research types of consultation, and had one of the most comprehensive programmes of such research in the country.

In summary, of the three case studies, force B perhaps embraced the reforms in the PMCA most rigorously. This was strongly related to the vision of the new command team, which conformed to the model of a 'performance-oriented' police force, with clear goals focused upon the core businesses as laid down in the national objectives and standard measures of performance. There was a good degree of consensus, both within the force and on the police authority, about what the police force was there to do, and how it should be held to account. The PMCA reforms certainly helped to clarify this and to focus the police force in this way. The downside of this was the danger, highlighted by divisional officers rather than members of the police authority, that some less quantifiable aspects of policing might be neglected in the drive to improve statistical performance.

Chapter 7

Case Study C: The Combined Authority Force

THE POLICE AUTHORITY AND FORCE

Force C area is 378,000 hectares, has a resident population of approximately 1.4 million, and has 108 miles of coastline and a major international airport. There are five major towns, and the area covers two administrative counties. The strength of the force in 1995 was 2931, though this was increased during 1995/6. The area is divided into nine divisions, and these are further sub-divided into sectors – there being 29 sectors in total. There are 10,000 neighbourhood watch schemes in the force area.

The police authority has 17 members. It applied to the Home Office for an increase – on the basis that the geographical area the authority covered was too large for nine elected members to represent effectively – but was turned down. Of the nine elected members, four are Liberal Democrats, three Conservative and two Labour councillors. The chairman is a Liberal Democrat. The police authority has a relatively small staff. The division of support is as before, with one county council providing clerking support to the police authority (clerk, deputy clerk/solicitor and a committee officer) and the other providing a treasurer and assistant treasurer. The police authority also employs a full-time community safety officer. The force employs a full-time principal committee officer whose job is to provide support to the force's senior management team in connection with their dealings with the police authority.

THE CHANGING ROLE OF THE POLICE AUTHORITY

Though there was variation in opinion, this was generally only at the margins and views about the effects of the new arrangements were marked by a high degree of consensus. In essence, the view was that the authority had always tended to work well, and cooperatively with senior officers, and that the recent changes had left this relatively undisturbed. Though some changes of emphasis and of procedure were visible, these had not affected the general running of the authority.

Again, this was a force included in our previous research on policing policy (Jones et al., 1994). At that time it was a 'combined police authority' covering two administrative counties, with the numbers of representatives from each council prescribed by the terms of the amalgamation order creating the force. Such authorities were wholly independent of the constituent councils upon which they levied a rate and, as such, were potentially less accountable than single county police authorities, which contained representatives who were also members of other committees and thus aware of the other demands being made on the local budget. Making choices among priorities in this manner is something that need not affect combined authorities. Lustgarten (1986) noted that combined authorities are most common in rural areas with Conservative majorities; force C was no exception. At the time of our earlier research the political distribution of councillors on the police authority was 13 Conservative, 4 Social and Liberal Democrat (as they were then called), and 3 Labour.

The police authority did not set up a new force-wide structure of consultative committees following Lord Scarman's recommendations. It had two general subcommittees of which the finance and general purposes committee (FGPC) was the more powerful. The members of this committee did not support the proposal to set up an authority-wide system of consultative committees. The chief constable's 1983 report stated that local consultative initiatives were already reasonably established in the region before Scarman, though these arrangements were reviewed in 1984. A report by the chief in 1985 noted that new formalised links between elected members and local crime prevention panels (CPPs) were widely viewed as a constructive development. According to the report, CPPs had been expanded so as to become more representative of the community.

In addition, the chief constable reported on arrangements in one of the region's two larger towns to establish a police and public safety subcommittee. He invited the police authority to recognise this forum as a suitable vehicle for consultation between the police and community in one of the major cities, and to regard it as appropriate for the purposes of section 106 of PACE. The police authority was initially rather reluctant, arguing that existing arrangements for consultation were sufficient. In the event, police support for the subcommittee meant that the police authority was forced to recognise it. Indeed, official reluctance extended even further. Conservative councillors from the borough council refused to take up their allocated places on the subcommittee because they felt it would become a forum dominated by left-wingers wishing to use it to criticise the police. According to senior police officers in the region, the Conservatives had hoped the police would have nothing to do with the subcommittee once they had pulled out, but this did not happen.

HMIC's 1991 report stated that its consultation arrangements were unsatisfactory and recommended the police authority review them. In particular, it was suggested that arrangements be made consistent between the two administrative counties, that steps be taken to improve public access to (and expand membership of) consultative groups, and that the police authority develop closer links with such groups. HMI strongly commended the police and public safety subcommittee's work.

During the course of the previous research there had been a significant debate in the authority about the efficiency of its structure. Some members felt that when subcommittee and full police authority meetings were added together there were too many meetings to attend every year. In addition, much of the paperwork discussed at subcommittee level was duplicated at full authority level. Another criticism, from a minority of members, was that the committee structure tended to hide issues, so that the police authority never properly and fully discussed important matters. Two alternative proposals for change were suggested. First, to abolish the subcommittees altogether and have six meetings of the full police authority each year or, alternatively, to create a more refined committee structure, including a smaller 'outputs' committee with some responsibility for monitoring policing policy. The new police authority created after the PMCA took elements of both these proposals.

Size and structure

The new police authority meets approximately six times a year in meetings that tend to last approximately two and half to three hours. The meetings are highly business like, with what are often very long agendas moved through efficiently and relatively swiftly. With the slimming down in size of the authority, the opportunity has been taken to deal with the bulk of business within meetings of the full authority and to reduce the number of committees that, according to the clerk, 'were an interference'. The authority retains an audit committee and an appointments committee for ACPO ranks.

A significant body of opinion among police authority members was largely positive about the new size and structure. The smaller number had the advantage, many argued, of allowing the authority to be more business like, and of enabling the chair to include all members in debates or discussions. Similarly, taking the bulk of business in full authority meetings, rather than in committee, was also felt to be advantageous.

On the other hand, in terms of representing constituencies there was something of a split. Officially, the line the authority takes is that all its members – elected or otherwise – have a role to play in representing the citizens of their local areas, or at least bringing the views of those citizens to the authority meetings. It was clear, however, that elected members saw their position as being qualitatively different from that of other members, including magistrates. They did not expect anything particular to flow from this, merely the recognition that they were *democratically elected representatives* of their local area, and thus their ties with that local area would, by definition, be different.

There was considerable concern that the size of the two counties meant that representation was inherently difficult. With only nine members to cover the whole area (and this anyway a number that could not be split evenly) there would inevitably be problems. The expectation was that, with the creation of a new unitary authority, the position would worsen rather than improve.

Attempting to achieve political proportionality – which is what is supposed to be achieved – would be especially difficult, particularly given that the new unitary authority would have almost twice as many councillors as its surrounding county council. The clerk took the view that a slightly greater variation ought to have been allowed and that this would have made a considerable difference: 'If the police authority, and it is a matter for the police authority and not its constituent councils, think that they should have a few more members, then there ought to be recognition by the Home Office that there should be greater flexibility.'

In the main, however, it appeared that police authority members and officers, as well as staff from the force, felt that the new, smaller authority was not hampered to any great degree by its size and structure. Indeed, most viewed it as a positive development. One of the elected members – who had been a member of the old and new authorities – described the new situation in the following way: 'I was concerned about that [the reduction in the size of the police authority] but in fact I think the business of the authority works very well with the number that we have. It's all the other things where people feel stretched, like in the police community consultative groups.'

Depoliticisation
Again, there was a large measure of agreement about the effects of the Act and its consequent changes on the role politics played in authority business. In summary, the view was that it was a much depoliticised forum (in the sense of diminished party politics). Most interviewees saw this as positive, though one or two offered more negative reflections. In part, the depoliticisation was felt to stem from the authority's new make-up and particularly from the fact that elected members were now only just in a majority. The absolute numbers of them had declined dramatically. The clerk also suggested that the presence of independent members had made a difference: 'The politics has gone out of it. Everyone's minding their tongues in front of the independents and wanting to include them, so that's a really big advantage.' Some of the elected members voiced a slightly more sceptical view of the impact of the changes:

> I think it's different because I think Michael Howard has achieved his objective. I think ... it has been neutered politically, in the sense that it was a party-political arena. Now, in some senses [the depoliticisation] is a good thing, and in some senses it's not. It was never a major confrontational battleground in [force C], as it has been in some areas, but what the atmosphere now is, is one in where whilst people are aware that there are political issues, with a small *p*, that are being raised, there is a great reluctance to turn that small *p* into a big *P*. There's a feeling that you should not really relate this to party politics or national politics, and to that extent I think Howard has achieved his objectives. ... This is not necessarily a good thing because it means that the debates are being held in a slightly unreal atmosphere. ... At the end of the day politics is about resource allocation. It's about making decisions as a local

community or national community about what to spend on A or B. You have to take those decisions. Nobody likes taking them but it's got to be done. And therefore the work you do in a police authority will relate back to your overall view of national priorities.

In this member's view, decreasing formal links with local councils meant that discussions of police priorities (with inevitably resource implications) tended to take place in isolation from discussions about resources available for other local services. Thus, even though the police authority was an independent precepting body prior to the PMCA, there were members who felt that the changes were reinforcing a relationship that was, in some respects, unrealistic:

> What you need to do as a community is understand that by spending X on the police, you are not spending it on something else. Now you might want to take that decision (to spend it on policing) but you shouldn't take it in isolation. The problem is that in the police authority now at the moment, the independent members and magistrates don't have that responsibility for other services, and it means those financial decisions are being taken in isolation from the broader spending picture. In other words it becomes a single function service. I think that is a mistake.

The chairman of the authority, himself an elected member, was more sanguine. He suggested that the new authority was 'totally different':

> It was immediately apparent right from the very first meeting of thc ncw authority. I don't really know exactly what it was due to. I think it was a mixture of being smaller, of having the five appointed members in, certainly of losing one or two hostile personalities – mutually hostile personalities who always set everybody off – and then there were conscious steps that I and the clerk took to change the format. Instead of meeting in big, formal council chambers-type setting, we moved them into committee rooms, all sitting on the same level, in a horseshoe or round a table, rather than the dais etc. . . . It's been much more cooperative, much more deliberative, much less knee-jerk and much more forward-looking.

The police authority's relationship with the chief constable

At the time of our previous research (Jones et al., 1994) we argued that this police authority was, in many respects, a somewhat ineffectual body in terms of its influence over policing policy in the county. The primary reason for this, we suggested, was that it circumscribed its own role by adopting an attitude of exaggerated deference towards the then chief constable and, on occasion, even complained that the force provided it with too much information.

To a person, every interviewee described the new police authority's relationship with the chief constable, and indeed with the force senior command team, as very positive and cooperative. This, it was suggested, had not been influenced by the change of authority – relationships had been just as positive before. That said, however, all respondents who had been members of both the old and new authorities commented on the different styles adopted by the current chief and his predecessor. Thus, although as our research showed, the authority had a long history of close relationships with its chiefs, there were some indications that the new authority was becoming clearer about its role.

A number of respondents described the relationship between the authority and the senior command team along the lines of 'close, but not too cosy'. One of the more outspoken members of the police authority said, 'I think it is a successful police authority. That is helped by having senior officers who, I think pretty much without exception, value consultation and involvement of members, often more than the members themselves in a few cases. There has been a tradition of consultation.'

Largely because of this, the transition between the old and new authority was perceived to be relatively smooth. It was suggested by people from across the authority and the force that there had been a general spirit of cooperation. Although the changes that were brought about by the Act were by no means universally approved of, it was suggested that the view was taken that once in place, it was incumbent on all parties to ensure that the new authority worked. Second, the new powers – especially the financial powers – were less dramatic in such a county because of its particular constitution. Being a combined authority, its relationship with local government was already significantly more distant than it was for many other authorities. Consequently, becoming a stand-alone body was not perceived to represent a dramatic change of circumstances. Finally, it was suggested both by authority members and the force, that the professionalism of the clerk's and treasurer's offices had enabled a smooth transition to take place.

The delegation of financial management from the police authority to the chief constable was predictably seen as having had some impact on the authority's business, but no interviewees viewed it as being a change for the worse. The powers delegated to the chief constable include administering and monitoring the force operational budget and being responsible for the management of the police estate, including the maintenance of property. It was clearly felt to impact on the treasurer's role. As the assistant to the treasurer put it:

> [Previously] as treasurer we would have a much greater role in what was going on at police HQ, and in terms of financial systems and their development. Now it's much more of an overview. In the past we would have been there saying 'well, should be doing this, should be doing this, should be doing that' and now, in the force I haven't got that clout. I can give the advice, and they may go with it. But it's a subtle change in that it's no longer for me to determine, it's for the force finance director. We support it, he'll bounce things off us. Before we would have been more proactive. We've had to allow them to be much more proactive because they've got the delegated responsibility now.

During the brief life of the new police authority one major event provided some sort of test of the relationship with the chief. That was the policing of the live animal exports demonstrations at a local port. There was considerable hostility in the county to the trade, and members of the police authority, both as individuals and as community representatives, both reflected some of this hostility though also recognising that the force had to deal with the public order issues which resulted. As one elected member put it: 'I think every member of the police authority had enormous sympathy with the demonstrators, but they know that the law has to be upheld.' The difficulty the authority faced – and the practical problem the chief constable faced – was that as a public order event there was a responsibility to provide a police presence, yet there was a clear public desire to have local police officers concentrating on local problems and not on a trade that lacked public support. One of the ACCs described the force's response in the following way:

> We spent an enormous amount of time during the [live animal exports] problem making sure the chairman and the authority were well briefed. . . . We eventually said that the amount of time that we spent on that problem compared with the other things we've committed ourselves to via the policing plan, and explained to the police authority that this was an issue of proportionality. It was an issue of what was reasonable in terms of demands on our services, and we made very clear why the chief constable was minded to take the course of action that he did do [to limit the police presence]. I think had we worked in an area where there might have been some political pressure to take that sort of action earlier, the chief would still have convinced the police authority that what we were doing was right. What happened, was that when we decided to take the course of action we did, some people perceived us as giving in to mob rule, and one or two members of the police authority were concerned about the precedent this might set. We did not leave it until the police authority meeting to try to convince members that it was sensible to do what we were doing. We wrote to them and involved them very much in the decision-making, basically looking for their support for the chief constable. In managing to do that we made our job a whole lot easier.

This was reinforced by the clerk who felt that the work that members had put in, in ensuring that their presence at the demonstration was visible, had been important in maintaining public confidence in policing:

> When things are going pear-shaped, say over [live animal exports], I think the police greatly value the contribution the police authority can make in making them accountable. It really was important to see that in action. We had members of the police authority going down there, seeing what was going on, making sure the police were working well as it were. There were police officers and members of the police authority speaking to meetings in pubs, things like that.

INDEPENDENT MEMBERS

The authority has the standard five independent members. A local advertisement was placed which elicited more than 100 responses. The candidate who was eventually appointed had not seen an advert and had only heard about the post by word of mouth. One of the issues that had been contentious during the passage of the legislation through parliament was the method by which independent members were to be selected. Although the selection method did allow for local involvement, both officers and members of the police authority remained steadfastly critical of the procedure. The amended selection procedure had gone a long way towards meeting fears about the extent to which there would be political interference in the process – though it did not do so entirely. People were now concerned about the appointments procedure being both cumbersome and inappropriate. For example, the clerk to the authority said:

> It is very long-winded and quite tortuous. I don't actually believe that the Home Office should have a role in it at all. It is more reminiscent of 1984 than 1994. If one goes back to the valuable role of independent members, that local community base and input, then I don't think you can justify the involvement of Whitehall in the selection process or, indeed, these checks they do on people which is part of the sifting, the process of reduction. That could well mean that if you are trying to get a balance of geography, a balance of all sorts of other qualities, gender, age, interest, involvement with the voluntary sector, whatever it is, it can make it very much a lottery. By the time you've got half the number back you can find it has destroyed what you were trying to achieve.

There are quite a number of issues here. The first is the opposition to Home Office involvement. This was widely expressed by members of the police authority and by police officers. More particularly, there was general concern about the possibility that political checks had been run on applicants. There was no feeling that the people who had eventually been selected brought with them any consistent political allegiance; but there was concern that the procedure provided a potential opportunity for political interference in the process. Second is the question of geography and representation. Apart from officers and members of the police authority feeling that 17 was too few to cover the whole of the area adequately, they worried that by not having complete control over which candidates were eventually appointed, their best efforts to ensure geographical coverage could be undermined. Indeed, they had been undermined, for several parts of the county had no representative on the authority. Though the impact had not been felt in the same way, the same was potentially true in relation to the gender and ethnic balance of the authority.

The professional backgrounds of those who were eventually selected were varied although, once again, there was a slant towards management and business. Two were involved in consultancy work, one was an ex-senior manager, and one was self-employed. The fifth had a background in teaching and community work, and one of the consultants also had a background in teaching. Of the original five, three were women and two men. The numbers are now four and one respectively.

Views about the principle of having independent members were generally fairly consistent and pragmatic. Most people interviewed took one of two positions. First, were those who either straightforwardly welcomed the idea of independent members or felt that, although they had some reservations, these had now largely, if not totally, been overcome. One of the senior command team, for example, said: 'In principle, I think there is some validity in bringing in members of the local community who are not councillors or magistrates, although their "brief" is very difficult to define.'

The second strand were those who disagreed with the idea of independents but nevertheless recognised it was a *fait accompli* and wished to make the best of it. Even the most outspoken members of the latter camp said they felt very strongly that independent members should become as fully integrated and as effective as possible. As another senior police officer said:

> They were very sensible our authority because they said we aren't going to fight these people. We'll welcome them into the fold etc etc. We haven't had the businessman earning £100,000 a year that Ken Clarke wanted because they're too damn busy elsewhere. You're obviously going to get people who can give the time. I don't notice any tensions in the police authority between the elected members and the independents or magistrates. They all get up, speak their view.

Other respondents were also asked about Kenneth Clarke's view that what independent members would bring was a set of skills not necessarily already available to police authorities. There was considerable scepticism about this. Perhaps the most critical opinion was voiced by one elected member:

> Some of the people who were appointed to the authority as independent members, really in terms of their previous experience and activities for the community, were not really in the same league as some of those elected members who were kicked off the authority. . . . People of great substance who had been working across a range of local authority activities, including caring about the police, were really rather ignominiously thrown off it . . . in order for the independents to come who, in terms of the experience they had, were really rather insignificant.

Another elected member was also sceptical about that particular rationale for the introduction of independent members:

> I think it was noticeable that the one experience they lacked, was the experience of the type of organisation that it is which is, not exactly modelled on local authorities, but has some links with the local authority model. The way that that was organised was probably rather unfamiliar to the majority of independent members, whereas of course it is very familiar to county councillors. Now whether that's a good thing or a bad thing is probably for others to say. . . . Now that they have had a year or two to get used to how it works, then I think it's working quite well.

In the main, however, although members and officers were critical of

Clarke's diagnosis, they were generally positive about the qualities the independent members brought to the authority and about how they had been working in practice. However, members and officers reported that, initially at least, the independents may have found their new role slightly perplexing, and were uncertain about what was expected of them. Although there were felt to be differences in the extent to which the five independents had settled in (one found that it was not possible to combine the time required with his own very significant commitments), in the main, most were felt to be working well. As one of the elected members put it: 'In the case of [this county] I think those who ended up being appointed are doing a good job and taking a great interest. I'm still not clear what the justification was for having them, but the particular people are fine.' The clerk's view was that: 'Our independent members work very well. When I referred to loneliness, it is not because they are being left out or not doing what they should be doing, most of them are working extremely hard, but they come to it without the trappings of having been involved in local politics or whatever it is.'

In talking of their experiences as new members of the authority, the independents reflected much that had been said about them. First, several talked of the strange 'go-stop-go' way in which they had been appointed. As one of them put it: 'I applied. Then, nothing. Then, all of a sudden you're told "yes, you're on", like tomorrow.' Moreover, applications did not include an interview and this came as something of a surprise to the applicants.

When they arrived, most of the independents found the experience strange – especially the more overtly political aspects of authority business. They all said, however, that in general they were made very welcome by the other members and any slight awkwardness was soon overcome. A degree of iso-lation and unfamiliarity did persist, however, and for a short period of time there was talk of the independent members meeting as a group. This did happen on a couple of occasions early on in the life of the new authority, but such meetings did not persist.

Observation of police authority meetings suggested that, in the main, inde-pendent members were both integrated into authority business and fully prepared to engage in any of the debates and discussions taking place. Predictably, individuals' contributions varied considerably in terms of content and frequency, though much the same could be said of elected and magistrate members. The independent member who chaired the audit committee was par-ticularly visible at a meeting at which some of that committee's business was discussed, and appeared already to have become both an active and important member of the authority. No titles were used in police authority meetings: elected members were not addressed as 'councillor' for example, and as a consequence there was no straightforward way of determining the status of the different members. The independent members did not stand out in any way.

LOCAL CONSULTATION

This is an area in which the changes brought about by the Act have, perhaps, been most visible. There is a sense, quite widely shared, that the police authority is now much more concerned about the whole issue of consultation than it had been under the old system. Members and officers were quick to point out that this should not be interpreted as meaning that consultation had been felt to be unimportant before, merely that the new responsibilities were being taken very seriously. That said, as we described above, our earlier research did in fact suggest that the old police authority had, at best, a mixed record in relation to community consultation, and it is hard not to see the efforts that were being put in by the new police authority as being very much in contrast to the position some years earlier.

The new police authority had made a concerted effort to reinvigorate the s.106 system. In part, this has meant trying to breathe new life into committees that were lying relatively dormant, or were merely perceived to be less active than they should have been. It also meant trying to set up new s.106 committees in areas where previously none existed. One of the ways in which this was done was by giving each member of the authority specific respon- sibility for consultation in a particular local area. Each member would then be expected to stimulate the development of a committee in the area if none existed or, where one did, to attend local meetings, often as chair, to endea- vour to ensure that meetings were publicised and that as broad a range of people attended as possible. They would then have this experience of public consultation to take back and to feed into police authority meetings.

The second method used to reinvigorate PCCGs arose partly from the financial settlement in 1995. The new funding formula for policing resulted in a 'relatively generous' settlement for the county and, as a consequence, accord- ing to the clerk, the police authority felt it could do 'something more in the community'. The police authority wanted an element of community part- nership. Consequently, it put forward a proposal early on that a sum of money should be made available for community projects. In the event, it was agreed that £300,000 should be used for community initiatives. One of the ACCs said that the police authority 'were very insistent on that and we were supportive of it'. The £300,000 was set aside specifically for community safety initiatives. Bids were to be invited for the money, half of which should come via the police and half via the PCCGs. The grants were to be pump-priming and aimed at crime prevention and community safety initiatives across the county.

In addition, in 1995 the police authority appointed a community safety coor- dinator. The job description for the post was wide-ranging, including liaison between the main local authorities in the region to ensure community safety and crime prevention initiatives are properly coordinated; liaising with the business sector to encourage sponsorship of such initiatives; working with local agencies to establish local priorities; assessing the resource implications of successful community safety and crime prevention projects and monitoring and appraising their effectiveness – a contrast with the situation in both the other case study forces.

In addition, though we return to this in the next section, the officer was expected to coordinate the actions of s.106 groups to ensure their adequate development and servicing. A subgroup of five police authority members, with the community safety coordinator acting as a consultant, made decisions about the disbursement of the money. In the first year of the crime prevention and community safety initiative, a total of 66 grants were made. The largest were three of approximately £15,000 (one to train victim support volunteers; one as part funding of a two-year youth project; and one a research project looking at the antisocial behaviour of young people on the street, under the heading 'Coalition for Youth'). The majority of grants were for £5000 or less and covered a very broad range of projects, from women's refuges, through youth diversion projects and mediation schemes to specific target-hardening schemes for the elderly or otherwise vulnerable people.

The coordinator said that the scheme had 'been a "bit" of a shambles' in the first year because it had not been possible to publish criteria sufficiently far in advance of the scheme. Providing the structure was therefore one of his first tasks, and having begun to put this into place he felt that the second year of the scheme – the police authority had unanimously agreed to continue it – was coming together much more successfully. He thought that the authority was now taking a much closer look at how the money was being disbursed and then used.

The force, as we said, was one of the forces that did not set up a new force-wide structure of consultative committees in the immediate aftermath of the Scarman Report. At that time the police authority had two general sub-committees, of which the finance and general purposes committee was the more powerful. Its members did not support the proposal to set up an authority wide structure for consultation. The chief constable's report for 1983 stated that local consultative initiatives were already reasonably established in the region before Scarman, and his 1985 report noted that new formalised links between elected members and local crime prevention panels (CPPs) were widely viewed as a constructive development (CPPs had been made 'more representative' and deemed to be consultative committees). In addition, in one town a police and public safety subcommittee had been established, and the chief constable invited the police authority to recognise this forum as a suitable vehicle for consultation – something the police authority only did after having been persuaded by the chief. The 1991 HMIC report on the force stated that the current consultation arrangements were unsatisfactory, and recommended they should be reviewed by the authority.

By the time of this research, the situation had changed. There were 21 PCCGs, with another due to be set up before long. The majority, however, were relatively new in this guise. As outlined above, one of the police authority's community safety officer's central tasks was to stimulate and coordinate the activities of local consultation groups. In practice, the community safety officer is also the line manager for the 12 clerks of the PCCGs. The coordinator said that when he took over the job the local consultation process was a little like 'a ship without a rudder' and, although it was envisaged that local consultation work would only be part time, he felt that it could quite easily be a full-time post in itself. Indeed, he felt that the expectations of the job in general were too great and that a decision would eventually have to be taken about what the priorities were to be. At the moment, one of the key tasks was maintaining the work of the existing s.106s, some of which covered very large areas, and attempting to stimulate some where currently they were absent. In practice, as in many parts of the country, the PCCGs are very variable. The majority are public meetings, most consultative groups meeting quarterly. Many are seeking new formats and attempting to encourage attendance and participation from previously absent groups – particularly young people. One of the independent members described the PCCG in her area in the following way:

> Ours has changed drastically in X because it was so boring. There was a new Superintendent and I was new. We stuck it out for two meetings and then I felt I can't handle this any longer. And as it coincided with a new directive from the Home Office about consultation and with the new police authority looking at how it did things, we used that as an opportunity to say, let's go and have a real open public meeting, and let's look at how we can do things differently. We did, and its a changed group now. I think it's getting more positive. . . . We've got new people on it, the attendance is better, people are participating more and we've got representatives from local schools coming along, some of the students.

One of the more innovative local consultative groups was the already mentioned and by now relatively long-standing Community Safety Forum in the main urban area. Initially, this was a subcommittee of the borough council (now a unitary authority) with elected members, though also recognised as an s.106 committee. It therefore had direct access to funds and to local authority decision-making structures. Its membership reflected the political balance on the council and, in addition, there were co-opted members and representatives from local residents groups, trades councils, and the voluntary sector. The police had long been supportive of the committee, and though there was some scepticism and resistance from the minority party on the council, the forum appeared to be well-respected and effective locally. It appeared from our research (Jones et al., 1994) that all those involved viewed the committee positively, though for different reasons. Both the then chief constable and the chair of the police authority described the committee as a useful device for defusing political problems. The chief also said the committee 'got things done', a view confirmed by local divisional commanders. It was contrasted favourably with what was described as the unquestioning and 'stifling' support of some police authority members for the police, and the police were keen to stress the changes in relation to domestic violence and crime prevention that had been brought about as a result of the committee's involvement.

Since the PMCA, there appeared to be increased enthusiasm in the county for consultative fora, and a guarded optimism about what might be achieved through them. However, there was also a pervasive sense that relatively little had been achieved so far. All respondents felt there had been a clear improvement in police community consultation in the past two years. One of the independent members of the police authority described the situation thus:

> They [PCCGs] differ tremendously. I found it interesting. They have a meeting of representatives of all the PCCG groups with the Chairman and Clerk and a liaison group of four of our members with overall responsibility for community liaison. . . . Our [local PCCG] has changed drastically. . . . It comes down to good communication between the various parties. . . . The Superintendent, Chief Inspector and I got together. The Superintendent has a training background. We've got a very good clerk and he was receptive to change. I've known the Chairman for a long time and so we met. We had the open meeting, I chaired it, we had all sorts of comments, and one of the driving things was that no-one actually knew that the PCCG existed. This was the first they really knew of it.

This quote encapsulates many of the things that appear to have taken place in the county. Though often somewhat moribund at the outset, local PCCGs were, by the time of the research, beginning to pick up. In part, this was down to the enthusiasm and work of police authority members. In turn, this was related to the new police authority now perceiving itself as being responsible for consultation in a way it did not as clearly before. This in itself is interesting, for police authorities have had a statutory responsibility for making arrangements for consulting with the public since PACE. However, it would appear, at least in this county, that PMCA had made a significant difference to the interpretation of this responsibility. In practice, it seems that clause 4A (3) of the Act has made the difference. This states that: 'Before determining objectives (i.e. local objectives) a police authority shall – (a) consult the chief constable for the area, and (b) consider any views obtained by it in accordance with arrangements made under section 106 of the Police and Criminal Evidence Act 1984'. While this may seem an unspectacular change, in reality the association between local objectives, the local policing plan and local consultation is the key. For perhaps the first time – at least for some police authorities – there is a clear reason for consulting the public and, moreover, a clear indication of why an authority might be seen to be failing in its duty if it had not attempted to comply. Crucially, the changing status of consultation appears to be bound up with the process the police authority was going through in attempting to find ways of establishing itself. As the clerk said:

> Where I think there is a difference, is that the members of the police authority – not all of them – are working harder in their communities, in their PCCGs, and in the areas which we say would you mind taking an interest in. I think there is far more effort going into making consultative committees meaning something and doing something. . . . There has been far more effort going into that, and that is part of the process of trying to establish the role of the police authority.

Both authority and senior police officers remarked on the extra effort being put into resourcing and stimulating PCCGs. These were moves of which they very much approved. However, there was some scepticism about the extent to which local consultative fora were, and even could be, productive. Indeed, one of the officers of the police authority commented that they were 'worried about the consultative process. There seems to be an awful lot of effort going on for very little result'.

Information from the PCCGs suggests that, for the most part, local concerns are considerably more parochial – and in some senses more 'minor' – than the strategic concerns that go to make up the local policing plan. For the period May–December 1996 (covering the time when the fieldwork for this study was being conducted) the major items raised at the PCCGs were local crime and nuisance issues, such as vandalism and minor criminal damage, traffic calming, cycling on footpaths, parking difficulties and also concern about drugs. Largely as a consequence of this focus, the view was quite strongly put forward both by police officers and by police authority members that it was more realistic to think of PCCGs influencing divisional service plans rather than the LPP. The problem was not simply that the concerns expressed at PCCGs tended to be far narrower than the more strategic issues handled in the LPP, but also the timing of the production of the LPP had, at least hitherto, provided little opportunity for PCCG input. As one independent member said: 'I think they are having impacts, some of them, on the local [divisional] service plans, but sometimes not as much as they could. Sometimes it's a case of getting them thinking about it early enough to have an impact, before it [the LPP] is too polished.' There was an indication that, in some areas, the fact that for 1996/7 there was an outline framework of the new LPP available fairly early on was providing an opportunity for the better organised PCCGs to at least consider the likely content of the new plan.

There were then generally positive views of the changes that were perceived to be being brought about in relation to PCCGs, though there was also some concern that the limitations of PCCGs were not always recognised. One divisional commander summarised his general view in the following way:

> I think it [the new police authority] came in with a lot of hype. And they started thinking 'what's our role, what's our role?', and there were initial difficulties there. They were very much led, understandably, by us. They wanted something they could actually grab hold of, that was theirs, where they could do some meaningful work. The one they settled on is s.106 committees and

community consultation. The one problem is that we have to hold them back. We have to point out that the s.106 committees might not be that representative of the community here. The other thing they wanted to do was give them too much say in the spending of money. They were making decisions about a £300K budget in support of initiatives from s.106 committees when they weren't really that well informed enough to make those decisions. The positive side is that it allowed us to bosh some 106 committees and to get into syndicate work and to push that through. We've done that under the mantle of change under the police authority. So we've used it as an opportunity to change the consultation models. It's great as a police commander because I don't have to say much except for in the question time at the end.

Finally, as is now the case in many areas, this force invests considerable resources in conducting surveys of public opinion locally. The organisation and development (O&D) department at police headquarters conducts numerous surveys of different parts of the local population, and of different sections of the police 'clientele'. Focus groups are also used increasingly. There was a strong body of opinion that the force's survey work was both important and influential and, more particularly as we will suggest below, was crucial in helping determine the objectives to be included in the local policing plan.

THE ANNUAL POLICING PLAN

1996/7 local policing plan

The 1996/7 plan is altogether glossier and more professional looking than its predecessor. It begins with an introduction from the chairman of the police authority and one from the chief constable. It sets out 'The [...] Police Standard' – mainly derived from the Statement of Common Purpose – and gives a brief description of the geography of the area and the policing sectors therein. In the overview of the plan, a 'commitment to preserving the peace' is reiterated. The chief constable opened his foreword to the 1995/6 plan with a statement that 'the prime function of the police is "maintaining the Queen's Peace". This has to be done before all other tasks.' He reiterated this point in the 1996/7 foreword. A medium-term strategy for the force was published in an appendix to the plan, which outlines aims for the year 2000. Also being planned were strategies focusing on crime, information technology published by the time of the 1996/7 plan and further documents on officer safety, estate, personnel, training, financial information, and risk management. The policing plan for 1996/7 was very similar in many respects to its predecessor. Some of the targets had been altered but, in essence, the structure, tone and basic content were almost identical.

Objectives and performance indicators

The structure of the body of the plan takes the key national objectives as the starting point. As one independent member put it: 'The objectives are largely based around the Home Secretary's. They come up through the police and then we tweak them and pass comments. I think that's the way. Because you've got to start from somewhere. You can't do it in Committee because you'd never get anywhere.' In any case, the general view was that the national objectives were unproblematic. A member of the force's senior command team summarised the position as follows:

> I don't have a great problem with the majority of the Home Secretary's objectives. The vast majority of them are not only predictable but are logical as well. Maintaining and if possible increasing the detection of violent crime. That is something that we in this force would wish to work on. Increasing the number of detections of domestic burglary. Absolutely, that's one of the things we know concerns and effects people outside. . . . Targeting and preventing local crimes . . . Absolutely. I'm firmly committed to that, so's the force. Responding promptly to the emergency calls from the public. Got to be able to do that. That's why we're here. High visibility policing so as to reassure the public. That's a difficult one. Probably pretty political. I'm not convinced about the Dixon of Dock Green image where there is the policeman on every corner and therefore that prevents crime. There is more than enough evidence to suggest that we need more police officers working, not so much undercover, but targeting well-known criminals and they do that best by working in plain clothes proactive units. So good criminal intelligence, targeting well-known offenders means by implication you are going to have more officers not in uniform. . . . But I do accept the importance of high visibility in certain areas.

In raising potential problems and issues of principle, the above senior officer went on to say that difficulties could arise if, for example, the national objectives were changed with any frequency, if they were added to all the time, or if they were added to by politicians looking to make political capital. There was broad agreement, however, that the current objectives were largely sensible or, as another senior officer put it, 'because they are broadly what ours would have been anyway there is not a problem with that'. However:

> If the Home Secretary had included something where as a force we felt it wasn't a priority, then we might have had more difficulty in handling it and so might the police authority. But because they [the current KOs] are the things that people tend to say they want us to do best on, like violent crime, getting to calls quickly . . . to date the Home Secretary's objectives have not given us a real difficult problem. Therefore one has to question, to some extent, both the theory of having them and the politics of it. Personally I'm uncomfortable with having Home Secretary's objectives unless they are so bland, as the current ones are, that you can all live with them.

This is an important point. The current objectives, arguably, are of such a general nature and, as ACPO put it to us, so 'mother and apple pie', that it is hard to imagine there being much objection to them. It might be argued, therefore, that it is unclear exactly what they are likely to achieve as a result. Nonetheless, printing them in the LPP is unproblematic, though in this area they are generally paired with a series of local objectives, which are presented as the specific interpretation of, and means of achieving, the national ones.

After the introduction, the plan's first substantive section is headed 'crime'. This opens with: 'We have fundamentally changed the way we tackle all aspects of crime prevention, investigation and detection. . . . We are working towards an integrated approach by all staff, targeting the criminal by using a blend of crime pattern analysis and intelligence provided both by our staff and by members of the public.' This echoes, very directly, the Audit Commission's recent strictures in *Tackling Crime Effectively* that an intelligence-based and offender-focused approach to policing should be developed. The plan highlights the importance of technological developments such as the national DNA database and the forthcoming trials of the national automatic fingerprint retrieval system in tackling crime. It suggests prioritising violent crime generally and domestic violence in particular. This force, one of the members of the senior command team argued, has a specific philosophy in relation to crime.

> We start with a philosophy of policing which is about protecting the peace, it is about public tranquillity, it is about feeling that [the area] is a good place to live and work. Whilst the objectives start from a crime perspective, there is this business beforehand of where we're coming from. Thus whilst our priorities, and how we look at resources, might start with preventing and then detecting burglary etc., that's within an ethos of if I see two yobs on the corner, I would have a word with them to say keep it quiet. Now that might be about crime, it might be about public tranquillity, but it is about us being part of the community, keeping the community peaceful and safe.

Consequently, any moves towards more intelligence-led policing are balanced, so it is argued, by a problem-solving approach. Senior officers suggest this is partly made possible by the relatively low crime rates in the county.

The plan stresses the importance of monitoring performance, but contains a number of comments on the limitations of measurement. Thus, it suggests that statistics should not be the only measure of quality, but that surveys of victims of crime are to be used increasingly in performance measurement. More particularly, the plan suggests there are a number of pitfalls in relation to crime detection rates: 'If there is an increase in the number of recorded crimes without a similar increase in the number of detections then the detection rate will fall.' It suggests therefore that the police authority will be provided with other information with which to contextualise police performance in this area.

The plan gave the impression of being fairly 'crime' oriented. Many respondents suggested this was deliberate. One independent police authority member said that in the county 'there was an HMI comment a bit ago that all sorts of other things were being done well in [the force], but they weren't handling the crime, so they switched their emphasis to crime. And when you look at the surveys of the population that's what they want and that's where their satisfaction areas are.' Under the heading 'crime', the plan then sets out the Home

Secretary's first four key objectives together with related local objectives and
a brief commentary. In relation to the Home Secretary's KO1 (to maintain,
and if possible increase, the number of detections for violent crime), the force
had a local objective of 70 per cent detections for violent crime in the 1995/6
policing plan, was set to achieve this and thus increased the local objective for
the following year to 75 per cent. In relation to KO2 (to increase the number
of detections of burglaries of people's homes), again a year-on-year improvement was being looked for; the local objective for 1996/7 was to increase the
burglary dwelling detection rate to 25 per cent (it had been 20 per cent the
previous year). It is noticeable that different indicators are used for local and
national objectives – *detection rates* for LOs, *numbers of detections* for KOs.
One of the criticisms of measuring performance according to a crude numeri-
cal account was that it would give a false impression of how a force had
performed compared with other forces:

> The problem with PI's for the police, for example, can be seen in connection
> with violent crime detections. If we detected every violent crime in [the
> county] we would still not appear above half way [in any league table] because
> we don't have that amount of violent crime. But actually that's rather good and
> we should be proud of our community that it is that low. And yet on the
> indicator we're not doing very well. The areas with a lot of violent crime
> appear to be doing very well, and yet we would say they are doing very badly
> because they have so much violent crime. If you increase the amount of crime,
> then you are likely to detect more which is a nonsense. So immediately you
> must question whether that is a legitimate target.

A further consequence of attempting to increase the arrests for certain
offences might, one senior officer suggested, be a significant deterioration in
relationships with the community:

> When you look at the Home Secretary's objectives that he has published so far,
> nobody's going to argue with them because any sane rational person will come
> up with the same ones. However ... some of [the KPIs] are damn silly. If you
> take drugs. The thing is to measure on the number of drug arrests per 1000
> population. That's damn silly. Drugs is a very important issue ... but that is a
> very silly measure. The fact that drugs is clearly a priority for the police is
> important. If you want to increase the arrests per 1000 population I could get
> out there tomorrow and the troops will clear them all off the streets and out of
> the pubs. I suspect we'll get all sorts of problems as a result.

A further four LOs were included under the KO3 general heading (to target
and prevent crimes that are a particular local problem, including drug related
criminality, in partnership with the public and other local agencies). The first
local objective was 'to increase the number of detections for offences of drug
trafficking by 10 per cent' and the second 'to achieve a detection rate of 30 per
cent of all crimes recorded'. Only the latter objective appeared in the previous
year's plan. In both years' plans, however, there were also two LOs on 'the

administration of justice'. The first seeks to maintain an efficient cautioning system ('of those offenders suitable for formal cautioning, to caution 60 per cent by way of instant caution') and the second aims to seek administrative efficiency – '80 per cent of guidance files (paperwork completed following the arrest of crime offenders) to be without error on first submission.'

The Home Secretary's KO4 (to respond promptly to emergency calls from the public) was also accompanied by four LOs. These were that 90 per cent of 999 calls to force C be answered within ten seconds; 90 per cent of non-999 calls be answered within 30 seconds; 90 per cent of grade one emergency calls be responded to within the relevant target time (ten minutes in urban, 20 minutes in rural areas); and all letters from the public be answered within ten working days. These were the same LOs as in the previous year's local policing plan.

The section of the plan dealing with public order and reassurance and encompassing the Home Secretary's KO5 (to provide high visibility policing so as to reassure the public) begins with the statement: 'Whilst crime and response to calls are again our joint priorities this year, these must be seen as a means to achieve our primary aim to preserve a peaceful society.' There are a further five LOs in this section:

- to release 25 police officers for operational duty (by eliminating or civilianising non-operational police posts;
- to maintain the level of one special constable for every five divisional police officers;
- to reduce the number of working days lost through sickness by 5 per cent;
- to recruit a further 35 police officers for community and patrol duties; and
- to provide an additional 15 support staff.

The plan goes on to say that it is not merely a question of providing more officers for patrol duties, but of ensuring that such resources are targeted effectively and are geared towards intelligence gathering. The authority's CCTV programme is highlighted as a positive example of police–public cooperation. What is unusual about the CCTV programme is that it is largely controlled by the police, and is used for the deployment of police resources, not simply as a means of attempting to prevent or detect crime.

Following the sections on crime, response to calls, and public order and reassurance there is a section devoted to community assistance. This suggests that community policing is integral to the policing of the county and refers to police community consultative groups, crime prevention panels, neighbourhood watch, links with county, town and parish councils, schools and victim support as examples of community links. There is also a section of the plan devoted to traffic. The plan states that the aim locally is to achieve the Department of Transport's target of reducing road accident casualties by one-third of the 1981–5 five-year average by the year 2000. Multi-agency working is to be encouraged, technological aids such as traffic lights and speed cameras introduced, and alternatives to prosecution for less serious offences encouraged so as to free up officer time.

As suggested above, the issue of how performance on community assistance should be measured had recently become an issue within the police authority. At a police authority meeting to discuss the contents of the draft 1996/7 LPP, one of the members pointed out that all the other key areas of the plan had measures attached to them, but not that one. By the time it was raised it was too late to do anything about it, but it was brought forward for discussion of the skeleton of the 1997/8 LPP and a suggested measure was put forward. The original suggestion was that the measures should be 'the number of PCCGs/ forums held per year and the number of members of the public attending' and 'to maintain or increase the number of calls to Crimestoppers and maintain or increase the number of people arrested as a result of Crimestoppers information'. Neither of these were considered by the authority to be particularly satisfactory though, perhaps not surprisingly, no alternatives were immediately forthcoming. One of the independent members who felt particularly strongly about the issue not only took it back to her local PCCG for discussion to see whether any ideas for an alternative measure might be offered, but also used it as an interview question when sitting as a member of the interview panel for a new ACC in the force.

The planning process

As most if not all police authorities experienced, the production of the first policing plan (1995/6) was a somewhat rushed affair and the authority played a very minor role in its production. As the inspector now in charge of drafting the plan put it: 'By the time anything got to the [police] authority it was about at draft nine. They said "hang on a minute". They wanted to be much more involved.' One member of the senior command team in the force held that:

> The policing plan we put together the first time round was probably one of the best examples of planning that I've seen the police service come up with for a long time. . . . The message that we have spelt out is clear, it's unambiguous, and it does not go into so much detail as to become a meaningless document and hopefully it will continue not to get bogged down in detail.

In reply to the question 'How has the policing plan process been in practice?' one of the elected members said, 'I think the chief constable produces a very good policing plan. What else can it be? The whole thing is in police-ese, its full of police jargon.' This latter comment was not made in a particularly critical manner; it merely reflected the member's belief that the process would inevitably be dominated by the police because of questions of timing, resources and expertise.

By the time the third policing plan was being considered, a more formalised and systematic process of consultation was in position. In theory, this system of consultation and drafting was to occur as follows. The plan is drafted by staff in the organisation and development department (headed by a superintendent responsible to the DCC), the process beginning in May. At this point, O&D circulates a 'blank sheet' consisting of little more than brief headings of what might be included in the plan to the heads of divisions and departments within the force and to police authority members outside. The accompanying note asks them to seek the views of s.106 committees. Responses are expected by July, at which point the first draft of the plan is produced. This goes to the senior command team and to heads of divisions and departments for comment. A second draft is then produced by the end of August or the beginning of September, and is circulated once again to these groups as well as going to police authority meeting in September. The hope is that once again the draft plan will be put before s.106s for comment.

Alongside this process, divisional commanders produce service plans to submit to chief officers and O&D in September, at which point they can be compared against what is in the draft local policing plan. Further drafts of the policing plan are produced and a new one prepared for the police authority meeting in November. This is also when the standard spending assessment and capital budget for the force are announced, thus allowing the chief officers to meet to discuss 'human resource' targets and budgets and reconsider capital bids made earlier in the year. Together with comments on the previous draft of the plan, this allows the LPP to be consolidated and then presented again to the police authority in time for its January meeting. The feedback from this meeting to chief officers allows a final draft to be produced, which is formally adopted, as is the budget, at the police authority meeting in February. The plan is presented formally to senior officers at a force conference in March; the summary and the full plan are also printed in March.

In planning terms, the aim was that the budget preparation and the police plan preparation ran along in tandem. Though the end point was two 'separate documents for two separate purposes', in practice they are closely linked. Within the force, divisional commanders are asked to estimate what they will need (or possibly what they would like) in terms of resources for the forthcoming year and, when put together, this allows the force finance team and senior command team to calculate an overall countywide budget. At the same time, the treasurer's team can make reasonably accurate forecasts about what is likely to be forthcoming from central government and what the implications of this are for force finances for the forthcoming year. Once an accurate figure is available, the treasurer and force management are able to establish a baseline against which divisional 'bids' can be assessed.

Divisional and departmental service plans are presented to a group chaired by the deputy chief constable in February. They can then be amended if necessary in March in time to begin implementation in April. Although the planning process was considerably more 'bottom-up' than in either of the other two case study forces, the local policing plan still had primacy over the divisional and departmental service ones. One of the senior officers in O&D said that 'he would prefer to see the service plans falling out of the LPP rather than the LPP falling out of the service plans'. In part, this was because what he called some of the 'givens' – by which he meant the national objectives and indicators that accompany them –were the prime determinants of the style and structure of the policing plan. The reason for this order of priority, in his view, was that, with so many different people in different places driving the process, there would be no overall coherence if it followed on from the service plans.

Consultation over the policing plan
How effective was consultation within and outside the force considered to be? What did it provide by way of input into the policing plan and would the plan have looked different without it? In relation to the role of PCCGs, we suggested above that the focus of local consultative fora rarely stretches far enough to encompass the more general strategic issues that are the stuff of local policing plans. Indeed, this was illustrated by the problems of terminology that were expressed with some frequency at police authority meetings. Many members of the police authority felt uneasy about the police authority's policing plan being referred to as a 'local policing plan'. Their difficulties arose, they said, because local people (those attending s.106 committees) considered 'local' policing to be about things that happened in their community, not what happened in one town if they happened to live in another. Though, by law, the police authority's plan has to be referred to as a 'local' policing plan, the solution suggested in the authority was that it might be referred to as 'X's local policing plan'. While this may get over the semantic problem, it does not overcome the essential problem of local consultation – the mismatch between local priorities and strategic concerns. Local commanders were convinced of the worth of local consultation; it informed their planning and decision-making, and influenced the divisional service plans. However, they thought it would be rare for the concerns they heard expressed to have much influence on the police authority's policing plan.

There was a suggestion that local consultation was constrained by its close association with and domination by the police. As one elected member put it:

> In my view [local consultation] is inadequate, and it always will be inadequate until it is independent of the police. There's a bit of a struggle. Not an overt struggle, but I think an implicit struggle; I want the police authority to do it, the police want to do it, and I don't think it will ever be really effective until the police authority really runs it properly and makes it accountable through all kinds of local democratic structures, be they local authorities or what have you.

This, however, was not a widespread view. The bulk of members saw the police authority's role in the management and conduct of local consultation as much more central and, as already mentioned, an independent member was closely involved in attempting to create PIs for such consultation.

Among police officers, there were different views of the impact PCCGs were perceived to have had on both LPPs and policing locally. From the more optimistic camp, one ACCs said that:

> They [106 committees] were very much involved [in the planning process]. We may not have got it right the first year round in terms of consultation, but they have been very supportive in terms of the way we have gone about preparing our policing plan. HMI was very complementary about the way in which we went about the policing plan, particularly as it relates to service planning in the rest of the organisation and the various different members of the police authority who have taken an interest in certain divisions now know not only what the policing plan is, but are keen to see how the service plan on division dovetails with that.

By contrast, both the divisional commanders interviewed were more sceptical. They reported considerable dissonance between what they heard about priorities locally, and what they saw reflected in the LPP. This applied particularly to local PIs. As one divisional commander said:

> The big dilemma is they [the PCCG] don't really care a jot about detection rates. They don't care a jot about numbers of detections. Which makes performance indicators set by government to be pretty irrelevant to people is my learning of the last four years here. We have a debate there. We simply pose things as questions ... they don't see the extra minute saved on response times as relevant ... their priorities are problem-solving, drugs ... violence against the individual, focusing on domestic violence and racial attacks.

Whatever the merits and demerits of consultation, it is clear that more time is being devoted to it now than previously. It is a time-consuming process. Consequently, though it is not costed, it is very expensive. It is rarely questioned as an activity and yet, given the limited impact it has on the planning process, the question of its worth is undeniably a valid one. Asked this question very directly, one member of the force senior command team replied:

> It is expensive, in terms of the effort put into supporting the police authority, to supporting us in preparing for a meeting, for helping the police authority know more about us, not just the meetings, the seminars. The paperwork cost is phenomenal. We have a person dedicated full-time ... if you costed it you'd be talking at least £100K I'd have thought, at least. That's just off the top of my head. Is it worth it? Depends on what worth is. If you costed and tried to produce a business case, you'd have some difficulty. If you were to say, on a political level if you believe in democracy and some form of accountability, yes. But having come from the Met where they didn't have a police authority, but they did have consultative groups, would it matter? I don't think you could stop them in all honesty.

This is perhaps the bottom of bottom lines. The reality of police consultation is that a huge amount of effort often goes in to sustaining it, and certainly a lot of staff time is used to this end. Yet, and understandably in many ways, there is some scepticism about precisely how useful it is to the police. Irrespective of how useful it is in practical terms, there appears to be complete acceptance that it has to happen.

Police authority influence over the plan

Certainly in the first year, the police authority had relatively little input into the final format and content of the policing plan. This, everyone seemed to agree, was largely to do with timing: there simply had not been enough warning. In the second year, most police authority members felt they had had much more opportunity to influence the plan. Nonetheless, the authority's input was still felt to be rather secondary. For the most part this was not meant as a criticism of the police, merely a sense of realism stemming from the recognition that the police were much better equipped to design a plan both in terms of expertise and experience. The third year's plan –being drafted at the time of the fieldwork – was, as we outlined above, delivered to the authority in skeletal form early in the year, in theory providing much greater opportunity for influence. All members of the police authority agreed that the police were the driving force behind the shape and the content of the plan. The following quote comes from one of the elected members of the authority:

> Although formally it is the authority's document, I am not convinced that the authority has had a great deal of influence over it, simply because we are lay people in that sense and we have to take advice from the professional side, and we have to take what we are offered. Well, we don't have to take what we are offered, but it's not that easy to fundamentally disagree with it. I think also this is where the role of the PCCGs across the two counties could have a bigger role in future. If there is genuine dissatisfaction with the priorities as set out in the plan, then that is the place where it (criticism) should start, and the local community can say well that's not what we see as being the priority in our area.

The widespread view – even among police officers – was that it was very difficult for the police authority to be especially influential. One member of the force's senior command team explained the reasons as follows:

> I think the shape of policing has been more affected by survey work (than by policing plans) and demonstrating to the police authority that the survey is as sound as any survey could be. And they've tested it themselves with their various mechanisms. Once we've said well that's what they're telling us and that's the batting order, I sense that that is more of a driving force, i.e. we have established common ground with the authority. To be honest what is the scope and scale for doing something very different? ... It's not very difficult to work out what [the public] want. It's how you achieve it that is the difficult bit. Once you have the logic that [the priorities] speak for themselves and [the police authority] are convinced of the logic, that seems to be driving the process more. Then you've got the difficulty of allying the resources to those, how you then

explain to the public that some things that are equally important to them at the time, don't get quite the priority, some things get done before them or not done at all.

In this view, some of the public consultation undertaken by the police – especially surveys – had been particularly influential. It had been influential not only in determining what the police service itself would put in the plan, but also in convincing the police authority that what the plan contained was what the public would wish to see it contain. This was reinforced, it was frequently argued, by the national objectives, which also tended to reflect both public priorities and police understanding of public priorities.

Costed policing plans

There was strong resistance from almost everyone to the idea of a costed policing plan. Police officers were particularly resistant. The force finance director described the situation as he saw it thus:

> In accountancy terms it's a very difficult concept, because costing in the strictest definition means that you cost activities and events in their full aspect: time, resources both fixed and variable. In the policing domain that is totally unacceptable and unrealistic. I know that some work has been done in terms of activity costing, but if you multiply that by the variety of ways in which officers spend their time on a daily basis, it would be an enormous task of data collection. What are you going to do with it when you get it? So the view we've taken in this force is produce a budgeted policing plan. We budget by function. In other words we know how much crime costs us, we know how much patrol costs us and so on. . . . We know what the descriptive elements of the costs are – pay, all the allowances – and we've got about 200 budget heads which we monitor constantly. That's all split up by division and department. What we haven't got in place is the costing of how our officers spend their daily time. We have sought clarification on that, put our view forward – that the word 'costing' is not actually in the legislation. However, we do have the resources in [this county] to cost up a particular event if we want to do so.

The county has one obvious example of costing policing – the policing of the major airport. This is negotiated on an annual basis and overheads are charged on it. However, the force finance director argued that there was an element of subjectivity to this, and that trying to apply the process force wide would be problematic. The general feeling among senior police officers was that attempting to cost local policing would itself be very costly; even if it were possible it would be unlikely to be economically worthwhile. One of the senior command team argued that, although there was still a lot of talk about costed policing plans and that such a thing was mentioned in the White Paper, the reality was that it was not a phrase that appeared in the legislation and therefore few would go down that road.

IMPLEMENTATION AT THE LOCAL LEVEL

The existence of a force-wide policing plan raises numerous questions about relations between the centre and divisions. To what extent are the objectives in the LPP flexible enough to take account of local variations in crime and policing? How do divisional and force-wide targets relate to each other? What is the role of divisional service plans? How much autonomy do local commanders feel they have in organising policing in their division? We visited two divisions, collected policing plans and interviewed divisional commanders.

Both divisional commanders spoke positively about the existence of the LPP, though they were sceptical about the extent to which it could possibly reflect local priorities. Nonetheless, the overall view was that the changes that had occurred were generally beneficial. One of the limitations of the changes, however, was in the area of finance. Delegation of budgets within the force is limited. As far as divisional commanders are concerned, there are both *devolved* and *delegated* budgets. Delegated budgets are those that are, in effect, controlled by those to whom they are delegated. Devolved budgets are still likely to be controlled by someone else, usually at headquarters. The divisional commander therefore sees the devolved budget – so knows how much it costs to run the division – but does not control it. In practice, overtime is totally delegated in the force, as is up to 20 per cent of the the division's total net budget. One divisional commander described the situation thus:

> I have a delegated budget which covers dedicated revenue such as overtime through to cleaning materials. That works out at about £600K. I have a £7m devolved budget which is salaries and all the rest of it. Now that is still controlled from the centre, albeit that I can tinker with the margins. I can hold some posts to create revenue which can then buy things, equipment, consultancy and so on. But there is a limit; I can hold three constable posts and two support staff posts. By holding three posts for six months I can buy IT systems which can free up more police time.

There was general scepticism, both among the senior command team and among divisional commanders about how far this process could go. Those at the centre gave the impression of wishing to proceed very cautiously in the direction of greater devolution of budgets. This was shared in divisions. As one divisional commander said: 'To give the whole payroll, one would have to ask why? How would we actually use it? I think it will go further, but I don't expect it to do so quickly.'

One of the key reasons divisional commanders viewed LPPs positively was, in their words, because of the developing 'performance culture' they felt characterised the force. Talking about KPIs, one divisional commander said:

> [They were] taken as tablets of stone in the policing plan, but we are now getting around to debating them. One of the things it did achieve though was that we have become far more performance focused. We'd actually started service

planning before the PMCA debates ... we've got better at it, and they are meaningful, they are drivers for us. As we learn, however, then the relatively simplistic stuff that comes from government in terms of KPIs becomes less relevant to us. As we build our networks up, and the police authority has done that in terms of meaningful consultation, the role of government should reduce. They could give general steers: 'burglary is a national problem, think about it, is it relevant to you?' ... The ACPO position in relation to KPIs seems to have been 'they weren't the ones we wanted, but they were the ones we could live with'.

There were some potential problems with force-wide indicators, though there were also indications of local flexibility. One divisional commander gave the example of response times. In the force, the target is a 90 per cent response to grade 1 calls (the most urgent) within ten minutes, yet in his division the achieved rate was about 85 per cent. He argued that to meet the target he would not only have to increase the number of vehicles capable of responding, but would also have to reassign 16 officers from the community beat section into cars. He consulted with s.106s and other bodies and found support for keeping the emphasis locally on problem-oriented policing, with a reduced emphasis on response times. Indeed, the s.106 groups had written to the chief constable requesting that the response times target be altered.

In fact, divisional commanders said that they had considerable flexibility within the LPP to organise policing locally the way they saw fit. One said 'I actually feel quite a degree of freedom within it, because we have the five core business areas, we have the targets within that, which are to meet the KPI requirements ... I actually feel not too constrained within it because community assistance really is very open to interpretation, it gives you a whole range you can work within.'

Another divisional commander presented a similar view, and provided a graphic example of how he had utilised the available autonomy:

> I don't believe in police houses in villages. That's a personal belief. I think it's outdated, outmoded, I think it's anti-equal opportunities because the only people who can have that job and serve in the community are the people who will live in the police house. They're an ever-diminishing breed. There's only 300–400 of those people left in the force. So you're fishing round in an ever-decreasing pool, can't fill the beats because there aren't the people there who want to move into a police house, and the people who live in police houses are not always the people that you want on a community beat. .... The only way [to get the best people for the job] was to get rid of the police houses. In [this area] we were committed to everyone living on their beat. So I sold all the police houses. One hundred and twenty of them. .... Internally I think it rocked [the senior command team] a bit, but by then it was too late. Scorched earth. All the contracts had been signed. .... So X division now has no police houses. I don't think a divisional commander should be responsible for maintaining and decorating people's houses. I'm not an estate agent. We're there to police. So I

sold the lot and produced cluster offices, like the model they use in North Yorkshire.

As a result of this action one division organised its community beat work entirely differently from the other seven divisions the force covered. This, the commander argued, was as clear an indication as one could get of the practical autonomy available to the divisional commander. Clearly, though what was undertaken was in certain respects contrary to general force policy, it did not go against the spirit or the detail of any of the five core areas outlined in the LPP; it was merely a different means of achieving stated objectives.

DIVISIONAL SERVICE PLANS AND LOCAL PERFORMANCE INDICATORS

The service plans include, geographic, demographic and functional profiles of the division. They provide a revenue expenditure statement for the previous year, a list of force and divisional targets together with the divisional results set against them, and a description of the planning process. It is worth repeating one of the latter in full as it outlines the full extent of consultation that typically takes place within divisions:

External
Each of the four s.106 groups in the division have contributed to this Service Plan. As not all parishes are represented on the s.106 groups a special meeting has been held in each sector to which all Parish Clerks and Chairs were invited specifically to put forward their views for the Service Plan. In addition the Public Opinion Survey has been used as well as the results of the Focus Group Pilot Study which took place on . . . division.

Internal
Firstly, the Divisional Management Team (every Inspector, Senior Support Staff and the Command Team) contributed to a SWOT analysis. The results of this analysis together with the results of the external consultation were given to each Inspector in hard copy. Each Inspector and Senior Support Staff then carried out a consultation process with staff in their area of responsibility. This comprised a 'brainstorm', having used the SWOT analysis as the base. The results of this input by all staff on the Division were brought together at a special Management Team Meeting.

One problem identified in the consultation process was a logistical and chronological one. One divisional commander complained of the difficulty of trying to marry timetables that were, in essence, incompatible. More particularly, he argued, whichever way one looked at it, the current situation was unsatisfactory because it neither provided a full means by which divisional consultation could be fed into the development of the LPP – because divisional consultation generally took place as the LPP was being put together – nor did it allow him, as a divisional commander, to ensure that the LPP and national objectives could properly be taken into account in producing a divisional plan:

Once we've got [the consultation] all together in the division, then of course you've got to embrace the LPP. The framework of that is being cooked up at the centre by O&D and by the police authority, and that's usually coming together in August or September. . . . The only unfortunate thing with that is that you might argue that you should get Home Office objectives first, what the force wants to do second, and what the division wants to do third. Thus, when I go out to my public as part of putting the divisional plan together we should know what the requirements are of the Home Office and what the requirements are of the force. We're actually doing it the other way around. Sometimes we've spent three months saying what we want to do, and then you get the force plan which changes the target. Last year [the] police [in this county] introduced a target on drugs trafficking . . . You've got a problem of ownership. Because I'm stuck in the middle. I've got total ownership in my plan from all of my staff. But then a target gets produced which none of them know anything about. It's just been whanged in from the centre. Now I've got to induce the whole culture of X division to believe in that target and to do something about it. Would you believe that it's the one that we're the least likely to achieve this year. I wonder why? Then you've got chief officers saying 'why aren't we getting this one?' Well I can say as a divisional commander, 'you haven't got ownership, you threw it in at the end, and it wasn't built in to the plan.' But that's about process. I think the LPP should be set first and then divisions know what they're about when they go out.

Nonetheless, in the main, divisional commanders saw the planning cycle as a positive and necessary process. It was felt both to aid internal management and accountability processes, and to underpin the autonomy divisional commanders felt they had. While broad parameters were set down to guide the philosophy and practice of policing in the county, within those, divisional commanders felt, in the words of one, 'pretty freed up'. That said, there was some criticism of the use of PIs that compared divisions. Although their purpose was to hold middle managers to account for the performance of their divisions, in some ways this was felt to be inappropriate. The central argument against the use of force-wide PIs was that they did not compare like with like. In general, this paralleled the arguments that have been used in relation to the publication of league tables of forces in terms of their performance in relation to KPIs. Why, critics ask, should what happens in, for example, one force, be compared with another. Similarly, divisional commanders ask why it is thought sensible to compare what happens, for example, in a largely rural division with what happens in a more urban one? As one divisional commander said: 'The down side is that PIs are compared division to division, when really we should be comparing ourselves with where we were before.' There was evidence, divisional commanders felt, that this was now changing so that the 'competitor' became the division's previous performance, rather than the performance of other divisions, but it was suggested that there was still some way to go.

One of the force senior command team said there had been a debate within the force about the existence and use of force-wide PIs and that the outcome of it was the acceptance that the bottom line had to be that they were a corporate organisation and that therefore it would continue to be important that force-wide targets existed. He argued that when divisions were being measured, it is not simply against the force-wide target, but also how divisions compared with each other, and how they were doing in relation to their own performance in previous months. He went on to argue that it was important not to take PIs in isolation. It was important to see how divisions were doing across the range of targets; that performing extremely well against one could not be offset against a poor performance against others. Even within this, he argued, managers must be careful about how they draw comparisons:

> One has to be very careful that one doesn't measure X division against Y division if they are totally different. But I should be looking at X in terms of how is it performing this year, compared with last year, and over the past 5 years. We do not draw up graphs for the public which show that X is there on burglary and Y is there (indicating different levels of performance), because we feel it is for X to demonstrate to its public how it has performed over time. But I might be saying to the Commander over at X 'I know you've got a very different community to Y, but Y has achieved what they have by doing this, is there anything in that for you? Now some might take that as inherent criticism – well, tough. If they can't learn from good practice elsewhere, then one has to say 'can't you even take the question?' They get paid a lot of money, they've got to come up with the performance.

CONCLUSION

The changes brought about by the PMCA were bedding down by the time of the fieldwork for this research. The police authority had settled down to its new method of operation and, though further changes were anticipated as a result of local government reorganisation, a new pattern of business appeared to have been established. The majority of respondents talked positively of the new police authority. Its reduced size was seen as largely positive in terms of getting business done. Members seemed pleased that the bulk of business was conducted in full meetings of the authority rather than in committee. There was, however, significant concern about the ability of an authority of 17 members to provide proper representation given the geographical area covered. It was anticipated that once the new unitary authority was created (and had two members on the police authority), the other two county councils would only have three and four members respectively. The authority was involving all its members in PCCG activity to ensure that the whole region was covered by consultative mechanisms. While this, it was hoped, would ensure some contact between police authority members and local communities across the counties, it would and could not overcome the 'democratic deficit' it was felt inevitably flowed from having so few elected members.

One consequence of the reduced elected component of the police authority, and of some other changes made to police authority business, was a significant *depoliticisation* of the authority. Members of the old authority were quick to point out that it too had been a largely apolitical body, in which party-political disputes were kept in check most of the time. However, it was still felt that politics had virtually been entirely removed from the business of the new authority. There was some disagreement about whether this was a good or bad thing. Some members, all authority officers and most police officers interviewed felt the reduction in political 'dialogue' was beneficial. They argued that it had been a distraction from the police authority's real business and that the new arrangements were a considerable improvement. On the other hand, several elected members of the police authority felt that the apparent inability to locate discussions of policing within their wider political and resource contexts was unhelpful and unrealistic. This frustrated some elected members.

The introduction of appointed members was one of the most controversial of the reforms. The general position appeared to be one of an objection in principle overtaken by accommodating realism – a desire to make the system work whatever might be felt about it. All respondents – including all three 'types' of police authority member, officers of the authority and members of the force – felt that the procedure for appointing independent members was overly cumbersome and overly centralised. The feeling was that if there were to be appointed members, then the authority ought to be trusted to appoint them. In relation to the background of the five appointees, although there was considerable scepticism about Kenneth Clarke's suggestion that appointed members would bring new skills to police authorities, most members felt that the new members had settled in well and were working hard at their new tasks. All the evidence was that they had been fully accepted as members of the police authority.

The consensus on the policing plan was that it remained a police document. Though the police authority was trying to increase its part in the production of the plan, it recognised the limitations of its position. The police authority was placing a significantly increased emphasis on local consultation and, while this seemed to be bearing fruit in terms of the activities of PCCGs, it seemed to hold out little real prospect of influencing the local policing plan. Of the three case study forces, force C had the most highly developed system of internal consultation within the force over objectives, performance measures and the construction/drafting of the plan. Officers found the system both transparent and generally satisfactory. External consultation, in terms of surveys, focus groups and so on, was quite highly developed and appeared to have been significant in the drafting of the policing plans. Creative ways of involving PCCGs in thinking strategically – such as the disbursement of community safety resources – were being followed, but there was clearly some way to go in bridging the gap between truly local concerns and the objectives contained in the police authority's plan. In some ways, this gap was also visible within the force. Though divisional commanders approved of the idea of a local policing plan, they too tended to feel that the strategic force-wide objectives were in some respects rather distant from their local communities' stated priorities. There was some difficulty in fitting very local concerns and needs to wider goals.

In financial terms, this force was one of those that had not been penalised when the new funding formula was introduced. Consequently, resources were available to set up a fund for community safety projects and, perhaps more important, it had not had to make any particularly difficult financial decisions in relation to policing priorities. When this does occur, as it inevitably must in the future, then the new police authority arrangements may be put under greater strain than hitherto. That said, the live animal exports demonstrations could easily have become an issue of dispute between members of the authority and the chief constable. That this did not occur, and that apparently the issue was handled to the complete satisfaction of both parties, is an indication of the level of trust that exists between the force and its police authority.

Chapter 8

Police Governance since the 1994 Act

In this chapter we draw together the study's main conclusions, locating them within the broader context of trends in the governance of the police in recent decades. At the beginning of the book we identified three themes that would run throughout the volume – centralisation, managerialism and the idea of democracy. We begin this chapter by focusing on the first two of these themes and consider the implications of the main findings of the study for the changing balance between local and national controls over the police. We then examine how far managerialism has been promoted by the reforms to the system of police accountability in England and Wales. In structuring this discussion, we look at each of the parties in the tripartite structure in turn, and consider how their role and function has altered since 1994. The main changes since the PMCA are then examined via the framework of democratic criteria outlined at the beginning of the book. We conclude the chapter with some general recommendations for the future structure for the governance of police.

MAIN FINDINGS OF THE RESEARCH

Local police authorities

Our analysis of local policing plans found that although most police authorities and police forces follow the guidance laid down in the Home Office circular 27/1994, a considerable amount of local variation remains in terms of presentation and content. Thus, while there are a number of central features that appear in most plans, in terms of length, presentation and content they are not uniform documents. While this may reflect variations in the roles of police authorities in producing the plans, it is more likely to be related to differing approaches on the part of police forces, which are the main players in the planning process. Within the broad framework of central direction about the content of the plans, and how they should appear, there is room for considerable local variation. Given that these are *local* policing plans, this is an important, though minor, achievement.

The survey of police authorities suggested the remodelled police authorities were often operating in what their clerks felt was a more 'businesslike' manner. This description could be applied in two ways. First, the smaller size of police authorities (with many now doing more work in the full authority and less in committees) and the depoliticization of their activities had led members to focus more tightly on the authority's 'business'. There was, it was suggested, less of a tendency to be distracted by peripheral matters. Second, as a result of the introduction of policing plans, national and local objectives and increased performance monitoring, authorities tended to focus more on organisational and management issues rather than the strategic policy issues governing the direction of local policing. To the extent that this was the case, it might properly be interpreted as continuing the trend away from 'explanatory and cooperative' accountability toward 'calculative and contractual' accountability (Reiner, 1993a).

One of the most controversial aspects of the reforms concerned the appointment of new independent members to police authorities. The original proposal had been that, as with other quangos, central government would appoint the new 'appointed members'. Even with the watered-down reform that eventually became law, there was concern in some quarters that the arrival of the new, independent members would dilute the powers of the local police authority. There appears to be little evidence that this has occurred in practice. How much of this is due to the way independent members have been working and how much to other aspects of the operation of the new police authorities is not entirely clear. Although there was initially widespread dismay about the process of appointing independent members and concern about central political interference, most clerks believed that the wishes of the police authority had prevailed in the end. Relatively few clerks suggested that their police authority was unhappy with the way the Home Office had shortened their shortlist.

In terms of managerialism, the backgrounds of the independents who were eventually appointed lends weight to the suggestion that experience in finance and industry would dominate. Almost half the independent members have backgrounds in business, commerce and management, compared with 6 per cent with backgrounds in central or local government. While Kenneth Clarke's suggestion that such members would bring skills to police authorities that had often previously been lacking would appear to be considerably overstated, it does appear that independents are, in the main, operating effectively after an initial period of settling in.

The situation in the three authorities studied in greater detail varied somewhat. In forces B and C, the general consensus was that the reforms had not diminished the power and influence of the authority *vis-à-vis* the other members of the tripartite structure. While there were differences in the way business was conducted, and the changed make-up of the authority had had some impact, there was little sense that the relationship between the authority and the chief had changed fundamentally. There was some concern that the Home Office had too much power in appointing independent members but, again, no sense that this had really mattered in practice. In force A, the metropolitan force, some respondents felt that the police authority had lost influence. This was felt particularly in relation to controls over the detailed financial management of the force. Consequently, authority members were trying to claw some of this back by asking detailed questions about such matters during police authority meetings. Similarly, there were differing views about the process of 'depoliticisation'. In force C, this was generally felt to have been a positive development and not one that impacted in any negative sense on the role of the authority. In force A, by contrast, some interpreted the process of depoliticisation as an indication that important matters concerning the wider context of policing were not being discussed.

There was a sense in all three police authorities that drawing up policing plans offered them an opportunity to increase their influence over policing locally. In terms of input, the three authorities were at different stages, with the former shire authority the most involved of the three. However, even here it was widely accepted that the force command team exerted the major influence over the shape of the plan. This led to the most focused of all the plans, not only among the case study forces, but probably in the whole of England and Wales. This plan clearly and explicitly embraced the national objectives and made a commitment to a focused, crime-oriented, performance management model of policing. In some respects, the plan of the former combined authority was not far behind this. It also articulated a clear model of policing, with detailed objectives and targets – the model being derived from the 'Policing Standard' introduced prior to policing plans being introduced. By contrast, the plan in the metropolitan area introduced local objectives that appeared to be aimed at balancing the enforcement orientation of some of the KPIs. Again it should be emphasised that the different approaches in these plans were not particularly related to differences in concerns among police authority members.

Chief constables

In practice, the new arrangements appear to have concentrated power further in the hands of chief constables, at least in the immediate term. Although the Act devolved significant management powers over finance and personnel to chief constables, this was intended to be offset by greater powers for the police authority and Home Office in setting strategic objectives. Thus, as articulated by a senior officer in one of the case study forces, police authorities and the Home Office were to be responsible for the 'what', and chief constables were to have greater freedom in deciding the 'how' (a view also put forward by Butler, 1996). In practice, national policing objectives have been broadly defined, and local policing plans have been largely dominated by the police service. Thus, chief constables have found themselves in a stronger position to determine both the 'what' and the 'how'.

Some local police authority members expressed a hope that they would move towards a position in which their 'ownership' of policing plans would be more fully reflected in their involvement in 'authorship'. Despite the nervous-ness of police forces on this issue, as police authorities become more attuned to the new arrangements, their involvement in planning and objective-setting will probably grow. However, this is likely to be a long-term process. Our analysis of local policing plan objectives reinforced the view that, at present, the police are the key driving force behind the substantive content of plans. The largest single subject category of local objectives concerned internal managerial and organisational objectives. It is unlikely that such objectives were proposed, unprompted, by police authority members. From this, we drew two conclusions. First, that the 'balance of power' within the tripartite structure continues to favour forces over police authorities. With the continued disturbance to police authorities caused by the reorganisation of councils following the local government review, it is difficult to see the balance being redressed in the immediate term. Second, either because of or despite this, the emphasis in local objectives is managerial rather than strategic. As we suggested above, there is some evidence that the drift towards 'calculative and contractual accountability' is continuing.

That said, the current arrangements are still some way from Reiner's (1993a: 19–20) estimate of how calculative and contractual accountability might operate in the future:

> Chief police officers will be accountable primarily through a market mechanism. They will be appointed on short-term contracts and receive performance-related pay. Their performance will be judged according to the achievement of a limited range of performance indicators. ... The combined effect of these changes is a new mode of accountability, side-stepping without displacing the constabulary independence doctrine, constables will remain formally free to exercise their powers according to their professional judgement in individual cases. They will be acutely aware, however, that their total performance must reach the required targets or they will suffer in the pocket and ultimately join the dole queues. This is likely to be the over-riding factor in their decision-making.

There is little evidence from this research that chief constables are finding their decision-making constrained by objectives and performance indicators in the way Reiner anticipated. Thus, while the setting and publication of national and local objectives has now become an accepted part of policing, there remain distinct limits to this form of managerialism. First, as we have shown, the national objectives are not remotely controversial and do not depart in any significant way from the general objectives chief constables might themselves have set. This is, in part, because they were involved in the setting of them. As we showed in some detail in our previous research (Jones et al., 1994) ACPO has become a significant 'player' in determining the national direction of policing policy. Few Home Office circulars on policing in recent years have not had a major input from ACPO before their release. The same is true of national objectives. When the Home Secretary was still reeling from the savaging of the Police and Magistrates' Courts Bill in the House of Lords, there was little appetite for further battles. Consequently (though this may have occurred anyway), there was considerable discussion between the Home Office and ACPO among others before the national objectives were published.

Not only are national objectives uncontentious, but the key players in setting local objectives still appear to be the police themselves. Evidence from the telephone survey tended to support the general picture drawn from the analysis of policing plans. In particular, it appears that the police are continuing to dominate the process of 'drafting' the plans. To describe the relationship between forces and authorities in the drafting process, we developed a three-fold typology: first, 'rubber-stampers', a minority of police authorities who appeared to have had little involvement in the policing plan; second, 'redrafters' — significantly over half of all authorities — who tended to be involved in the process much earlier than the 'rubber-stampers' and were able to become more involved in the process of consultation; and third, 'junior partners', who became involved even earlier than the redrafters and where it was suggested that chief constables went to some lengths to involve the police authority before the appearance of the first draft. It is worth noting, however, that even authorities with the greatest involvement in drafting their policing plan must still be characterised as 'junior partners', with the force retaining by far the more senior position. In dominating the drafting process and, in particular, in being central to the setting of LOs and PIs, chief constables are no doubt careful not to produce targets that, individually or collectively, are likely to cut against the grain of local policing philosophies and practices. The result is that chief constables, though having to 'have regard' to national and local objectives, and thus invest considerable resources promoting knowledge of the objectives within their forces, are nonetheless still able to operate in ways that are not vastly changed from pre-PMCA practices.

There are other indications of the current limits to managerialism. One of the central intentions behind the introduction of policing plans was to provide the basis for a finely-graded costing of policing services. All the evidence so far suggests that there has been considerable, and successful, resistance to such a move. There is no obvious enthusiasm from either the police or from police authorities for producing plans in which the objectives are 'output costed'. As a consequence, little has been done to develop either the technology or other means for achieving such an end. The majority of existing financial information systems are simply not sophisticated enough for complex activity analysis and costing. Notwithstanding that performance is now measured in much more sophisticated ways than even five years ago, compared with the full-scale managerialist model, current measuring techniques remain fairly crude. Most authorities and forces are a long way from being able to tie the performance of discrete functions to expenditure. In most cases, unless some further central pressure is brought to bear, it is hard to see this situation changing markedly in the near future.

A crucial question about future shifts in the tripartite structure will therefore be how far police authorities will move from being junior partners towards being genuinely equal partners in the production of a policing plan. One of the most significant limitations on the role of local police authorities in the past has been their own reluctance to take advantage of the powers at their disposal. As one clerk suggested to us, many authorities still operate in a form of 'compliance culture' where members either find it extremely difficult or simply do not wish to challenge the chief constable or other senior officers. In the absence of information that will allow police authorities to increase their consideration and analysis of local policing, and without sufficient resources to do all the work necessary to play a full role, it is unlikely that many police authorities, if any, will become anything more than 'junior partners'.

Home Office

Although national objectives are incorporated fairly centrally into the vast majority of policing plans – as is legally required – we found no clear evidence that plans are, as yet, becoming dominated or driven by central concerns. A large number give national objectives considerable prominence, but even more do not do so and are careful to balance national objectives with local ones, or even to give local ones priority. Indeed, some plans appeared to rephrase or revise the national objectives to change their emphasis. Moreover, some authorities argue that the apparent priority they give to national objectives is because the national priorities simply reflect what were found to be the main local concerns. Although it could be argued that this was merely some form of *post hoc* rationalisation, the widespread arguments of both police authority members and senior police staff that the national objectives were both self evident and uncontentious tended to provide some support for this position.

One of the main concerns some commentators raised when the reforms were first proposed was that performance objectives and performance indicators might impact in a negative way on the nature and style of policing. More particularly, there was concern that the 'model' of policing outlined in the White Paper on Police Reform (Home Office, 1993) would be brought about through the imposition of national objectives that stressed 'crime-fighting'. Our functional analysis of the published national and local objectives provided little clear evidence of a marked shift towards enforcement. Although it is impossible to infer actual priorities from published objectives, it was nevertheless significant that a number of police authorities/forces identified local objectives concerned with crime prevention/reduction, public order and reassurance, and traffic. In general, the published objectives were more in line with a broader functional than a narrow 'crime-fighting' model of policing. Furthermore, although we could not systematically examine shifts in policing on the ground, there was no substantial evidence from the case studies that there had been a large-scale skewing of emphasis within policing towards crime and, in particular, enforcement-type functions. However, some officers feared that this would be the ultimate result of the introduction of performance management systems.

The changes that have been made to the structures for police accountability in England and Wales have not been nearly as far-reaching as first anticipated. In particular, it is not yet clear that the power of the centre has been radically increased. If anything, it would appear to be the security of the chief constable that has been cemented. This may, however, be temporary. There are signs that some of the potential that exists for local police authorities to begin to exercise more influence may be taken advantage of in the future. Though traditionally police authorities have generally been reluctant to exercise fully the powers available to them, the clarification of their role may have changed this. There are indications that police authorities are beginning to explore ways of becoming more involved in the drafting of policing plans, that they are interested in exploring the potential for new performance indicators, and that they are taking their responsibilities for local consultation more seriously than in the past. At present, all is relatively quiet and there have been few major disputes between authorities and their forces. However, the potential exists for some highly significant confrontations.

There are numerous possibilities, but two examples will suffice. First, such battles could occur between police authorities and the Home Office over the treatment of national objectives in local policing plans. Although national objectives are widely perceived to be written in tablets of stone, according to Earl Ferrers in the House of Lords, a chief constable will be free not to meet KOs or any related performance targets if other operational considerations are of overriding importance. Given the very wide definition of operational matters that appears to be used in practice, this amounts virtually to a *carte blanche* for chief constables to do their own thing should they wish. In reality, of course, chief constables would be reluctant to engage in such confrontations, but the time is bound to come when, if new and less acceptable objectives are introduced, such a confrontation will occur. When it does, the real impact of this part of the legislation will become clearer. One subsidiary benefit of such a conflict could be the legal clarification of the idea of 'operational independence'.

The second major possibility is that substantial differences may emerge between chief constables and their police authorities either over the content of the local policing plan, or in relation to their perceived response (or lack of one) to that plan. In the first of these two, it is fairly easy to see how conflicts might arise in the future if police authorities attempt to become full co-authors of local policing plans. At the moment, conflict is clearly absent because there is little challenge to the 'police view' of how local policing should be presented and measured. The second possibility is a parallel of the potential conflict that could exist between local police authorities and the Home Office. In other words, although there are both national and local objectives within the local policing plan, the chief constable only has to 'have regard' to such objectives and can claim that operational considerations mean that it is impossible to address one or more of the objectives properly. Again, this might have to be tested in court and it would be interesting to see whether, as in the past when such matters have been tested, the courts rule in favour of the police.

DEMOCRATIC FRAMEWORK OF CONTEMPORARY POLICE GOVERNANCE

The idea of 'democracy' has been central to much academic discussion and analysis of police accountability. More particularly, the changes Kenneth Clarke originally proposed to the tripartite structure were perceived – particularly by local government associations – as a direct attack on democratic influence over policing. In our previous work (Jones et al., 1994), we argued that insufficient thought had been given to what the term 'democracy' means in these circumstances and, more particularly, that there is a tendency to conflate or elide the terms 'democracy' and 'elected representation' and, consequently, to focus on political institutions at the expense of the normative content of democracy. We have argued for a focus on the 'values' inherent in the notion of democracy and, to that end, have outlined seven criteria underpinning our understanding of this idea. In the this section these criteria are used as a framework for analysing the changes to police governance that have resulted from the implementation of the PMCA.

Equity

In this context, equity means that service-delivery and law enforcement functions are applied fairly by the police across all groups and individuals. However, given that it is now well-established that the bulk of crime is committed locally and that it is also very unequally distributed – it is concentrated in the poorest areas – policing services will inevitably be unevenly distributed. Given the different roles the police play, this can be seen both as unequal distribution of enforcement and/or as uneven distribution of protection. Perceptions of a service as equitable or otherwise are likely to determine how much legitimacy it has. We have found little evidence so far of national objectives for policing shifting policing away from prevention and toward enforcement and detection. However, if the fears of some commentators, including some senior police officers, are realised and such a shift does occur, the potential impact on equity is significant. If the enforcement model being used is the 'intelligence-led' one that prioritises 'hot-spots' and 'frequent offenders' or, alternatively, adopts some of the cruder aspects of what is currently described as 'zero tolerance', then policing may be even more skewed towards the control of the already disadvantaged.

On the other hand, there are early indications that the introduction of local objectives (LOs) may be making some policing policies more equitable. Some police authorities and forces have set objectives that have as their focus more responsive policing of certain particularly disadvantaged groups, such as victims of racial harassment and racial attacks, and victims of domestic violence. Indeed, there is an overlap here between this and the next of the 'democratic criteria': delivery of service.

LOs that place the emphasis on the quality or nature of service delivery to marginalised or relatively powerless social groups have the potential effect of enhancing the degree of equity in local policing policy.

Delivery of service

A central facet in the reform of the police service in the 1990s has, as with other public services, been an emphasis on the 'customer' and on providing both value for money and quality in the delivery of policing. However, there are a number of problems in applying such a philosophy to policing. First, there is the problem of agreeing to a definition of the objectives and second, of deciding how effectiveness is to be measured. What counts as 'good perform-ance' is a crucial question in this regard. Moreover, policing is not a politically-neutral 'technical' exercise, as governments in the late 1980s and early 1990s often implied. As argued previously, discussions about policing are inevitably 'political' in that they concern collective decisions about priorities. Published policing objectives may look uncontentious and measur-able, but may also imply a particular model of policing, and not one that necessarily meets the wishes of most local residents.

There are many unanswered questions about performance measurement. What is to be measured? How can it be done? There is also a fairly sizeable difference between systems of performance measurement that are focused enough to work, and those that can adequately capture the interlinked complexity of tasks that make up policing. Notwithstanding the pressures to develop 'hard' measures of performance, there remains much in policing that is not easily measured or captured via routine indicators. Though the Home Office, Treasury and ACPO are working on the design of performance indicators that will allow even more complex aspects of police work to be measured, we are still far from having an effective monitoring system for the delivery of policing services.

A question that goes to the heart of accountability and governance issues is that of who manages and oversees the systems for measuring performance once they are introduced. During the case studies, a number of senior police officers emphasised the need for an ingrained understanding of the nature of police work as a prerequisite for the sensitive introduction of performance measurement systems. In this regard, the British police service is at an advan-tage in having senior police managers who themselves started as constables. Such officers would be more likely to know 'the tricks of the trade' regarding recording manipulations and so on. In other countries, such as the Netherlands, senior police officers are recruited directly to an officer class, which, it has been suggested, has contributed to a wider gulf of understanding between managers and lower-ranking officers (Jones, 1995). On the other hand, in some respects local police authorities, independent of the police force, are better placed to set objectives and monitor performance. At the moment, they have neither the information nor the staff they need to take on that level of responsibility.

Responsiveness

In determining the order of priorities for policing, resource allocation between different activities and objectives and choice of policing methods to be used, the police should be 'responsive' to the views of representative bodies and individuals. In relation to the discussions above, three levels of responsiveness can be identified.

First, let us consider the Home Secretary. Although responsiveness to the centre has arguably been increasing for several decades, it was suggested that this process would be advanced and entrenched by the PMCA reforms. Crucial in this has been the introduction of national objectives which, though largely uncontested, have become significant drivers of policing. Senior officers and police authority members argue that such is their predictability that they would have been policing objectives anyway. Nonetheless, having now been established, the introduction of more contentious objectives in the future cannot be ruled out. How chief constables and police authorities would respond to them is a moot point, but it is undeniable that the mere setting of police priorities from the centre represents, if not an increase, then a formalisation of the Home Secretary's powers.

There are other dangers in setting national objectives. First, apart from retrospective questioning of the Home Secretary in the House of Commons, the setting of such objectives is not open to democratic scrutiny. At the moment, decision-making appears to be undertaken by an *ad hoc* Home Office committee. Though so far this has been largely unproblematic because of the uncontentious nature of objectives, there is a danger that, with increasing 'politicisation' of law and order in general, and policing in particular, objectives may be set for ideological reasons. Second, setting objectives at the centre may introduce other 'players' into the governance of the police structure. It offers an opportunity for other government ministers and departments to proffer suggestions about priorities for the police (as the Department of the Environment unsuccessfully did over traffic policing). The spectre of internal horse trading between government departments over policing budgets and priorities is one that must be considered. Third, it is important to balance opportunities to change unsuitable or no longer appropriate objectives, with the need for stability. The fact that national objectives are set annually introduces the danger that the thrust of the objectives could change from year to year. Although this has, in the event, not happened, such a destabilising development remains more than a theoretical possibility.

The second level of responsiveness we might identify is responsiveness to police authorities. When introducing the reforms to police authorities, government ministers argued that the changes being proposed would increase their effectiveness and make local police forces more responsive to them. We argue that there is some evidence that this has indeed been a consequence of the Act. Although there have been no radical realignments between authorities and their forces, some of the reforms appear to have had the effect of making police authorities clearer both about their role and their responsibilities. However, there are also some caveats we would raise here. First, most police authorities have clearly been bit players in the production of policing plans. They remain some distance away from being primary drivers of police activity at a local level. Although there is evidence that authorities are now becoming more active and informed, there remain significant limits to this and, in addition, a problem of overlapping responsibilities with their forces, which are yet to be clarified. The role and identity of the police authority, as a body distinct from, and yet working with, the police force has yet to be firmly established. There appears to be a division opening up within the ranks of police authorities, between those that continue to identify closely with their local government roots, and those that wish to emphasise their independence from the local authority structure. Second, as far as local objectives are concerned, there is a problem about what is meant by 'local'. While, from the Home Office perspective, police authority areas no doubt look like relatively small areas that could, potentially, be organised to give rise to objectives that summarise 'needs' for the areas. However, the reality is that most police authority/police force areas are internally differentiated to a considerable degree. Consequently, while at a 'basic command unit' level it is often feasible to apply practical objectives, these may be all but meaningless at the force or police authority level. Put another way, police authorities are at a good level for strategic objectives, but not such a good level for local practical objectives, which are more connected with the level of the neighbourhood.

The third level of responsiveness is to PCCGs and other local fora. It follows from the above that consultation at the 'neighbourhood' level is unlikely to have any great impact on local policing plans. Aside from the difficulty of distilling broader strategic objectives from the work of these groups, a number of other well-known difficulties also limit their work. In the main, such groups are unrepresentative and thus in a poor position to speak for the 'community' from which they are drawn. Even at the more local level, they have shown little willingness to get involved in the business of producing clear measurable objectives. The reforms brought about by the PMCA have, nevertheless, increased to a considerable degree the emphasis placed on local consultation, and have in many parts of the country led to a significantly increased commitment of resources to such activities. It remains to be seen what effects these developments will have on operational policing.

Distribution of power

One of the key themes themes running through this book has been the question of whether the distribution of power between the key actors in the tripartite structure has shifted as a result of the PMCA. An important objective of the study was to examine whether the PMCA was a continuation of the process of centralisation of power over policing, or whether it was an Act of devolution. Predictably, perhaps, no clear answer is yet apparent. As outlined above, there has clearly been some enhancement and formalisation of the Home Secretary's role and influence, and also some reinforcement of the power of chief constables. The Act also contains the potential for increasing the sphere of influence of local police authorities. At present though, this remains very much a potential rather than an actual development.

In relation to centralisation, the political control over national objectives has been influential. However, it is difficult to find examples of police authority members or officers complaining that the KOs are forcing them to prioritise things they would not otherwise be prioritising. KOs have certainly increased the potential for exercising central powers, but this has yet to become visible in practice. There is no evidence of forces being penalised for not performing against the KOs, though again the potential is there. In reality, the pressure is likely to be more indirect, via criticism from Audit Commission and HMIC. Exactly how tightly defined national objectives are, and how strictly the centre pressures forces to follow them, will be vital factors in the future development of the nexus of control over policing. The other alleged aspect of political influence – the appointment of independent members – would now be a rather ineffective mechanism of central control. Although a few police authorities perceived the invisible hand of central political interference, most accepted that the rather arcane process of selecting independent members allowed few opportunities for such behaviour.

As for local influences, the evidence is rather mixed. First, most police authorities appear to be publishing policing plans that contain local objectives for policing. However, the evidence is that these objectives are, in the main, being set by the police themselves. Within forces, the freedom of local commanders to set divisional objectives and respond to them depends on two key factors. First, how far forces continue to delegate financial and policy-making power down the organisation, and second, the tightness of the force-wide performance objectives system. Like the Home Office, most senior police officers are treading carefully at the moment.

The influence of police authorities might also have been thought to have been increased via their establishment as independent precepting bodies. In one sense, this increased autonomy reinforces the police authority's role and function. On the other hand, it also potentially drives a wedge between police authorities and those other bodies with which they increasingly need to work if coherent community safety policies are to be implemented. Some police authorities, such as that in force C, and some metropolitan authorities, are making efforts to establish links with councils in their area, and are positioning themselves as a lead body for community safety strategies. The fragmentation of the local government system following the local government review makes this kind of activity even more important. The proposals in the Crime and Disorder Bill for placing a statutory responsibility on local authorities to produce community safety plans, and to work with the police in doing so, will further reinforce such activity.

It is difficult to reach a straightforward conclusion at this stage about the effect of the reforms on the balance of power within the tripartite structure, for many grey areas persist. At the moment, it seems that chief constables have been net gainers of influence though, depending on the response of police authorities, some of this may be clawed back. The main reasons for this state of affairs are, first, police authorities have devolved powers to chief constables and, second, the latter have yet to take full advantage of their new powers and responsibilities. If, however, the Home Office becomes more assertive in its selection and pushing of national objectives then, as was the case over Clarke's original proposals for reform, we may see develop a new, closer relationship between police authorities and chief constables in defence of local autonomy. The campaign against the Act showed that they can be powerful allies against the centre. Although it is possible to see such a relationship being conceived and sustained for as long as campaigning was necessary, it is more difficult to see it developing without a 'common enemy' being discovered. Should such a relationship develop, it is likely to result in considerable difficulties for police authorities effectively attempting to hold chiefs to account.

Information

Our earlier research (Jones et al., 1994) found that information on the funding, expenditure, activity and outputs of policing has hitherto been quite inadequate. However, the PMCA has accelerated the trend towards increased public availability of general performance information. This is being used to try to enhance political accountability. But similar concerns apply here as we raised in relation to the question of delivery of service. Information remains largely controlled by the police. Thus, the information that is available, and the way it is presented, is inevitably the result of a political process of decision-making, usually by the constabulary whom it is hoped to hold to account. Although the current approach is to present such information as politically neutral, technical and self-evident in interpretation, it is generally none of these things.

The case study in force A suggested that the flow of information was, if anything, too great. There are so many performance objectives, indicators and measures that the 'rational consumer' – even if such a thing existed – would most likely be overwhelmed by the variety. Moreover, the 'consumer' of policing is not a 'rational consumer' in the sense that somebody purchasing private goods or services is. There is a case for improving levels of standard performance information, but in many ways this seems to have gone beyond the point where it clarifies matters for the citizen, and is actually in danger of confusing the citizen. With HMIC, Audit Commission, ACPO, and now KPI (plus local PIs) being published, there is arguably a case for rationalising the amount of information being produced. The question that remains, therefore, is what information is needed? The answer to this should be informed by what was said earlier about the process of defining objectives and 'good' performance. Careful thought needs to be given to the 'audiences' for performance information. The information needs of police managers and police authority members clearly overlap in a number of important ways, and better performance information should help improve both police management and the process of political accountability. It is important to remember that political and managerial accountabily are different things with different information requirements. This study has shown how political and managerial accountability are becoming increasingly blurred, with a resulting confusion of roles between police forces and police authorities.

It is therefore appropriate to consider the type of information, the level of detail, and the mode of presentation depending on the audience in question. For example, it is likely that the level of detail about performance for police managers should be greater than that provided for the police authority and should certainly be significantly greater than that provided to the wider public.

While it is proper that full information should be provided as a matter of course to a police authority, there are pitfalls in publishing large amounts of relatively 'raw' information for the public, without giving adequate thought to how it is to be used. The twice yearly publication of criminal statistics valuably illustrates this problem. A huge amount of political attention is devoted to scrutinising what are unanimously seen by informed commentators as rather crude criminal statistics. In just the same way that criminal statistics retain an inflated importance in public debate, so similarly unexplained or unqualified information about detections per 100 officers or other crude measures of police 'performance' may also have negative effects. It is important not to lose sight of the fact that there is no necessary correlation between the overall amount of information that is available and how enlightened people will be as a result.

There remain suspicions about the 'political' uses to which performance information might be put. As we outlined in our summary of the debates surrounding the Sheehy Report, there was considerable concern within the police service that the introduction of performance-related pay and, more importantly, fixed-term contracts, together with proposed increases in the power of the Home Secretary and police authorities to direct police forces as to their priorities, would place chief constables in a very uncomfortable position. There remains considerable scepticism about the value of FTCs and, as a consequence, some reluctance wholly to embrace PIs.

A final point relating to information concerns the fact that, with one or two exceptions, police authorities have neither the expertise nor the support of a sufficiently large secretariat to deal with the vast body of performance information that is now being produced. Though information is central to democratic control, it is only valuable if it can be properly interpreted and acted upon.

There remains considerable variation in the size of staff to support police authorities, which are still largely dependent on their police forces for the delivery of performance information. For example, of our three case studies, the metropolitan police authority had a significantly larger body of support staff than either of the other two police authorities. However, significant differences in police authority input to the policing plan, for example, were not immediately apparent. While it was not within the scope of this study to consider in detail the impact of the differing sizes of police authority secretariats, such analysis would be useful. The lessons learned could then inform recommendations for best practice in England and Wales. That said, there seems to be a case for top-slicing police grant and laying down minimum levels of police authority support, which are greater than the levels that currently exist in most police authorities.

Redress

Potentially, both FTCs and PRP reinforce the element of redress that exists in the police system of governance. This was certainly the intention of the Sheehy Committee, and it represents part of the 'contract culture' more typical of the private sector, but increasingly a part of the public sector in the UK. Not only have senior officers been wary of the consequences of this 'contract culture', but police authorities themselves have exhibited a reluctance to consider PRP and, though under an obligation to place new ACPO-rank appointments on FTCs, have not sought to introduce them for all existing senior officers. Moreover, in the way they have been introduced, many FTCs have taken officers beyond their retirement date, and therefore have little bite, or potential bite, in practice.

Participation

This has been the democratic criterion that has formed the focus for most debate about the realities of police accountability. The Act reduced democratic input into police authorities in terms of the proportion of elected representatives. The more extreme of Kenneth Clarke's proposals would have seen elected representation shrink to just half of authority membership and authority chairpersons appointed from the centre. Though depoliticised police authority meetings appears to be one consequence of the changes, there is little evidence so far that the democratic deficit is having particularly deleterious effects on the police authorities' work. Moreover, some of Kenneth Clarke's objections to previous arrangements *do* stand up to scrutiny. In interview, he outlined three central criticisms of police authorities – they were relatively ineffective, 'exercising no effective control over the service at all and taking very few real decisions'; the relationship between police authorities and 'local government allegedly gave democratic accountability, but in practice ... was mythical'; and 'the average member of the police authority did not regard himself or herself as being accountable to the public for any of the things they did.' While some of the criticism may contain an element of the politician's rhetorical flourish, a substantial body of evidence suggests that the old police authorities were relatively ineffective. Moreover, given the low turnout in local elections, the general 'invisibility' of police authorities to the majority of the public, and the undeniably low level of public interest in police authority business, it is hardly conceivable that the number of elected representatives on a police authority was *the* key issue in determining how effectively the police could be held to account.

At the local neighbourhood level, there is some evidence that the reforms have had a positive impact on participation. Though local consultative fora are developing slowly, the PMCA undoubtedly reinforced the police authorities' responsibility to ensure that communities are consulted and, perhaps even more important, gave police authorities a reason to consult the public. Though the mismatch we described above between neighbourhood concerns and strategic issues at the force level will not easily be overcome, the statutory responsibility to consult the public as part of the process of producing a policing plan will almost certainly lead to much more innovative thinking in this area. At the strategic level, the growth area appears to be public satisfaction surveys, and in a few force areas, the development of 'consumer panels', focus groups and other market research methods.

Despite attempts to reinvigorate local consultative mechanisms, determining a meaningful 'public view' about policing still presents a fundamental difficulty with participation in police policy-making. Though it is vital that mechanisms for public participation in discussions about policing policy exist, it should not be assumed that the outputs of such consultation represent the 'public' or 'community' view. Without doubt certain geographical areas, and certain groups of people will still disproportionately come into conflict with the police and, moreover, most of the time they will be the least likely to enter into formal consultation. In part, this can be addressed by developing new ways of attracting 'hard-to-reach groups', but more fundamentally it requires those involved in policing and its control to consider means of addressing some of the roots of public disaffection.

THE WAY FORWARD

Our earlier research identified a number of characteristics of the tripartite structure that required reform (Jones et al., 1994). We argued that:

- police authorities were relatively ineffective in part because their statutory powers were insufficient, but also because they engaged in self-limiting behaviour; all too often police authorities were reluctant to use or exploit the powers that were available to them;
- police authorities suffered through lack of information about policing and lack of expertise in analysing and responding to what they were given;
- police authorities were too large and unwieldy;

- given the shortcomings of police authorities there might well be a case for having co-opted members or independent members on police authorities, so long as elected representation was not significantly diluted (Jones and Newburn, 1995);
- given its financial stake in policing, the significant Home Office role in the tripartite structure was seen as inevitable. However, we were concerned that the mechanism of accountability for the exercise of these major powers was insufficient; and
- it appeared to be the case that chief constables were generally only held to account locally with their consent and they were, in the main, much more attuned to central pressures. Prior to the PMCA reforms, the key relationships appeared to be those between ACPO and the Home Office, and national bodies such as the Audit Commission and HMIC.

In this study, we have examined the impact of the reforms on these issues. In summary, it is our view that:

- the PMCA has enhanced the statutory role of police authorities. There are some indications that the very process of redefinition has focused the attention of authorities on the need to become more effective bodies;
- though the 'performance culture' being encouraged in relation to policing is leading to an increased emphasis on accessible information about policing, it is not clear that authorities are better placed yet to take advantage of such changes;
- the new smaller police authorities do appear to be benefiting from the streamlining that has taken place. There remain concerns, however, that some authorities have too few members to allow proper representation from across the force area;
- the introduction of appointed independent members has not diminished the capacity of police authorities to hold their forces to account. We believe that the role of police authorities could be enhanced, but that in the majority of cases this remains a potential and is not yet an actual consequence of the PMCA;
- there remains confusion about the proper role and identity of the police authority. Many police authority members and officers appear to subscribe to a model that sees the police authority as independent and constructively critical of, yet working with, its police force. However, overlapping responsibilities between forces and authorities due to grey areas in the legislation are causing confusion and may in the future lead to tensions between chief constables and their police authorities;
- the Home Secretary's role has been reinforced, but this has not been accompanied by a significant increase in the transparency of decision-making at the centre. It is difficult to see a justification for continued Home Office involvement in the appointment of independent members; and

- at the time of the passage of the PMCA there were some strategic realignments among the members of the tripartite structure. More particularly, there was a degree of rapprochement between ACPO and the local authority associations, and a temporary cooling of relations between ACPO and the Home Office. There is some evidence that the improved relationship between ACPO and local government has been carried over into the post-reform period, and that this has been paralleled by a recovery in the relationship between ACPO and the Home Office.

Policy recommendations

In responding to the shortcomings they identify in the structures for the governance of police, many authors have attempted to outline how the system might be radically overhauled (see *inter alia*, Jefferson and Grimshaw, 1984; Loader, 1996). Our aim here is the rather more modest one of suggesting some relatively small changes that will address a number of the problems outlined above. Needless to say, they are not intended as a panacea for police accountability, merely some practical suggestions for what we see to be improvement.

First, we feel that there should be greater flexibility in the use of the Home Secretary's power to sanction increases in the size of police authorities. While we would not see widespread significant increases in police authority sizes as a positive development, there is a case for modest increases to ease some problems of political representation.

Second, Home Office involvement in the appointment of independent police authority members should end. Appointments should be made entirely locally, though following guidance laid down by the centre.

Third, the diminished representation of elected members on new the smaller police authorities could be addressed if magistrates were no longer to take up three of the 17 police authority places. We recommend that in 17 member authorities, there should be 12 elected members (the existing nine plus three new members replacing magistrates) and five independent members. This is not intended to devalue the extensive experience and contribution of magistrate members to many police authorities. However, a key justification for the inclusion of magistrates on police authorities was that they were 'independent' of the party-political structure, and would therefore provide a buffer against partisan control over policing. The appearance of independent members on police authorities makes the magistrates' role somewhat redundant. Critics of such a recommendation might argue that police authorities would lose the expertise derived by magistrate members from their direct contact with the criminal justice system. We would respond that this would not necessarily be lost to police authorities. Magistrates would be free to apply to become independent members themselves.

Fourth, minimum levels of secretariat support for police authorities ought to be established and laid out by the centre. Unless this is done, increases will be resisted by chief constables in some areas. How exactly this would be done needs considerable thought. We would suggest that the Home Office and Department of Environment, in consultation with representatives of the police authorities and ACPO, should lay down recommended minimum levels of support in terms of particular posts. This would help police authorities meet more effectively their expanded statutory responsibilities.

Fifth, because the quantity and quality of performance information is still largely controlled by forces (although HMIC and the district auditors do have a role in validating the reliability and checking systems), there may be a case for an independent national survey of public satisfaction along the lines of the Police Monitor survey in the Netherlands (see Jones, 1995). This could be used as a basis for comparing forces against standard satisfaction measures (rather than relying on internally-generated measures). Moreover, the possibility of using the district audit service – or similar – as a source of independent information for police authorities should also be explored.

Sixth, more imaginative approaches to consultation are needed from police authorities. At the moment, the market-research style innovations are nearly all coming from forces. Police authorities should be encouraged to look to universities and market research companies to undertake work on their behalf. New structures for consultation also need to be developed, and focused particularly on areas and groups with difficult relationships with the police. We suggest that the police authorities' representative body at the national level – the Police Authorities Committee – address consultation as a priority, and disseminate advice and good practice among local police authorities. At the moment, what advice there is tends to come from force research departments.

Seventh, the grey areas in which roles and functions overlap need to be clarified. We identified three areas of 'joint responsibility' that could become sources of tension. These were financial and personnel management, community consultation, and the production of the annual policing plan. On top of the confusion this causes by blurring lines of accountability, this represents considerable financial costs in terms of duplication of effort and opportunity costs.

Eighth, a strong theme from the case studies concerned fears about the use of national objectives as a 'political football' both for reasons of democratic integrity (local areas having irrelevant or unpalatable objectives imposed on them), and for effectiveness (the danger of yearly changes in the number or nature of the objectives). We would argue that while KOs are useful in providing a national framework for policing, their number needs to be limited, and their method of selection made more transparent and laid down in statute. There is a danger, in the words of a senior Home Office official, of other government departments wanting to 'hang baubles on the Christmas tree'. We favour the creation of a formal advisory body, consisting of representatives from HMIC, the Audit Commission, other government departments, local police authorities, and ACPO, which would report to the Home Secretary and make recommendations about KOs and allied performance measures. Furthermore, given the point we made earlier about the possibility of destabilising year-on-year changes in key objectives, we recommend that such objectives be set for a longer time period, possibly three years.

Ninth, it is clear that some of the difficulties in police force–police authority negotiations arise because of confusion (and over-interpretation) of the idea of constabulary independence. A definition of 'operational independence', and the implications of the definition for the role of police authorities, should be provided. We stop short of recommending that this be incorporated in statute, but suggest rather that consideration be given to providing Home Office circular guidance on this issue.

Finally, we would recommend (in line with Kenneth Clarke's original suggestions) that a standard police authority with elected representation should be introduced for the Metropolitan Police. Given its position as the country's largest and most influential police force, we would argue that such a reform would considerably enhance the accountability and perceived legitimacy of the police service in London.

CONCLUDING COMMENTS

When the reforms that eventually led to the PMCA were first put forward, they aroused considerable criticism because of their supposed threat to the 'local democratic accountability' of the police service. However, as we argued in Chapter 1, this system of accountability was severely flawed and was already centralised in many important respects.

This book contains the first detailed information about the emerging effects of the Police and Magistrates' Courts Act 1994. Given that the reforms are still relatively new, it is hardly surprising that we have not yet seen the dramatic effects that some commentators predicted. Incremental change rather than dramatic transformation was a clear theme of both the case studies and the telephone survey. Most forces, some in conjunction with their police authorities, have been setting policing objectives and developing strategic 'business plans' for some years. Similarly, the content of the national objectives was largely seen as uncontentious and conformed to those areas the chief constables and their police authorities would probably have prioritised in any case.

In sum, a major shift in the tripartite structure has yet to occur. Prior to the reforms, some commentators argued that central government in the form of the Home Office would henceforth exercise far more control. Others suggested that the new arrangements might tip the balance back towards the local police authority. So far, it appears that neither of these has happened. In a context of largely uncontentious national objectives (strongly influenced in any case by ACPO), and of police authority passivity in setting local objectives, it is the position of chief constables that has been strengthened. How long this situation will continue is unclear. The PMCA has clearly given police authorities a number of important tools with which to enhance their input into the development of local policing policy. At present, the most visible changes in the operation of police authorities are 'managerialist' in nature. Aided and abetted by the Audit Commission, HMIC and the 'privatisation mentality' of recent governments, the PMCA moved the focus of police authority business closer to performance measurement and general management, and away from questions of policing style and operation. In addition, the PMCA introduced a number of grey areas and overlapping responsibilities, which, combined with the 'compliance culture' that has traditionally characterised many police authorities, has meant that the new tools available to police authorities have yet to be employed to their full potential. However, our research has suggested that this is likely to change. As the new police authorities become more established, more experienced in dealing with the planning process and more sophisticated in monitoring performance information, we may well see police authorities play a more prominent role in the system of police governance in England and Wales.

References

ACPO (1993) 'Police reform: the government's proposal for the police service in England and Wales', London: ACPO (unpublished)

Association of Metropolitan Authorities (1994) *Changing the Face of Quangos: A Discussion Document*, London: AMA

Audit Commission (1989) *Improving Vehicle Fleet Management in the Police Service*, Police Paper No. 3, London: HMSO

— (1990a) *Calling all Forces: Improving Police Communication Rooms*, Police Paper No. 5, London: HMSO

— (1990b) *Footing the Bill: Financing Provincial Police Forces*, Police Paper No. 6, London: HMSO

— (1990c) *Taking Care of the Coppers: Income Generation by Provincial Police Forces*, Police Paper No. 7, London: HMSO

— (1991a) *Effective Policing: Performance Review in Police Forces*, Police Paper No. 8, London: HMSO

— (1991b) *Reviewing the Organisation of Provincial Police Forces*, Police Paper No. 9, London: HMSO

— (1991c) *Pounds and Coppers: Financial Delegation in Provincial Police Forces*, Police Paper No. 10, London: HMSO

— (1992) *Fine Lines: Improving the Traffic Warden Service*, Police Paper No. 11, London: HMSO

— (1993) *Helping With Enquiries: Tackling Crime Effectively*, Police Paper No. 12, London: HMSO

— (1994) *Cheques and Balances: A Management Handbook on Police Planning and Financial Delegation*, Police Paper No. 13, London: HMSO

— (1996) *Streetwise: Effective Police Patrol*, London: HMSO

Baker, K. (1993) *The Turbulent Years: My Life in Politics*, London: Faber & Faber

Butler, A. (1996) 'Managing the future: a chief constable's view', in Leishman, F., Loveday, B. and Savage, S.(eds) *Core Issues in Policing*, London: Longman

Chatterton, M., Humphrey, C. and Watson, A. J. (1996) *On the Budgetary Beat*, London: Chartered Institute of Management Accountants

Day, P. and Klein, R. (1987) *Accountabilities*, London: Tavistock

Dunleavy, P. and Hood, C. (1994) 'From old public administration to new public management', *Public Money and Management*, 14 (3)

Home Office (1993) *The White Paper on Police Reform*, London: HMSO

— (1995) *Report of Police Core and Ancillary Tasks*, London: Home Office

Horton, C. (1995) *Policing Policy in France*, London: Policy Studies Institute

Independent Committee of Inquiry Report into the Role and Responsibilities of the Police (1994) *Discussion Document*, London: Police Foundation/Policy Studies Institute

— (1996) *Final Report*, London: Police Foundation/Policy Studies Institute

Inquiry into Police Responsibilities and Rewards [The Sheehy Inquiry] (1993) *Final Report*, London: HMSO

Jefferson, T. and Grimshaw, R. (1984) *Controlling the Constable: Police Accountbility in England and Wales*, London: Muller

Jenkins, S. (1995) *Accountable to None: The Tory Nationalization of Britain*, Harmondsworth: Penguin

Johnston, L. (1996) Policing diversity: the impact of the public–private complex in policing. In Leishman, F., Loveday, B., and Savage, S. (eds) *Core Issues in Policing*, Harlow: Longman

Jones, T. (1995) *Policing and Democracy in the Netherlands*, London: Policy Studies Institute

Jones, T. and Newburn, T. (1995) 'Local Government and Policing: arresting the decline in local influence', *Local Government Studies*, 21 (3) 448–60

— (1997 forthcoming) *Private Security and Public Policing*, Oxford: Clarendon Press

Jones, T., Newburn, T. and Smith, D. (1994) *Democracy and Policing*, London: Policy Studies Institute

— (1996) 'Policing and the Idea of Democracy', *The British Journal of Criminology*, 36 (2), Spring, 182–98

l'Anson, J. and Wiles, P. (1995) *The Sedgefield Community Force*, University of Sheffield: Centre for Criminological and Legal Research

Lloyd, C. (1985) 'National Riot Police: Britain's third force?' In B. Fine and R. Millar (eds) *Policing the Miners' Strike*, London: Lawrence & Wishart

Loader, I. (1996) *Youth, Policing and Democracy*, Basingstoke: Macmillan

Loveday, B. (1987) 'Joint Boards for Police in Metropolitan Areas: a preliminary assessment', *Local Government Studies*, 13 (3)

— (1991) 'The New Police Authorities', *Policing and Society*, 1 (3)

— (1994) 'Police Reform: problems of accountability and the measurement of police effectiveness', Institute of Public Policy, Department of Management, University of Central England

— (1994) 'The Police and Magistrates' Courts Act: the impact of police reform on local policing in England and Wales', Paper presented at the AMA Conference, Newcastle-on-Tyne

— (1995) 'The new police authority', Unpublished paper for IIR conference, *A new age in policing*, April 1995

Lustgarten, L. (1983) 'Beyond Scarman: Police accountability in Britain'. In, Glazer, N. and Young, K. (eds) *Ethnic Pluralism and Public Policy*. London: Heinemann, 236–57

— (1986) *The Governance of Police*, London: Sweet & Maxwell

Marshall, G. (1978) 'Police accountability revisited'. In D. Butler and A. H. Halsey (eds), *Policy and Politics*, London: Macmillan

Morgan, R. (1986) 'Police consultative groups: the implications for the governance of the police', *Political Quarterly*, January–March, 83–7

— (1987) 'The local determinants of policing policy', in Willmott, P. (ed.) *Policing and the Community*, London: Policy Studies Institute

— (1992) 'Talking About Policing'. In D. Downes (ed.) *Unravelling Criminal Justice*', London: Macmillan

Morgan, R. and Maggs, C. (1985) *Setting the PACE: Police Community Consultation Arrangements in England and Wales*, Centre for the Analysis of Social Policy: University of Bath

Morgan R. and Newburn, T. (1997) *The Future of Policing*, Oxford: Oxford University Press

Morgan, R. and Swift, P. (1987) 'The future of police authorities: members' views', *Public Administration*, 65 (3)

Pateman, C. (1985) *The Problem of Political Obligation: A Critique of Liberal Theory*, Cambridge: Polity Press

Poulantzas, N. (1980) *State, Power, Socialism*, London: Verso/New Left Books

Rawlings, P. (1991) 'Creeping privatisation? The police, the Conservative government and policing in the late 1980s'. In Reiner, R. and Cross, M. (eds) *Beyond Law and Order: Criminal Justice Policy and Politics into the 1990s*, London: Macmillan

Regan, D. (1983) *Are the Police under Control?*, London: Social Affairs Unit

Reiner, R. (1991) *Chief Constables*, Oxford: Oxford University Press

— (1992) *The Politics of the Police* (second edition) Brighton: Harvester

— (1993a) 'Police Accountability: principles, patterns and practices'. In Reiner, R. and Spencer, S. (eds) *Accountable Policing: Effectiveness, Empowerment and Equity*, London: Institute for Public Policy Research

— (1993b) 'Accountability and Effectiveness'. In Dingwall, R. and Shapland, J. (eds) *Reforming British Policing: missions and structures*, Faculty of Law: University of Sheffield

Reiner, R. and Spencer, S. (eds) (1993) *Accountable Policing: Effectiveness, Empowerment and Equity*, London: Institute for Public Policy Research

Rogerson, P. (1995) 'Performance Measurement and Policing: Police Service or Law Enforcement Agency?', *Public Money and Management*, 15 (4), October–December, 25–30

Royal Commission on Criminal Justice (1993) *Report*, London: HMSO

Schumpeter, J. A. (1961) *Capitalism, Socialism and Democracy*, London: Allen & Unwin

Shattock, D. (1995) 'The new style police authorities', *Policing Today*, February

Smith, D. J. (1987) 'The police and the idea of community'. In Willmott, P. (ed.) *Policing and the Community*, London: Policy Studies Institute

Stratta, E. (1990) 'A lack of consultation?', *Policing*, 6, 523–49

Weatheritt, M. (1993) 'Measuring police performance: accounting or accountability? In Reiner, R. and Spencer, S. (eds) *Accountable Policing: Effectiveness, Empowerment and Equity*, London: Institute for Public Policy Research

— (1996) 'Policing plans: a members' guide', London: AMA/COLPA

Index